MANU FORTI

A HISTORY OF THE HEREFORDSHIRE REGIMENT

MANU FORTI

A HISTORY OF THE HEREFORDSHIRE REGIMENT

Lt Col T.J.B. Hill MBE, KSLI

ALAN SUTTON PUBLISHING LIMITED

First published in the United Kingdom in 1996
Alan Sutton Publishing Limited · Phoenix Mill · Far Thrupp · Stroud · Gloucestershire

Copyright © Lt-Col. T.J.B. Hill MBE, KSLI, 1996

British Library Cataloguing in Publication Data

ISBN 0-7509-1182-4

Typeset in 10/12pt Times.
Typesetting and origination by
Alan Sutton Publishing Ltd.
Printed in Great Britain by
Butler & Tanner, Frome, Somerset.

Contents

List of Illustrations

Maps

Foreword

Col. Sir Thomas Dunne KCVO
Lord Lieutenant of Herefordshire

As the Lord Lieutenant of Herefordshire and the honorary colonel of 5th Battalion the Light Infantry, the successor regiment to the Herefordshire Light Infantry and 4th King's Shropshire Light Infantry (KSLI), I am delighted to write a brief introduction to this history of the Herefordshire Regiment.

It is the first time that a book has been published recording the magnificent services of this purely volunteer regiment, which had a continuous period of service from its inception as the Rifle Volunteers in 1860 until its disbandment as the Herefordshire Light Infantry in 1967. The history indicates how well the regiment emulated the proud tradition of former Herefordshire regiments, including 36th Herefordshire Regiment of Foot, the Herefordshire Militia and the Herefordshire Volunteers. Together with the Regimental Museum Collection at the TA Centre, Harold Street, Hereford, this book should help to preserve a record in the greatest traditions of the Light Infantry.

Acknowledgements

I wish to acknowledge the considerable assistance provided by the *Historical Records of the Herefordshire Regiment*, compiled by G. Archer Parfitt of Shrewsbury, in particular for the material on the Hereford and Radnor Rifle Volunteers, which is based on the historical records.

Thanks are due to Capt. Ashworth, whose diary on the 1914–18 period provided the basis of the First World War chapter, and also to Pte Edwards of Llandrindod Wells, for his personal recollection of Gallipoli.

The chapters on the 1939–45 war are in the main based on the war diaries and the historical records. My grateful thanks to the many who have assisted me with information and advice.

Lt-Col. T.J.B. Hill

ABBREVIATIONS

A/	Acting	NCO	Non-Commissioned Officer
ASC	Army Service Corps	NRA	National Rifle Association
BAOR	British Army of the Rhine	OTC	Officers' Training Corps
Bt	Baronet	QMR	Quartermaster
CQMS	Company Quartermaster Sergeant	RAMC	Royal Army Medical Corps
CSM	Company Sergeant-Major	RAPC	Royal Army Pay Corps
Dmr	Drummer	RFA	Royal Field Artillery
FM	Field Marshal	RFC	Royal Flying Corps
GSO	General Staff Officer	RRVC	Radnorshire Rifle Volunteer Corps
HRVC	Herefordshire Rifle Volunteer Corps	RSM	Regimental Sergeant-Major
IOM	Isle of Man	RV	Rifle Volunteers
KLI	King's Light Infantry	RVC	Rifle Volunteer Corps
KOSB	King's Own Scottish Borderers	RWF	Royal Welsh Fusiliers
KSLI	King's Shropshire Light Infantry	SWB	South Wales Borderers
LCI	Landing Craft Infantry	TD	Territorial Decoration
MID	Mentioned in Despatches	TF	Territorial Force
MM	Military Medal	VSC	Volunteer Service Company
MTS	Motor Transport Ship	WO1	Warrant Officer Class 1

Introduction

This book sets out to record the history of the volunteers and territorials of Herefordshire who from 1860 to the present day formed the Herefordshire Rifle Volunteers, the Herefordshire Regiment (TF), and the Herefordshire Light Infantry (TA). It does not cover the earlier Regular Regiment, 36th (Herefordshire) Regiment of Foot, which was associated with Herefordshire in 1782 and in 1881 became 2nd Battalion the Worcestershire Regiment. The historical records of 36th Regiment of Foot can be found in the book compiled by Richard Cannon, published by Parker, Ferninal and Parker of Charing Cross, London.

The continuous history of the Herefordshire Regiment dates from 1860 when eight Volunteer Rifle Corps were raised in Herefordshire and three in Radnorshire, and joined as 1st Administrative Battalion Herefordshire Rifle Volunteers.

The Volunteers were more closely formalized as a battalion in 1880 when they were titled 1st Herefordshire Rifle Volunteer Corps (HRVC) (Hereford & Radnor). At the same time the War Office listed regular regiments and reorganized the areas of control of Regular Regimental Districts, and the Volunteers and Militia of Herefordshire came under the control of 53rd Regimental District Shrewsbury and Depot of the KSLI.

During the South African War (1900–1902), Volunteer Service Companies were raised from the Rifle Volunteer Corps and Militia to serve with their associated county regiments. In the case of Herefordshire and Shropshire, two Volunteer Service Companies were raised and went out to South Africa to serve with 2nd Battalion KSLI.

In 1907, Mr Haldane, Secretary of State for War, introduced major reforms to the organization of the Reserve Forces. These reforms were enacted in the Territorial and Reserve Forces Act of 1907. The Militia ceased to exist, a new special reserve was created, and the Volunteer Yeomanry and Rifle Volunteers became the Territorial Force, organized in war formations of brigades and divisions. Under the reorganization the Herefordshire Rifle Volunteers became 1st Battalion the Herefordshire Regiment (TF) and part of 159 Infantry Brigade of 53 Welsh Infantry Division.

During the Great War (1914–18), the Herefordshire Regiment was mobilized with 53 Welsh Division and served with that formation in Gallipoli, Egypt and Palestine. At the conclusion of the Palestine Campaign they returned to France and served with 34 Infantry Division until the end of the war. A 2nd Battalion was raised in August 1914 and served in the UK as a training and draft forming unit until April 1918, when it was absorbed by 4th Reserve Battalion KSLI. A 3rd Line Battalion of the Herefordshire Regiment was raised in the autumn of 1915 and this unit was amalgamated with 4th Reserve Battalion KSLI in November 1917.

In 1920 the Territorial Force was reconstituted as the Territorial Army and in 1921 1st Battalion the Herefordshire Regiment was reformed as part of 159 Welsh Border Infantry Brigade of 53 Welsh Division. With the increasing threat from Germany in April 1939, a 2nd Battalion of the Herefordshire Regiment was raised by dividing the old 1st Battalion and increasing recruitment; both battalions were made up by trainees from the conscription to the new Militia formed in May 1939.

During the Second World War (1939–45), both battalions were mobilized: 1st Battalion with 53 Infantry Division; 2nd Battalion with 38 Infantry Division. In April 1940 53 Infantry

Division was concentrated in Northern Ireland – a precaution against a German invasion. In May 1942 159 Infantry Brigade was selected to become part of 11 Armoured Division as a lorry-borne brigade, and 1st Battalion the Herefordshire Regiment landed in Normandy with 11 Armoured Division and served through France, Belgium, Holland and Germany until the end of the war in Europe. In recognition of this service, the regiment was granted the Freedom of the City of Hereford on 29 September 1945. In January 1946 11 Armoured Division was disbanded and 159 Infantry Brigade returned to form part of 53 Welsh Division on occupation duties in the Ruhr. At the end of June the battalion returned home for demobilization.

The Territorial Army was reformed on 1 January 1947. The Herefordshires were reformed as 1st Battalion the Herefordshire Light Infantry as part of the Light Infantry Group, which became the Light Infantry Brigade on 21 June 1951. On reformation of 1st Battalion the Herefordshire Light Infantry, it became part of 159 Infantry Brigade of 53 Welsh Infantry Division.

In the Territorial Army reorganization of 1967, 1st Battalion the Herefordshire Light Infantry was disbanded, and the TA battalions of Shropshire and Herefordshire were joined together as the Light Infantry Volunteers. In 1972 the latter became 5th Battalion the Light Infantry (Volunteers) with two companies in Herefordshire: one at Hereford, one at Ross.

PART I: THE RIFLE VOLUNTEERS, 1860–1908

CHAPTER I

The Early Volunteer Units Before 1860

The close association between the Herefordshire Militia and the Herefordshire Volunteers has on occasions caused the histories of the two forces to be confused. Any attempt to achieve continuity in lineage of the Herefordshire Light Infantry by reference to the Volunteer element in the Herefordshire Militia cannot be justified, for it merely confuses the lineage with that of the old Constitutional Force of the county. The Herefordshire Regular Militia, a quite separate organization which had its roots in the Fyrd or General Levy of the county, became 4th Militia Battalion KSLI in 1881.

It will be appreciated that Volunteers were accepted in aid of the ballot for the Militia, first as individuals and then as separate companies, but those separate companies formed part of the Militia. However, following the outbreak of the war of the French Revolution in 1793, Volunteer Corps were raised independently of any Act and in addition to the Militia, and it is these Volunteer Corps that are the true predecessors of the Herefordshire Light Infantry.

Before considering the Volunteer Corps it is necessary to note that in 1797 the Militia in England and Wales was augmented by Supplementary Militia, and in 1798 this force was embodied by Royal Warrant. The Supplementary Militiamen were incorporated into the Regular Militia, and drafts joined the Herefordshire Regular Militia, at that time serving outside the county.

During the period 1808–1816, a force of Permanent Local Militia was raised to replace the Regular Militia when they were embodied, and in place of the infantry volunteer companies. Into this local militia men transferred from the Volunteer Corps of Herefordshire. In view of this relationship, the local militia is sometimes confused with the Volunteer Corps.

During the French Revolution and Napoleonic Wars, Volunteer Corps of infantry were raised in Herefordshire, and in 1794 an Act regulating the Volunteer Corps decreed that such Volunteers were exempted from liability to serve in the Militia. The Volunteer Corps were thus distinct from the Militia, and can justly claim to be the true predecessors of the Herefordshire Regiment. This Act expired at the Peace of Amiens in 1802, when many of the Volunteer Corps were disbanded.

In Herefordshire the corps raised at that time were:

Gentlemen and Yeomanry Cavalry of Hereford
Hereford Volunteer Infantry
Moccas Volunteer Infantry

Leominster Loyal Association Cavalry
Leominster Loyal Association Infantry

The peace was short lived, and in 1802 another Act was passed, authorizing the raising of yeomanry and Volunteer Corps. The threatened invasion by Napoleon caused the rapid formation of a large number of Volunteer Corps, and, in Herefordshire, three troops of yeomanry cavalry and thirty-eight companies of infantry were raised in 1803.

Details of these units were given in the well known chart by James Willson, entitled 'A view of the Volunteer army of Great Britain in the year 1806'. The strength of these units shown in that chart were:

Herefordshire Cavalry	243
Herefordshire 1st Regiment	806
Herefordshire 2nd Regiment of two battalions	2088
Archenfield Infantry	605

The regimental colour of 1st Regiment the Herefordshire Volunteer Infantry (1803–1808) is in the possession of the Herefordshire Regimental Museum, to which it was presented by the Trustees of the Royal Hampshire Regimental Museum in 1960. The colour was purchased by the Royal Hampshire Regiment in 1938 from a London showroom, with the effects of a descendant of a former commanding officer of 67th South Hampshire Regiment of Foot; it was erroneously believed to be the colour carried by 2nd Battalion the 67th Foot at the Battle of Barosoa in the Peninsular War.

The colour is of green silk, being the facing colour of the regiment with the union in the upper canton. Painted in the centre of the field on a circle within a gold frame is the coat of arms of the city of Hereford, with crest and supporters above a three-part scroll bearing the motto *Invictae fidelitatis praemium*, all within the union wreath of roses, thistles and shamrocks. The size of the colour was originally 6 feet 6 inches flying, and 6 foot deep on the pike, the pike being 9 feet 10 inches, inclusive of the spear and ferrule. The cords and tassels were of silk, crimson and gold mixed.

The Herefordshire Regimental Museum also possesses a side drum, believed to have belonged to the Ledbury Company of 1st Herefordshire Volunteers (1804). The shell is painted yellow and emblazoned with the badge, which comprises a lion rampant on a red ground, within a circle bearing the title 'Loyal British Rangers', all surmounted by the Georgian Crown and ensigned with the cypher 'GR'. It is unusual to find the shell painted other than in the facing colour of the regiment, therefore the drum may have seen prior service, but no regiment styled the Loyal British Rangers has been traced.

It will be realized that while mention has been made of the Hereford Yeomanry Cavalry and the Leominster Association Cavalry in order that the statement of the Volunteer corps in the county during this period will be complete, these cavalry units do not form part of the lineage of the Herefordshire Light Infantry.

The Herefordshire and Radnorshire Volunteer Rifle Corps, 1859–60

Following the downfall of Napoleon, the foot Volunteers, with only two exceptions – the Honourable Artillery Company and the Duke of Cumberland's Sharpshooters – were disbanded.

However, in 1859, in consequence of the hostile tone of the French Army and Government and the defenceless state of Great Britain, they were revived as Volunteer artillery and rifle corps.

The establishment of the Volunteer Force was sanctioned by a War Office circular dated 12 May 1859, signed by Gen. Peel, Secretary of State for War. The main points stipulated that Volunteer corps should be formed under officers holding a commission of the lord lieutenant of the county; that all members would take an oath of allegiance; that the force should be liable to be called out 'under arms' in the case of invasion, appearance of an enemy force off the coast or in the event of rebellion arising out of those causes; that while so under arms, the members of the force would be subject to military law and entitled to pay 'in like manner as the Regular Army'; that officers disabled in service under those conditions should be entitled to half pay, while non-commissioned officers and men would be entitled to the benefits of Chelsea Hospital; and finally that members should not 'quit the corps' when actually on service, although they could do so at other times by giving fourteen days notice, and that they would be considered 'effective' on completion of eight days training in each quarter or a total of twenty-four days 'drill or exercise' each year.

In consequence of this circular, meetings were held in all of the principal towns in Herefordshire and Radnorshire with a view to forming Volunteer Rifle Corps, the services of which were to be offered to Her Majesty Queen Victoria.

It would appear that the initiative was taken by Nathaniel Kyrle Collins in Ross, where the services of the Ross Volunteer Rifle Corps (RVRC) were offered in November 1859. However, as they were not officially accepted until March 1860, the precedence of the Herefordshire Rifle Volunteers (RV) dates from that time. The Herefordshire Light Infantry is directly descended from the Herefordshire RV, and by virtue of this fact it celebrated its centenary in 1960.

In 1860 eight Volunteer Rifle Corps were raised in Herefordshire, and three in Radnorshire. The names of these VRCs, the dates when they were raised and the names of their commanding officers are listed below. The precedence number of the HRV was 69th, and that of the Radnorshire RV was 85th, as stated in the Army List of 1860.

The units raised were as follows:

VRC	Date of formation	Commanding officer
Hereford City	April 1860	Capt. Fieldon, Robert
Ross	March 1860	Capt. Power, Kingsmill Manley
Ledbury	May 1860	Capt. Somers, the Earl
Bromyard	May 1860	Capt. Hopton, H.
South Archenfield	May 1860	Capt. Partridge, Edward Otto
Leominster	May 1860	Rt. Hon. Rodney, Robert D.
Kington	May 1860	Capt. Coke, John*
Hereford (Oddfellows)	October 1860	Capt. Arkwright, Richard
Presteign (1st Radnorshire RV)	March 1860	Capt. Mynors, Robert Baskerville R.
Knighton (2nd Radnorshire RV)	April 1860	Capt. Green, Richard
New Radnor (3rd Radnorshire RV)	August 1860	Lt. Mynors, Thomas Baskerville

*Capt. Coke, later Maj.-Gen. Sir John Coke KCB, raised 1st Punjab Rifles, later 1st Battalion Frontier Force Rifles Indian Army ('Coke's Rifles')

The uniform of the Volunteer Rifle Corps of Herefordshire and Radnorshire differed in style for each county but they were both grey with black facings, and the head-dress was the kepi.

CHAPTER 2

1st Administrative Battalion Herefordshire Rifle Volunteers

Lord Bateman and Sir John Benn Walsh Bt, the lord lieutenants of Herefordshire and Radnorshire respectively, together with the original officers, were responsible for the success which attended the formation of the Volunteer Rifle Corps in the two counties. Initially these eleven VRCs were entirely independent of one another, but, as a consequence of War Office circulars dated 24 March and 4 September 1860, they became components of 1st Administrative Battalion HRV. Nevertheless, they retained a great measure of individuality and independence.

The object of the formation of an Administrative Battalion was to unite the different corps composing it under one common head, to secure uniformity of drill among them, and to afford the advantage of the instruction and assistance of an adjutant. It was not intended to interfere with the financial arrangements of the separate corps or with the operation of their respective rules, or to compel them to meet together for battalion drill in ordinary times, except with their own consent. Furthermore, an establishment was laid down providing a staff for a rural battalion in accordance with the number of companies or corps administered by it. To warrant a lieutenant-colonel, a major and an adjutant, it was necessary to have at least ten companies, while less than four could not stand alone.

As Herefordshire had eight corps of company strength and Radnorshire had only three, one of which, New Radnor, was only of half company strength, a union between the Volunteer corps of the two counties was of obvious mutual advantage. Furthermore, this merger was fostered by the fact that not only did the border share a common history, but also Presteign, the county town of Radnorshire, fell within the diocese of Hereford. Therefore, by 1863 the Army List showed the RRV as united with 1st Administrative Battalion of the HRV. This connection with Radnorshire continued to 1920, and to an extent was revived with the formation of the Home Guard in 1940.

In view of the historic relationship between the military forces of Hereford and Radnor it is pleasing to note that the history of the Radnorshire Militia was written by Lt-Col. Gilbert Drage DSO, who commanded 1st Battalion the Herefordshire Regiment during the First World War (1914–19).

On the formation of 1st Administrative Battalion the HRV in 1860, Capt. Robert Fieldon of Hereford City VRC was appointed lieutenant-colonel to command the battalion, with Capt. Daniel Peploe as the first adjutant. Capt. Peploe, late of the Dragoon Guards and afterwards known as Peploe Webb, resigned the adjutancy in 1867 and continued in the battalion as a junior major, later becoming an MP. In 1865 Capt. Thomas Heywood of Ledbury VRC became the first, and then the only, major in the battalion, and he succeeded Col. Fieldon to command in 1874.

For all purposes except that of uniting for battalion drill, the command and financial control of the several corps remained in the hands of the captains.

Following the Royal Commission on the Volunteer Forces of 1862, the force was placed on a proper footing by the Volunteer Act of 1863 (26 & 27 Vict c 65), which superseded all previous

The Volunteer Rifle Corps HBS Team, photographed at Gloucester on 31 October 1864. Back row, left to right: Capt. Webb (Adjutant); Capt. Suter; Pte. Stanway; Cpl. Luntley; Lt. Fowler; Pte. Seymour; C/Sgt. Taylor; Pte. Sayby; Cpl. Proudman; Pte. Hughes; Pte. Adams; Pte. Yates; Sgt-Maj. Sye; Pte. Hayward; Sgt. Grigg. Front row: Pte. Newton; Pte. Llewellyn; Pte. Butcher; Sgt. Dodd (Champion, 1863); Pte. Adams (Champion, 1864); Pte. Levason (Honorary Secretary); Cpl. Wormington; Cpl. Treen; Capt. Collins.

Acts, and which provided, *inter alia*, for a permanent staff, a standard of efficiency and a capitation grant for the subsidy of each corps. This statute, together with the Volunteer Forces Regulations of 18 September 1863, caused the Volunteer Forces to be reorganized and to become a valuable auxiliary to the British Army as a means of defence.

In the early days there was no government grant; the expenses had to be borne by public subscription and all ranks found their own uniform. The uniform selected was a medium grey with black facings, set off with scarlet piping and worn with black belts. This continued until 1875, when it was replaced by a scarlet uniform with black facings.

The HRV were typical of the Volunteer Force as it existed in rural areas, where the towns were small and scattered, and the population depended largely on agriculture. The company drills necessary for efficiency were completed by the several corps in their own localities, and the only battalion drills were those that were ordered four or five times a year in the various county towns. Much time was wasted in travelling, and the attendance at battalion drill rarely exceeded 250 officers and men.

After the passing of the Volunteer Act of 1863, through which the War Office laid down a standard of efficiency, the percentage of 'efficients' to 'enrolled', with an average enrolled strength of 750, ranged between 70 and 78 per cent, and in 1870 it fell to 67 per cent. Nearly every battalion, but especially country battalions covering large areas, had the same experience, and it is difficult to understand why so many of them held on to the old system of battalion drills instead of adopting camps when they were first authorized in 1861.

The 1st Bn Herefordshire Rifle Volunteer Corps, commanded by Col. R. Fieldon, at camp on Broomy Hill, Hereford, in 1872. (From a contemporary photograph)

The Herefordshire Rifle Volunteers went into camp for the first time in 1871 at Broomy Hill, near Hereford, and thereafter attended camp for a week every summer, except for that of 1888. The early camps were voluntary on the part of the men, except for three battalion drills necessary for efficiency and inspection. At that time there was no government camp allowance dependent on regular attendance. The effect of the change was immediately felt, for the percentage of 'efficients' rose in 1871 to 74 per cent and in 1872 to 80 per cent.

In 1875 the percentage rose to 91 per cent, the number enrolled being 723 with 664 efficients, and in 1879 it reached 96 per cent with 911 enrolled. Year by year the attendance at camp for the whole week increased, but the number of those who 'marched in, stayed the whole time, and marched out' never exceeded 450. At the same time the daily attendances throughout the week gradually increased until the number present usually reached between 800 and 850 officers and men.

A magazine was published called *The Grasshopper in Camp*, and a bound copy of the first twelve issues (1871–4) is contained in the Museum of the Herefordshire Light Infantry. From this publication the nickname 'The Grasshoppers' was derived.

In the early years the battalion attended reviews at Gloucester in 1861, Bristol 1862, Oxford 1863 and Windsor 1868, and each year it sent representatives to the National Rifle Association (NRA) meeting at Wimbledon and/or Bisley, and obtained several badges. In 1864 Sgt Dodd of Ross won Sir John Bennett's forty guinea prize; and in 1868 Pte Packwood won the 'Windmill' 1st prize.

The 1st Administrative Battalion was gradually reorganized, the weaker corps becoming defunct and being replaced by more active companies. Thus in 1874 the South Archenfield VRC, 5th HRV, then known as 5 (Goodrich) Company, was disbanded, together with the half company forming the New Radnor VRC, 3rd RRV. In 1875 8th HRV (Oddfellows) was increased to a strength of one-and-a-half companies, making good the loss of the New Radnor Corps, while in 1878 2nd HRV (Ross VRC) was increased in strength to form two companies, later known as B and E, to replace the Goodrich Corps. Meanwhile, in 1875, 2nd RRV (Knighton VRC) had become defunct, and in their place was raised in 1878 a new 10 Company at Rhayader, Radnorshire, by Capt. Stephen W. Williams, who later commanded the battalion during the years 1894 to 1899.

The resultant organization of 1st Administrative Battalion Herefordshire Rifle Volunteers (Hereford & Radnor) was as follows:

Corps	Name
1st	Hereford (City)
2nd	Ross (increased to form a second company (5) in 1878)
3rd	Ledbury
4th	Bromyard
5th	South Archenfield/Goodrich (disbanded in 1874 and replaced by 2nd Ross in 1878)
6th	Leominster
7th	Kington
8th	Hereford (Oddfellows) (increased to one-and-a-half companies)
9th	Presteign
10th	Knighton (disbanded in 1875, replaced by Rhayader Company in 1878)
11th	New Radnor (disbanded in 1874)

CHAPTER 3

1st Herefordshire Rifle Volunteer Corps (Hereford and Radnor), 1880–1908

To appreciate the reasons for the changes in the regimental title and organization which took place within this period, it is necessary to consider briefly the events which preceded them.

On 19 April 1870 the various military districts in Great Britain were rearranged, and Herefordshire and Radnorshire became part of the 2nd Western Sub-district, having its headquarters in Bristol, and being part of No. 4 Western District, with headquarters at Devonport. The general officer commanding the district was given command of the volunteer units in his district. By the Regulation of the Forces Act of 1871, the Militia, Yeomanry and Volunteers were transferred from the jurisdiction of the lord lieutenants of the counties to the War Secretary, and thereafter commissions in the Auxiliary Forces were by grant of the Sovereign direct, instead of through the lord lieutenant. Furthermore, the Act made the volunteers subject to the Mutiny Act and Articles of War when assembled with the Militia or Regular Forces. The Auxiliary and Reserve Forces Circular of 21 April 1873 stipulated that the Rifle Volunteers should be attached to the infantry sub-district brigades, as constituted under the Cardwell Reforms introduced in 1872.

Herefordshire then came under 22 Brigade Depot, with headquarters at Worcester. The organization comprised brigade, sub-district and brigade depot, as follows:

29th Worcestershire Regiment of Foot
36th Herefordshire Regiment of Foot
(67) Worcester Militia of two battalions
(110) Hereford Militia
(39) 1st and 2nd Administrative Battalions Worcestershire RV
(69) 1st Administrative Battalion Herefordshire RV
(85) Radnorshire Rifle Volunteers united with 1st Administrative Battalion Herefordshire RV

In January 1879 the committee on the Volunteer Force recommended, *inter alia*, that the Rifle Volunteers should form an integral part of the Territorial brigade in each sub-district, and that the force should be consolidated into a smaller number of battalions. Thus on 1 April 1881 the Regulations of 1878 were repealed and from that date the administrative battalions ceased to exist, being replaced by consolidated battalions in which the old corps became companies.

The consolidation of 1st Administrative Battalion HRV was completed by 1 November 1880. The battalion was renamed 1st Herefordshire Rifle Volunteer Corps (HRVC) (Hereford & Radnor).

The organization of 1881 was as follows:

Battalion Headquarters Hereford

Company	Location	Old corps
A	Hereford	1st HRV
B	Ross	2nd HRV
C	Ledbury	3rd HRV
D	Bromyard	4th HRV
E	Ross	5th HRV
F	Leominster	6th HRV
G	Kington	7th HRV
H	Hereford	8th HRV
J	Presteign	1st RRV
K	Rhayader	2nd RRV

(E Company gradually merged with B Company, and a new E Company was formed in 1889 at Weobley)

In the meanwhile, far-reaching reforms were also taking place in the Regular Army. In 1876 Col. Stanley's committee recommended that the connection should be more clearly drawn between the line battalions of a brigade and the Militia battalions of a sub-district. It decided that this would be best effected by their being treated as one regiment, such regiments bearing a Territorial designation – the line battalions being the 1st and 2nd and the Militia the 3rd and 4th of such a Territorial regiment, with the depot being common to all. In February 1881 Sir C.H. Ellice's committee, on the formation of Territorial regiments as proposed by Col. Stanley's committee, made suggestions regarding the affiliation of regiments and their title.

In Herefordshire, Worcestershire and Shropshire the result was as follows: 29th Worcestershire Regiment of Foot and 36th Herefordshire Regiment of Foot to be the Worcester and Hereford Regiment; 43rd Monmouthshire Light Infantry and 53rd Shropshire Regiment of Foot to be the Shropshire Regiment (Light Infantry).

In 1881 Mr Childens, Secretary of State for War, carried the scheme to its logical conclusion by the amalgamation of the linked battalions. This merger was authorized by General Order 41 of April 1881 but, surprisingly, certain changes took place on 1 July 1881, resulting in the following formations:

Regimental district 29, Worcester

Worcestershire Regiment:
1st Battalion late 29th Worcestershire Regiment of Foot
2nd Battalion late 36th Herefordshire Regiment of Foot
3rd Battalion late Worcester Militia
4th Battalion late Worcester Militia

Regimental district 53, Shrewsbury

The King's (Shropshire Light Infantry):
1st Battalion late 53rd Shropshire Regiment of Foot
2nd Battalion late 85th King's Light Infantry
3rd Battalion late Shropshire Militia
4th Battalion late Herefordshire Militia

The 6th Hereford Rifle Volunteers at Camp in 1890

It will be noted that, as from 1 July 1881, the sub-district was replaced by the regimental district, having the same precedence number as the first battalion of the regiment. At this juncture it should be mentioned that, immediately prior to this reorganization, the Herefordshire Militia and the HRV (Hereford & Radnor) had severed connection with 22 Brigade Depot at Worcester to join 25 Brigade Depot at Brecon. Herefordshire now severed its connection with Worcester and Brecon and became part of 53rd Regimental District, with the depot at Copthorne Barracks, Shrewsbury.

Although General Order 41 dealt only with Regular and Militia forces, the Volunteer Force was also affected by the scheme, and the RVCs soon became Volunteer battalions of their Territorial regiment, the affiliation being dealt with by War Office circulars as individual cases arose. The RVC of 53rd Regimental District were as follows:

1st Shropshire RVC
2nd Shropshire RVC
1st Herefordshire RVC (Hereford & Radnor)

The Radnorshire companies of 1st HRVC were placed in a peculiar position, as their county was part of 24th Regimental District, with the depot at Brecon. Nevertheless, they continued their association with Herefordshire.

By the authority of a General Order of 1 December 1887, 1st and 2nd Shropshire RVCs assumed the titles of 1st and 2nd Volunteer Battalions K(SLI) in 1888. The RVC (Hereford & Radnor) did not adopt the title 3rd Volunteer Battalion K(SLI) but was such in everything but name.

In 1889 E Company was reformed by Capt. W.E.A. Walker in the old parliamentary borough of Weobley, and this had the effect of keeping ten-and-a-half companies on the establishment.

These changes in organization resulted in greater efficiency and made possible more advanced methods of training. The discontinuance of battalion camps held in the county of Hereford and the substitution of brigade camps at a distance proved most popular, as it provided the Volunteers with an opportunity to travel. This fact, coupled with the increased difficulty of returning home at will, had the result of very greatly increasing the numbers attending the camp for the whole period. Thus, in the years 1890, 1891 and 1892 the numbers attending were 597, 675 and 803 respectively. The numbers enrolled during these years were 908, 912 and 975, with 'efficients' at 867, 871 and 927 respectively. This represented 95 per cent efficiency for each year. The battalion joined the Welsh Border Brigade in camp at Towyn in 1890 and at Conway in 1892. In 1891 and 1893 it was attached to 3 Infantry Brigade at Aldershot. The battalion had sent two companies to summer drills at Aldershot in 1882 under Maj. Suter, and in 1883 a company under Capt. Scobie attended the Easter manoeuvres at Brighton.

Brigade Bearer Company

Up to 1889 there were only two-and-a-half companies (A and H) at headquarters, but in that year, when the battalion was detailed as part of the Welsh Border Infantry Brigade, in which Surgeon Maj. Peter B. Giles of the RVC was appointed brigade surgeon, he specially recruited a third company to act as brigade bearer company. For all practical purposes it was a separate company, but technically it was at first designated part of A Company, as permission had not been obtained to increase the establishment of the battalion to eleven-and-a-half companies.

The Volunteer Medical Staff Corps was first authorized by the Volunteer Regulations of

1887, but how to provide efficient bearer companies for the various brigades was a very difficult problem for each of the brigade surgeons to solve. Surgeon Capt. Sleman of the Artist's Rifles stated in an article which appeared in July 1892 that the best solution to the difficulty was made by the Welsh Border Brigade, and subsequently by the East London Brigade, where in each case a bearer company was raised from specially enlisted men. The Welsh Border Brigade Company did not wear the uniform of the Herefordshire RVC but that of the Volunteer Medical Staff Corps, with brown belts. Brigade Surgeon Lt-Col. P.B. Giles and the company were therefore the pioneers in the organization of brigade bearer companies, and experience showed the practical advantages of their method over that whereby each battalion in a brigade was required to contribute a certain number of men per rifle company to form a bearer company when in brigade camp. The hospital of the Welsh Border Brigade had the services of men specially trained for the purpose, occupying their own site in the brigade camp, and having their own cooks, who had been taught to supply appropriate foods for the patients. The stretcher-bearers of the various battalions in the brigade drilled together in camp with the bearer company under the command of the brigade surgeon. The Bearer Company became a separate unit and was known as the Welsh Border Bearer Company Royal Army Medical Corps (RAMC), of which a considerable number served in the South African War. On the formation of the Territorial Force in 1908 it became the South Wales Mounted Brigade Field Ambulance RAMC, under the command of Maj. J.R. Raywood, and was part of the South Wales Mounted Brigade in the Western Command.

The Cyclist Section

The RVC, in addition to pioneering the organization of bearer companies, also pioneered the formation of infantry cyclist sections, which were later authorized for the Volunteer Force as a whole in the Volunteer Regulations of 1893, with an establishment of 1 officer, 2 NCOs, 20 privates and 1 bugler. The Cyclist Section of 1st HRVC was formed in 1888 by Maj. Scobie. In 1888 it took part in the Cheshire manoeuvres in the neighbourhood of Reading under the same officer. In the autumn of 1889, Maj. Scobie obtained leave from the War Office to form a cyclist camp at Tintern, and this is claimed to have been the first authorized by the War Office. Cyclist Sections from 1st Volunteer Battalion K (SLI), 2nd Volunteer Battalion SWB and 3rd Glamorganshire Volunteer Artillery joined the Herefordshire section, all of which were commanded by Maj. Scobie. The Cyclist Section was later commanded by Lt. F.H. Leather.

In this connection may be mentioned a reference in Von Lobell's annual *Reports (German) on Military Progress* (Vol. XXV), an able precis of which by Lt-Col. E. Gunter appeared in the *Journal of the United States Institution* in 1900. Alluding to the evolution of the military cycle, the writer states that, in England, Lord Wolseley, Col. Savile of 26th Middlesex (Cyclists), Col. Stracey of the Scot's Guards, Maj. Scobie of 1st Herefordshire and Lt. Eustace Balfour of the London Scottish were the first to take it up.

It has been noted that the first commanding officer was Col. Robert Fieldon. He was succeeded in 1874 by Lt-Col. Thomas Heywood, who held command until 1893, being followed in succession by Lt-Col. T.H. Purser, Lt-Col. S.W. Williams in 1894 and in 1899 by Lt-Col. Mackay J.G. Scobie. From 1871 onwards the HRVC took every advantage of the annual eight-day camps. From 1890 to 1902 it was one of the six battalions forming the Welsh Border Brigade; from 1903 to 1906 it was one of the four comprising 30 Field Army Brigade (and as such trained in camp for fifteen days), rejoining in 1907 its old brigade, which had been renamed the North Wales Border Brigade. During those years it attended camps in Aldershot; Towyn and other places in Wales; the emergency camp of 1900 at Fleetwood; camps in the Isle of Man and Salisbury Plain, gaining much praise for its memorable route march in 1906 from Southampton; and at Scarborough, where in 1907 the North Wales Border Brigade was commanded by Lt-Col. M.J.G. Scobie in the absence of the brigadier.

From 1891 the financial arrangements of the battalion had been completely under the control of the finance committee, the quartermaster, Mr Mason Akerman, acted as secretary to both the finance and the clothing committees. In 1897 a general consolidation of finances took place, which finally relieved the company officers of all financial responsibility, after which time the battalion was completely administered by the commanding officer.

With regard to clothing, the whole battalion was provided with greatcoats and equipment, and the Government allowances were supplemented by funds raised by bazaars held for the purpose. In 1891 the battalion adopted a new clothing scheme whereby articles of uniform were issued regularly throughout the battalion at stated intervals. The effect of this was a uniformity of appearance which did much to improve the smart appearance of the men. In 1891 kerseys were issued, in 1892 helmets, and in 1893 trousers. To this end a fixed sum per head was deducted from the capitation grant and credited to the clothing fund, which was administered by the clothing committee.

In the table of precedence of VRCs the position of the Volunteer battalions of Herefordshire and Shropshire was as follows:

Date	1st Volunteer Battalion K(SLI)	2nd Volunteer Battalion K(SLI)	1st HRVC
1898	169	170	199
1900	172	173	204
1901	173	174	205
1901	174	175	206
1903	175	176	207
1904	176	177	208
1904	176	177	207

With regard to shooting, the battalion sent representatives every year to the NRA meeting at Wimbledon or Bisley, where they obtained several badges for the Queen's Sixty, the Hundred and the St George's. The following is a brief record of some of the principal prizes gained. Sgt Fowler tied in 1881 for the first prize of the St George's, but lost it to Sgt Heiton by one point when shooting off. In 1883 the battalion team won the Belgium Cup for volley firing, and in 1889 Sgt Corey won first prize in the All Comers Aggregate. Corey also shot in the English Twenty at Glasgow in 1886 for the National Challenge Trophy, and four times won the bronze medal, presented to the county by the NRA.

The proprietors of the *Hereford Times* presented the battalion with a very fine challenge cup, valued at 40 guineas, for the encouragement of individual, team and class firing. It was to be held for a year by the winning company. No company of less than sixty strong on 31 March was allowed to compete, and the number of men in the teams varied with the strength of the companies, each team consisting of one man for every ten men in the company.

Each team fired three competitions, and the team with the best aggregate average score won the cup. Badges for the winning team and prizes in money for the best individual scores were given by the Herefordshire and Radnorshire Rifle Association. As an incentive to class firing, none but first class shots were allowed to compete in the teams.

The outlying companies had small armouries and quarters in addition to ranges. At

Leominster the armoury and quarters were in the old borough gaol. At Ross they started off at the old dock in 1889, then moved to Wilton Road in 1896 and to Cantilupe Street in 1897. The headquarters at Hereford were houses acquired in 1890 by Maj. Scobie (A Company), Capt. Morris (H Company) and brigade surgeon Lt-Col. Giles (Bearer Company). They were later purchased by the battalion under the Military Lands Act of 1892. The site was a square with a block of buildings on one side containing the orderly room, stores, reading and lecture room, and the armourer sergeant's house. On another side was a strong building used as an armoury and store for the Headquarter Companies, and facing it on the opposite side was a large drill shed, 120 feet by 60 feet, made of corrugated iron in a single span, and erected at the expense of Maj. Scobie, Capt. Morris and Lt-Col. Giles. The barrack square was enclosed by a brick wall, with marks painted on it for aiming drill, and the Bearer Company had a special iron building for medical stores.

The Hereford companies drilled either on the barrack square or in the drill shed, but during the long summer evenings they had the permission of the city council to drill on the Castle Green.

By 1893 the battalion was well organized and highly efficient, having a Signal Platoon under Cpl Dolby, supplied by Hereford and Kington companies. A Pioneer Platoon under Sgt Biddle was supplied by the Leominster company, and the battalion band at headquarters in Hereford was supported by a band fund, raised by means of the authorized percentage on the Battalion Capitation Grant. Bandmaster St John Jones was in charge for many years, and his son, Band Sgt Jones, superintended the buglers of the battalion, who formed a bugle band in camp. E (Weobley) and G (Kington) companies, with the Lugwardine Platoon of H Company (Hereford), united in providing the battalion with a drum and fife band, so that on all occasions martial music was readily available.

The efficiency of the battalion was evidenced by the fact that it was one of the 27 out of 223 in the United Kingdom selected to form part of the Field Army, a new departure introduced in 1903. However, prior to that members of the HRVC had experience of warfare while serving in 1st and 2nd Volunteer Service Companies (VSC) KSLI, which joined 2nd Battalion KSLI on active service in South Africa, and won for 1st HRVC the battle honour 'South Africa 1900–1902'. The Herefordshire detachment of 1st VSC was under the command of Lt. J.F. Cutler, serving in 1900 and 1901, while Lt. Percy Anthony commanded the second detachment, serving from 1901 to 1902. Other officers of the battalion served in South Africa attached to other regiments, notably Maj. J.R.L. Rankin with Rimington's Guides and Capt E. Kenworthy with Robert's Horse. There is an account of the war services of the VSC in the South African Campaign (1900–1902) in Chapter 4.

Cadet companies were authorized in the Volunteer Force Regulations of 1863, but it was not until after the South African War that 1st HRVC had a Cadet Company. In 1902 Hereford Cathedral School instituted practice with the Morris tube rifle and applied to the War Office for permission to form a Cadet Corps. Authority was received on 24 December 1902 and the corps was raised in January 1903. The Hereford Cathedral School VRC was affiliated to 1st HRVC (Hereford & Radnor) and the first commissions appeared in the Army List of 28 March 1903: Capt. Edward V. Martin, Lt. Norman Hathery and 2/Lt. Percy J. Lewis.

The cadet corps became the Hereford Cathedral School Officers' Training Corps (OTC) in 1908. In that year the HRVC became the Herefordshire Regiment in the newly formed Territorial Force and so ended the Volunteer Force in Herefordshire.

To a large extent the strength and efficiency of the battalion was due to the NCOs, and a large proportion of them held the District Inspector of Musketry's Certificate. Foremost among these was Col.-Sgt William Wigley (1st Corps Hereford), late sergeant in 11th Hussars and a veteran of the Crimean War. He gave the battalion the benefit of his experience for twenty-three years.

The record of service of Col.-Sgt Griffin of Ross is typical of the Volunteers. He enlisted in 1889, was made L/Cpl in 1891, joined the Cyclist Section in 1893 and qualified as a sergeant on 24 April 1896. He volunteered for the Service Company, which went out to South Africa to 2nd Battalion KSLI in January 1900, returned in May 1901, and was made colour sergeant in 1904. He was still serving when the Volunteers were converted into the Territorial Force.

CHAPTER 4

The Herefordshire Detachments of the Volunteer Service Companies KSLI in the South African War, 1900–1902

1 st HRVC took part in the twenty-eight day emergency camp at Fleetwood, Lancashire, in 1900, and detachments from the battalion formed part of 1st and 2nd Volunteer Service Companies KSLI, which served with 2nd (Regular) Battalion KSLI in South Africa during the years 1900 to 1902. 2nd Battalion KSLI formed part of 19 Brigade of 9 Division.

The numbers volunteering for these detachments far exceeded the requirement, and this enthusiasm was indicative of the fighting spirit of the battalion. The first detachment was under the command of Lt. J.F. Cutler, who served from 1900 to 1901, while the second detachment served under Lt. Percy Anthony from 1901 to 1902.

The restriction on numbers accepted for active service with the VSCs caused some disappointment, and it was mentioned in Chapter 3 that two officers of 1st HVRC offered their services individually: Maj. J.R.L. Rankin served with Rimington's Guides and Capt. E. Kenworthy with Roberts' Horse, two of the irregular units raised in South Africa during the war, and which greatly distinguished themselves.

Maj. Rankin was the author of the well known history of Rimington's Guides: *A Subaltern's Letters to His Wife*. It is of interest that the adjutant of the Guides was Capt. C.H. Rankin of the 7th Hussars. The unit, commonly known as 'Rimington's Tigers' from the piece of leopard skin worn around the slouch hat, became famous when one of its patrols discovered the main Boer Force under Cronje on the western border of the Free State. This discovery led to the capture of Cronje's force at Paardeberg on 27 February 1900, one of the first successes of the war, and one of the proudest battle honours of the KSLI.

1st VSC, having sailed for South Africa on 3 March 1900 on board the SS *Ninevah*, joined 2nd Battalion KSLI at Jacobsrust in the Orange Free State on 2 May 1900, and participated in the march to Pretoria and the advance on to Barberton. It received its baptism of fire at Zand River and fought at Vredfortweg, Rhenoster Spruit, Howling Spruit, Krugersdorp, Oliphants Nek and Barberton. They marched for more than a thousand miles and shared fully in the engagements of the battalion.

1st VSC left 2nd Battalion KSLI at Belfast in the Transvaal on 18 October 1900 under the command of Lt. B. Head. After serving in the Transvaal, Orange Free State and Cape Colony, it sailed for home on 9 April 1901, arriving on 10 May. On the departure of 1st VSC Maj.-Gen. Smith-Dorrien published a Special Brigade Order on 18 October 1900, in which he 'thanked the Company for their hard work and wished them a safe and speedy journey home'. Lt-Col. James Spens, commanding 2nd Battalion KSLI, gave them an excellent report: 'From the time the 1st

VSC joined my Battalion it has shared equally with the other Companies . . . and it has come out of the campaign with flying colours.'

2nd VSC sailed for South Africa in March 1901 and disembarked at Cape Town for duty with the 2nd Battalion KSLI on 29 April 1901. It spent its year of active service occupying the sections of blockhouse line, escorting trains and guarding baggage. It left 2nd Battalion KSLI on 24 April 1902 and returned home on 4 June 1902.

On this occasion, Maj. C.T. Dawkins CMG, who was commanding the battalion, published a letter recording his 'appreciation of the patriotic spirit shown by the members of the Company in volunteering for active service at a time when the original excitement raised by the war had to a great extent subsided'.

The Bearer Company was also eager to render help in the urgent demand for stretcher-bearers, and a number of volunteers from the Welsh Border Bearer Company RAMC served in the South African War.

Casualties

Killed in action or died of disease:
1st VSC 2
2nd VSC 2

Battle Honours

South Africa 1900–1902
(emblazoned on the regimental colour)

Campaign Medals

The Queen's South Africa medal with clasps:

1st VSC	*2nd VSC*
Cape Colony	Cape Colony
Orange Free State	Orange Free State
Johannesburg	Transvaal
South Africa 1901	South Africa 1901
	South Africa 1902

The conditions under which the services of members of the Volunteer Force were accepted for duty in South Africa were set forth in an Army Order issued by Lord Wolseley, Commander-in-Chief:

1. A carefully selected Company of 116 of all ranks may be raised for each line Battalion serving in or about to proceed to South Africa from the affiliated Volunteer Battalions. This Company will be attached for service to the line Battalion in South Africa and placed under the Commanding Officer of that Battalion.
2. An equal number of waiting Companies may be maintained at home.
3. The 5th (Irish) Volunteer Battalion, Liverpool Regiment, will furnish the Company for the Royal Irish Regiment, and the 16th Middlesex (London Irish) for the Royal Irish Rifles.
4. The strength of each Company will be one Captain, two Subalterns, one Sergeant-Instructor to act as Pay Sergeant, four Sergeants, two Buglers, five Corporals, ninety-nine Privates and two Stretcher Bearers. Total: 116.

5. The selection of Officers and the composition of each Company will be controlled by the Officer Commanding the Regimental District in which it is raised. In the case of line Battalions having several affiliated Volunteer Battalions, Companies will be formed from about an equal number of men from each Battalion, as the Officer Commanding the Regimental District may decide. No Volunteer Battalion will be allowed to contribute less than one complete section.

6. The following will be qualifications for service:
   a. Every Volunteer must enlist for one year, or for the War. In the event of the War being over in less than one year he will have the option of being discharged at once or of completing his one year's service.
   b. He must be not less than twenty nor more than thirty-five years of age.
   c. He must be a first class shot under volunteer rules.
   d. He must have been returned as efficient during 1898 and 1899.
   e. He must be of good character.
   f. He must be up to the physical standard of an Infantry recruit as laid down in the Recruiting Regulations for the Army. No relaxation of standard will be allowed.
   g. He must be medically fit for active service.
   h. Preference should be given to unmarried men or widowers without children. Married men should be accepted only in the event of an insufficient number of single men or widowers without children volunteering.

7. When a Volunteer Commanding Officer has received application from not less than a Section of Volunteers, he will so inform the Officer Commanding the Regimental Depot to which his Battalion is affiliated, who will then – if they are to form part of the Service Company – have them medically inspected and, if fit for service, attested.

8. After attestation they will join the Regimental Depot until required for embarkation. In the event of there not being sufficient barrack accommodation available, they may be billeted.

9. Volunteers accepted for the waiting Companies will be attested and passed to the Reserve at once for the unexpired portion of their engagement, or until required for permanent service. During the time they are in the Reserve they will receive Reserve pay and they will be liable to carry out the training laid down in the Reserve Forces Act of 1882.

10. General Officers Commanding will arrange for all Volunteers to receive, after enlistment, as much instruction in musketry, including range practice, as is possible, prior to embarkation.

11. Every Officer and man must be clothed and equipped under Regimental arrangements exactly as those of the Regular Battalions which they are to join, except that the numerals on the shoulder cords will be as laid down in the Volunteer Regulations. For these purposes a special capitation grant of £9 will be granted to the Corps for each Volunteer.

12. Each Volunteer will receive from the date of enlistment pay and allowances of his rank as a regular infantry soldier, rations and clothing. Should a married man be accepted his family will be entitled to separation allowance.

13. On completing his period of service he will receive a gratuity of £5 in addition to any gratuity given to the troops at the end of the war. If discharged in consequence of wounds, injuries or disability received or contracted while on active service he will be entitled to pension in accordance with the Royal Warrant for Pay etc. of the Regular Army.

14. On the departure of a Company from the United Kingdom the Officers and Volunteers composing it will be considered supernumerary to their Corps.

15. Service in one of these Companies will entitle an Officer or Volunteer to be considered efficient for the year, and the Corps will receive capitation grant accordingly for each Volunteer actually enlisted.

1st Volunteer Service Company

1st and 2nd Volunteer Battalions KSLI and the Herefordshire RVC (Hereford & Radnor), being the three volunteer battalions of 53rd Regimental District, each provided a detachment for the VSC KSLI, which was formed at the depot of the KSLI, Copthorne Barracks, Shrewsbury, in 1900.

1st VSC of 116 all ranks was commanded by Capt. W.H. Trow (1st Volunteer Battalion KSLI) and the subalterns were Lt. B. Head (2nd Volunteer Battalion KSLI) and Lt. J.F. Cutler (1st HRVC). The sergeant-instructor was Col.-Sgt William Lee of the Oswestry Company 2nd Volunteer Battalion KSLI. The waiting company was commanded by Lt. H.P. Harris Edge of 1st Volunteer Battalion KSLI, and he and his men later joined 1st VSC in South Africa on 30 July 1900 following the death of Capt. Trow, who died of enteric at Kroonstadt.

1st VSC was stationed at the barracks, but owing to the shortage of accommodation some of the volunteers were billeted in the town. The men were clothed in khaki field service dress with the Wolseley helmet and equipment. After being formed, equipped and trained, 1st VSC sailed for South Africa on 3 March 1900 on board the SS *Ninevah* and joined 2nd Battalion KSLI (Late 85th KLI) at Jacobsrust in the Orange Free State on 2 May 1900. 2nd Battalion KSLI was commanded by Lt-Col. James Spens, and it formed part of 19 Brigade, commanded by Maj.-Gen. H.L. Smith-Dorrien, which was in 9 Division. The battalion had been on active service since 1 December 1899 and had taken a prominent part in the Battle of Paardeberg on 27 February 1900, in which Gen. Cronje and his entire Boer Force were captured.

Maj.-Gen. Smith-Dorrien DSO, in addressing the regiment at Pretoria on 5 June 1900, said:

Colonel Spens, Officers and men of the King's Shropshire Light Infantry. I had no intention of speaking to you this morning, but after giving me such a hearty welcome I feel that I must say something. The first time that I saw you under fire was at Paardeberg, and I was much struck by the magnificent way in which the leading Companies opened out for the attack – which at once showed you thoroughly understood the art of skirmishing. The next time was at Poplar Grove, and I asked Colonel Spens if he could advance to take up a certain position. This was over an open piece of ground, commanded on both sides by Kopjes occupied by Boers with guns. This required a great deal of dash and determination, but it was done. The Boers were driven out and a gun captured by you, and whenever we met the enemy, and I knew the Shropshires were in front, I was certain of the best results. You are now going to Veseeniging where the Boers are reported to be threatening but not attacking. You have been specially selected for this, on account of your good work during the campaign, and I hope you will shortly join me again at Johannesburg. And lastly I must commend you on your good conduct and smartness, both in the field and camp, which has been everything desired. With regard to my own feelings I may add that whatever praise or credit I get is due to Colonel Spens and the Shropshires.

The following is a press cutting from the *Hereford Times*, dated May 1901:

THE DOINGS OF THE SHROPSHIRE VOLUNTEERS IN SOUTH AFRICA

Now that the men have returned, it will be interesting to quote what the commanding officers under whom they have served have said as to their conduct in the field, and also to give a brief summary of their doings.

Capt. N.A. Matthews, A Coy, 1 Bn HRVC, pictured in his full dress uniform, c. 1905.

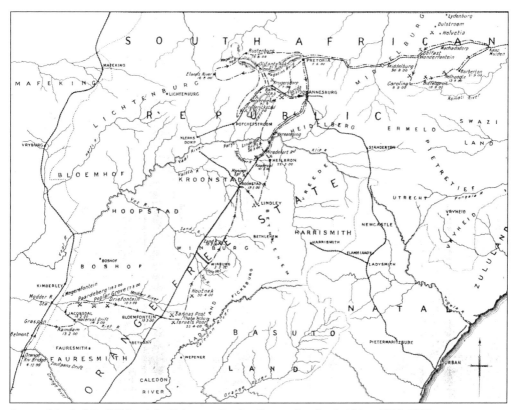

Route of the 2nd Bn KSLI and the Volunteer Service Companies, South Africa, 1900–1902.

At the commencement of June last, the 19th Brigade was made up of the Duke of Cornwall's L.I., the King's Shropshire L.I., the Gordon Highlanders, and the Canadian Infantry, and on the 5th of that month, the Brigade Orders contained the following: 'The 19th Brigade has achieved a record of which any infantry may be proud. Since it was formed on the 12th February, 1900, it marched 620 miles, often on half rations and seldom on full. It has taken part in the capture of 10 towns, fought in 10 general engagements, and on 27 other days. In one period of 30 days it fought on 21 of them, and marched 327 miles. Casualties between 400 and 500. Defeats nil. (By order), C.P. Higginson, Capt. and Adjt.'

Lieut.-Col. James Spens, commanding the 85th King's Shropshire Light Infantry, in his report of the Volunteer Company attached to his Battalion, after the period named, says: 'They [the Volunteers] accompanied the Battalion from Pretoria on 6th June, and whilst on outpost duty at Vredefort Weg on 10th June, were attacked by the enemy, and one man was slightly wounded by shrapnel. On 11th June, another engagement took place under Lord Methuen near Rhenoster Spruit. No casualties. On 14th June, at Rhenoster, General De Wet attacked the camp occupied by the Battalion, and the Volunteers acquitted themselves creditably in its defence. From Rhenoster, they were ordered to Katsbosch, on detachment duty, under Capt. W.S.W. Radcliffe, where they were attacked on 22nd June, 1900, being subjected to a heavy shell fire for six hours and a half, but having previously entrenched thoroughly, no losses were sustained by the Shropshire Light Infantry, although the Canadian Mounted Infantry lost two men killed, and one officer and three men wounded. The company next proceeded to Krugersdorp, taking part in a stiff engagement at Sterkfontein. On the 30th July, their strength was augmented by the arrival of Lieut. Harris-Edge, in charge of 20 non-commissioned officers and men, who joined at Fredericksstad, their arrival being marred by a railway accident to the train on which they were travelling, it having been wrecked by the Boers, three Volunteers were killed and four injured. The Company afterwards took part in forced marches under Lord Kitchener, covering 244 miles within a fortnight, in an abortive attempt to capture De Wet, and they eventually reached Pretoria for the second time on 25th August, 1900. They also marched from Belfast to Carolina, and formed part of General French's force operating from the latter place to Barberton. This ended the active part of their services with the Battalion, and it must be admitted by all ranks that each individual performed his arduous duties, marches and fatigues in a manner highly creditable to their country and themselves.'

Lieut.-Col. Spens adds: 'From the time the Volunteer Company joined my Battalion, it has shared equally with the other companies every duty which they have been called upon to perform, and whether in camp, on the march, or in action, it has come out of the campaign with "flying colours".'

The Ross men who have been under Lieut. Cutler, speak highly of the bravery which he always exhibited under fire, and Lieut. Col. Spens says of him 'that he has carried out his duties to my satisfaction'.

Most enthusiastic welcomes awaited members of 1st VSC on their return home, and in every town an official reception was arranged.

The chairman and members of the Kington Urban Council presented an illuminated address to the following volunteers from G Company of 1st HRVC:

Number	Rank	Name
7311	Col.-Sgt	Lewis, L.
7321	Pte	Cox, G.
7414	Pte	Taylor, A.
7334	Cpl	Lewis, J.
7323	Pte	Davies, E.
7329	Pte	Giles, J.

Pte G. Cox was in the leading section of 1st VSC on 27 May 1900 when 2nd Battalion KSLI marched to and crossed the Vaal River at Boschbank Drift, the Volunteer Company being given the honour of leading the battalion into the Transvaal. FM Lord Roberts of Kandahar VC, on noticing Cox's unusual Volunteer shoulder title, 'HF', asked what regiment he belonged to. Cox proudly replied: 'Herefordshires, Sir'. Pte Cox later acquired a pet monkey named Jacko at Barberton, which accompanied the Herefordshire detachment home. It was ultimately presented by Lt. Head to London Zoo.

The roll of honour of 1st VSC is displayed in the County Buildings, Shrewsbury. The nominal roll is reproduced in Appendix II.

1st VSC qualified for the award of the Queen's South African Medal with clasps for the following campaigns:

Cape Colony
Orange Free State
Johannesburg
South Africa 1901

A rapturous welcome awaited the 1st Bn Volunteer Service Company at Shrewsbury Station on their return from the Boer War, 10 May 1901.

The following is the roll of officers, NCOs and men of the HVRC present at the distribution of the South African War Medal at Shrewsbury on 19 October 1901:

Number	Rank	Name	Number	Rank	Name	Number	Rank	Name
	Lt	J.F. Cutler	7325	Pte	England, A.	7351	L/Cpl	Morgan, L.
7316	Pte	Adamson, P.D.	7326	Pte	Evans, A.	7349	Pte	O'Neil, W.
7404	Sgt	Badham, B.	7327	Pte	Farmer, E.	7335	Pte	Palfrey, D.
7317	Pte	Beavan, W.E.	7328	Pte	George, W.	7336	Pte	Powell, A.
7352	Bgr	Bethell, W.	7329	Pte	Giles, J.	7413	Pte	Price, J.
7344	Cpl	Brookes, E.	7330	Pte	Godsell, W.	7337	Pte	Price, S.
7318	Pte	Cheshire, C.	7312	Sgt	Griffin, F.	7338	Pte	Pyart, E.
7320	Pte	Corfield, C.	7345	Pte	Groves, C.	7339	Pte	Reeves, A.
7321	Pte	Cox, G.	7331	Pte	Hayward, W.	7340	Pte	Small, T.J.
7313	Cpl	Dalby, G.	7332	Pte	Howells, G.	7414	Pte	Taylor, A.
7409	Pte	Davies, C.	7333	Pte	Jenkins, G.	7341	Pte	Taylor, M.
7323	Pte	Davies, E.	7311	C/Sgt	Lewis, L.	7342	Pte	Williams, A.
7324	Pte	Drew, A.	7334	Pte	Lewis, J.	7343	Pte	Wynn, S.
7348	L/Cpl	Drew, G.						

The same men, with the addition of Maj. J.R.L. Rankin, who had served with Rimington's Guides, received the clasps from HRH The Princess Henry of Battenberg on Tuesday 13 May 1902.

2nd Volunteer Service Company

1st VSC having enlisted for one year, and this period being nearly completed, it was necessary to raise a second company to replace those who had gone to the front in 1900. The war fever had cooled down and it was not likely that there would be any important battles, and living in block-houses or moving about the country in small detached columns did not appeal to that martial spirit which was so much in evidence twelve months earlier.

1st and 2nd Volunteer Battalions KSLI and VSC 1st HRVC again each provided a detachment for 2nd KSLI, which was formed at Copthorne Barracks, Shrewsbury, in 1901. The company of 116 all ranks was commanded by Capt. B.W. Treasure (1st Volunteer Battalion KSLI) and the subalterns were Lt. Percy Anthony (1st HRVC), who commanded the Herefordshire detachment, and Lt. H. Mansell (1st Volunteer Battalion KSLI). 2nd VSC was stationed at Copthorne Barracks, Shrewsbury, but a large number were billeted in the town, including some at the Lion and Pheasant Inn, Wyle Cop, Shrewsbury.

The company was clothed in khaki service dress with slouch hats. Once trained, it sailed for South Africa in March 1901, and disembarked at Cape Town for duty with 2nd Battalion KSLI on 29 April 1901.

During this period a new type of warfare was introduced. Until then the battles had been fought with the object of occupying positions, but, now that the British Army was in possession of the whole railway system and most of the large towns, nothing was to be gained by driving the Boers from positions which it was not afterwards intended to hold. Success in the future was to be judged by the numbers of Boers killed or taken prisoner. 2nd VSC therefore spent its year of active service occupying sections of block-houses, escorting trains and guarding baggage. 2nd VSC left 2nd Battalion KSLI on 24 April 1902 and returned home on 4 June 1902.

2nd VSC left the battalion for England after a year's service in South Africa. The following letter was published by Maj. C.T. Dawkins CMG:

> On the occasion of the departure of the 2nd Vol Service Coy for England after a years service at the front, the C.O. wishes to place on record his high appreciation of the patriotic spirit shown by the members of the Coy in volunteering for Active Service at a time when the original excitement, raised by the war, had to a great extent subsided, and also of their excellent behaviour while attached to the 2nd Bn. The work which they have been called upon to do has been of a hard and uninteresting nature, but they have carried it out with credit to themselves and to the Regiment; and the C.O. desires to thank Captain Treasure and the Officers, NCOs and men of the Coy for the consistent support they have afforded him. In bidding the Coy goodbye the C.O. hopes the experience they have gained in the field will not be lost, and that the recollection of the days spent in South Africa will tend to strengthen the ties which bind together the various Line, Militia and Volunteer Battalions of the Counties of Shropshire and Herefordshire.

2nd VSC received a warm welcome on its return home, and the roll of honour of this company is also displayed in the County Buildings, Shrewsbury. A copy of the nominal roll is given in Appendix II.

2nd VSC qualified for the Queen's South Africa Medal with Clasps for the following campaigns:

Cape Colony
Orange Free State

Transvaal
South Africa 1901
South Africa 1902

The regimental South African War memorial is situated at St Chad's Terrace, Shrewsbury, on which the roll of honour of each battalion is displayed. The following relate to the Herefordshire Militia and the VSCs.

4th (Herefordshire Militia) Battalion KSLI

Rank   Name

Killed in action:
Pte   Goodwin, A.

Died of wounds or disease:
Pte   Gingell, A.
Pte   Mountain, D.
Pte   Russell, J.
Pte   Tinson, G.
Pte   Vicerage, W.
Pte   West, C.

1st Volunteer Battalion KSLI

Number	*Rank*	*Name*	*Company*
Died of wounds or disease:			
	Capt.	Trow, W.H.	1st VSC
7553	Pte	Beddall, J.	2nd VSC
7388	Pte	Giles, W.A.	1st VSC
7273	Pte	Maddox, W.	1st VSC

2nd Volunteer Battalion KSLI

Number	*Rank*	*Name*	*Company*
Killed in action:			
7370	Pte	Gough, W.T.	1st VSC
7363	Pte	Jones, H.	1st VSC
7358	Pte	Wright, J.	1st VSC
Died of wounds or disease:			
7023	Sgt Instr.	Lee, W.	1st VSC
7290	Pte	Connor, A.	(at sea) 1st VSC
7300	Pte	Kenyon, J.	1st VSC

1st Herefordshire Volunteer Battalion

Number	Rank	Name	Company
Died of wounds or disease:			
7589	Cpl	James, A.	2nd VSC
7315	Pte	Adams, E.A.	1st VSC
7347	Pte	Oakley, F.	1st VSC

At the end of 1904 the Regular Forces engaged in South Africa received permission to have additional distinctions recorded on their colours, and for the first time volunteers were accorded similar honours. The units of the Volunteer Force did not carry colours, so the words 'South Africa 1900–1902' were only emblazoned on the drums, badges and appointments.

The following is an extract from Army Orders dated 21 December 1904:

Army Order Special.
War Office, 21st December 1904.

The following instructions are promulgated to the Army.
Honorary Distinction.

His Majesty The King has been graciously pleased to approve of the following Corps of the Regular and Auxiliary Forces being permitted in recognition of services rendered during the South African War 1899–1902 to bear upon their Colours or appointments the words specified in each case [amongst other Battalions]:

1st Vol Bn King's Shropshire Light Infantry
2nd Vol Bn King's Shropshire Light Infantry
1st Herefordshire Rifle Volunteer Corps.

'South Africa 1900–02'

PART II: THE HEREFORDSHIRE REGIMENT (TF) 1908–19

CHAPTER 5

1st Battalion the Herefordshire Regiment, 1908–14

In 1905 the troops in Herefordshire came under the command of the headquarters at Chester and 53rd Regimental District at Shrewsbury. They consisted of the following:

Militia – 4th Battalion KSLI (Herefordshire Militia)
Volunteers – Welsh Border Brigade, comprising:
    1st Volunteer Battalion Royal Welch Fusiliers (RWF)
    2nd Volunteer Battalion RWF
    3rd Volunteer Battalion RWF
    1st Volunteer Battalion KSLI, Shrewsbury
    2nd Volunteer Battalion KSLI, Newport Salop
    1st Herefordshire (Hereford & Radnor) RV, Hereford
    Bearer Company RAMC, Hereford
    Army Service Company

The general anxiety as to the practical efficiency of the Auxiliary Forces of the Crown, the Imperial Yeomanry, the Militia and the Volunteer Force led to the appointment of a Royal Commission in 1904, known as the Norfolk Commission. Its terms of reference were to 'enquire into the organization, numbers and terms of service of our Militia and Volunteer Forces, and to report whether any, and if any what, changes are required in order to secure that their forces shall be maintained in a condition of military efficiency and at an adequate strength'.

The commission reported that the Volunteer Force fell short of the desired standard and recommended, *inter alia*, that the force should be organized in its war formation of brigades and divisions. In consequence of this recommendation, on 25 February 1907 Mr Haldane, Secretary of State for War, introduced the Territorial Reserve Forces Bill, which became law in the Territorial and Reserve Forces Act of 1907 (7 Edward VII c9).

Under the authority of this Act, the Militia ceased to be raised in the United Kingdom. The greater number of the existing units were converted to units of the newly constituted Special Reserve and the remainder were disbanded. It has already been recorded that 4th Battalion KSLI (Herefordshire Militia) was disbanded on 13 April 1908 in consequence of this Act.

The Imperial Yeomanry and Volunteer Force ceased to be raised as such, and the existing units were transferred to the newly created Territorial Force.

On 1 April 1908 the HVRC (Hereford & Radnor) became the Herefordshire Battalion KSLI, but four months later the title was again changed to 1st Battalion the Herefordshire Regiment, which, while remaining within the corps of the KSLI, had separate mention in the Army List.

The Herefordshire Regiment thus became one of the four 'County regiments' of the Territorial Force, the others being the Monmouthshire, Cambridgeshire and Hertfordshire regiments.

At the date of conversion, 1st HVRC comprised eleven companies, with a numerical establishment, inclusive of enrolled members of the Hereford Cathedral School Cadet Corps, of 1,280, and a strength of 1,029. Nine of the eleven companies underwent such compression as was necessary to transform them into the eight companies authorized for the Territorial Force Battalion, while the cadet company severed its connection and became an officers' training corps. The eleventh company, E Company (Weobley), was transformed into the headquarters company of the Welsh Divisional Transport and Supply Column, Army Service Corps.

The organization of the new battalion was as undernoted, and after belonging to the 'army troops' attached to the division it later formed part of the Welsh Border Brigade of 53 (Welsh) Division:

Battalion headquarters	Harold St, Hereford
Honorary colonel	Col. Heywood, T. VD
Lieutenant-colonel	Lt-Col. Scobie, M.J.G. VD
Majors	Maj. Rankin, J.R.L.
	Maj. Gilbert-Harris, J.H.
Captains	Wood-Roe, W.B.
	Carless, W.T.
	Matthews, N.H.
	Mortlock, H.
	Boulton, A.H.
	Pope, A.W.W.
Lieutenants	Anthony, E.A.
	Capel, E.A.
	Giles, P.B.
	Smith, H.J.C.
	Porter, T.H.
	Edwards, D.L.I.
	Yates, R.G.
	Greenly, J.H.M.
	Lester, F.
	Hughes, H.
	Cazalet, G.L.
	Holman, A.V.
Adjutant	Capt. Stanton, R.W.S. KOYLI
Quartermaster	Capt. Phillips, W.J.
Medical officers	Capt. MacMullan, J.N. RAMC
	Lt. Green, A.L.B. RAMC

New company	Headquarters	Old Company	Old Corps
A	Hereford	A	1st
B	Ross	B	2nd
C	Ledbury	C	3rd
D	Kington and Presteign	G & J	7th & 1st regiments
E	Ruardean	M	
F	Leominster and Bromyard	F & D	6th & 4th regiments
G	Radnorshire (Rhayader & Knighton)	K	2nd Regiment
H	Hereford	H	8th

1st HVRC was the parent of three distinct territorial units: the Herefordshire Regiment, the Headquarters Company of the Welsh Divisional Transport and Supply Column ASC and The South Wales Mounted Brigade Field Ambulance RAMC. Reference was made in Chapter 3 to the singularly efficient Bearer Company, originally part of 1st HVRC, which later became the Welsh Border Bearer Company RAMC (Volunteers), and which in 1908 became the South Wales Mounted Brigade Field Ambulance. Mention has already been made in this chapter to the fact that the Weobley Company (which had acted as the 'Transport Company' in the volunteer brigade) was converted in 1908 to the Headquarters Company of the Welsh Divisional Transport and Supply Column ASC. The commanding officer of the column was Lt-Col. T.P.B. Giles, and Maj. F.H. Leather was in command of the Headquarters Company stationed at Weobley. The Honorary Colonel was Sir J.R.G. Cotterell Bt.

The new regiment was proud of its rich martial heritage and jealously sought to retain the former traditions. Permission was obtained to adopt the grass-green facings of the old 36th Herefordshire Regiment of Foot, which had become 2nd Battalion the Worcestershire Regiment in 1881, and to wear gold lace and brass appointments. The old Herefordshire Militia, which as 4th Battalion KSLI had been disbanded on 13 April 1908, was kept in remembrance by the adoption by the officers of buttons bearing the old Militia badge (a sprig of apple), while the collar badge was that of the Volunteers: the Herefordshire lion.

In view of the fact that the motto, 'Firm', of the old 36th Foot had been adopted by the Worcestershire Regiment in 1881, the Herefordshire Regiment (Territorial Force) obtained permission from HM King Edward VII to adopt the motto *Manu forti* ('with a firm hand'). This is the motto of the Clan Mackay to which the then commanding officer Lt-Col. J.G. Scobie VD belonged. The motto was shared with the East Coast Battalion of the Auxiliary Force India until partition in 1947. This battalion was descended from the Godavari Rifle Volunteers and the Vizagapatam Rifle Volunteers, raised in 1885.

The regiment chose as its march 'The Lincolnshire poacher', a traditional country tune based on the Lincolnshire folk song of the same name. This march is also the regimental march of the Royal Lincolnshire Regiment, and it had been used by 36th Foot. By General Order of 6 April 1744, Lincolnshire, Leicestershire and Bedfordshire comprised the regiment's recruiting areas prior to its becoming 36th Herefordshire Regiment in 1782.

The king's and regimental colours were provided by the ladies of the counties of Hereford and Radnor, and were presented by King Edward VII at Windsor on 19 June 1909. The officers of the colour party were 2/Lt. E.A. Capel and 2/Lt. R.G. Yates. It will be appreciated that prior to 1947 the colours of territorial battalions were not provided from public funds. The colours were as follows:

The king's colour
The Great Union Flag is in silk, in the centre of the St George's Cross the Territorial designation of the regiment, 'The Herefordshire Regiment' on a crimson circle, with the battalion numeral 'I' within, the whole ensigned with the imperial crown.

The regimental colour
This flag comprises a field of green silk (being the colour of the facings of the regiment), in the upper canton the battalion numeral 'I', in the centre of the colour on a crimson ground the regimental badge, 'a lion passant guardant holding in the dexter paw a sword', within a crimson circle inscribed 'The Herefordshire Regiment', all within a union wreath of roses, thistles and shamrocks and ensigned with the imperial crown. The motto *Manu forti* is on a scroll placed across the tie of the union wreath, and below all is a scroll inscribed 'South Africa 1900–02'.

The colours of the Herefordshire Regiment, presented on 19 June 1909.

The size of the colours is approximately 3 feet 9 inches in width and 3 feet deep on the pike, exclusive of the fringe. The battle honour 'South Africa 1900–02' borne by right of the parent Volunteer Battalion and was won by the Herefordshire detachments of 1st and 2nd VSCs, as recorded in Chapter 4.

These colours are still in service with 1st Battalion the Herefordshire Light Infantry. (Following the First World War, ten out of the regiment's sixteen battle honours were emblazoned on the horizontal arms of the Cross of St George. A further ten of the regiment's sixteen battle honours awarded for the Second World War have been emblazoned since.)

These colours were authorized for 1st Battalion the Herefordshire Regiment in accordance with War Office Memo 100 of 3 September 1908. The drawings were prepared by the Heralds College on 10 May 1909 and approved by the AD Dress & Clothing Quartermaster-general at the War Office on 11 May 1909. Copies of the coloured drawings are displayed in the TA Centre, Harold Street, Hereford. The Inspector of Regimental Colours was then Sir Henry Farnham Burke KCVO CB, then Somerset Herald and later Garter King of Arms.

At this stage in the historical records it is necessary to mention the territorial associations, which, as an intrinsic part of the 1908 organization, have played, and continue to play, such an important part in the life of the regiment. In fact, under the authority of the Territorial and Reserve Forces Act of 1907, the County associations were established to raise and administer, but not to command, the Territorial Force.

The Territorial Force associations of the counties of Hereford and Radnor administered the following units:

Hereford:
1st Battalion the Herefordshire Regiment (headquarters and seven companies)
Welsh Divisional Headquarters Company, Transport and Supply Column ASC
South Wales Mounted Brigade Field Ambulance RAMC

Radnor:
D Squadron the Montgomeryshire Yeomanry
G Company (Knighton & Rhayader) the Herefordshire Regiment

The object of the Territorial associations was to foster and maintain the territorial concept of the Haldane Reforms, and it was intended that each association would consist, *inter alia*, of a committee of commanding officers of the Auxiliary Forces concerned, together with the district brigadier general, who would furnish the necessary link between the Territorial Force and the general staff. Furthermore, each association would appoint a secretary, and the lord lieutenant of the county would act as president, thereby ensuring a continuity in the traditional responsibility of the lord lieutenant for the military administration of the county. (It will be remembered that by the Regulation of the Forces Act of 1871 the lord lieutenant was dispossessed of much of this responsibility.)

The Auxiliary Air Force and Air Force Reserve Act of 1924 (14 and 15 Geo V C15) modified the Act of 1907 and permitted, *inter alia*, the formation of county joint associations to perform the duties of associations under the Act of 1907, as regards both the Territorial Army and the Auxiliary Air Force.

Hereford Territorial Force Association

Chairmen:

Col. Middleton, D.R.	1908–1919
Col. Scobie, M.J.G. CB TD VD	1919–1929
Col. Pateshall, H.E.P. CB DSO TD DL	1929–1947
Col. Tomlinson, S.C.	1947–1949
Brig. Carver, R.T. TD	1949–1955
Brig. Copland-Griffiths, F.A.V. DSO MC	1955–1960
Maj. Singleton, G.M. MC TD DL	1960–1967

Secretaries:

Col. Wood, C.K. OBE	1908–1922
Lt-Col. Henry, V. CB	1922–1931
Lt-Col. Ffrench, K. MC DL JP	1931–1945
Maj.-Gen. Gattie, K.F.D. DSO MC	1945–1950
Lt-Col. Hope, J.W. OBE	1950–1967

Radnor Territorial Force Association (after 1920 no longer connected with Herefordshire)

Chairman:	
Coltman-Rogers, C. (Lord Lieutenant)	1908–1929
Secretary:	
Capt. Shrimpton, S.N.	1908–1944

1st Bn Herefordshire Regiment on parade at Bow Street Camp in 1910.

1st Battalion the Herefordshire Regiment carried out a 'counties march' in 1908 to attract recruits. This was most successful and by 1911 the battalion strength was 900 out of an establishment of 1,009.

In 1909 a circular announced the proposed formation of a Territorial Reserve, a Technical Reserve and a Veteran Reserve. The formation of these auxiliary organizations commenced the following year. With the exception of the Veteran Reserve, they did not attain great strength, but the Veteran Reserve under the revised title of the National Reserve reached a strength of 5,464 officers and 185,372 other ranks by 1 January 1913. It was not intended that the National Reserve should form a 'last stand' third line army, but its members undertook to maintain their military efficiency in time of peace and to be prepared to rejoin the colours on mobilization. The national Reserve was well supported in Herefordshire. In 1910 Lt-Col. Sir J.R.L. Rankin assumed command of the battalion, and he was followed in 1912 by Lt-Col. J.H. Gilbert-Harris.

By 1913 1st Battalion the Herefordshire Regiment was well established and the following extract from the register of the Welsh Border Infantry Brigade is of interest:

1st Battalion the Herefordshire Regiment

Honours	South Africa 1900–02
Motto	*Manu Forti* (with a strong hand)
Uniform	Scarlet, facings grass green
Headquarters	The Barracks, Hereford
Honorary colonel	Col. Heywood, T. VD
Lieutenant-Colonel commanding	Lt-Col. Gilbert-Harris, J.H.

Majors		Maj. Wood-Roe, W.B.	
		Maj. Carless, W.T.	
Adjutant		Capt. Legge, R.G. Lieutenant in the Devon Regiment	
Quartermaster		Hon. Lt. and Qmr Morgan, A.	
Instructor of musketry			
Officer in charge machine-gun section			
Signalling officer			
Officer in charge scouts		Capt. Holman, A.V.	
Transport officer			
Medical officer		Capt. MacMullan, J.N. RAMC TF (att'd)	

Company	Headquarters	Commander	Subaltern(s)	Sgt Instr(s)
A	Hereford		Lt. Capel, E.A.	Act-Sgt-Maj.
			Lt. Wallis, O.B.	Roberts, R.
B	Ross	Capt. Yates, R.G.	Lt. Nott, F.T.	Col.-Sgt Barrett, J.
C	Ledbury	Capt. Holman, A.V.	Lt. Hughes, H.	Sgt Barnham, J.H.
D	Kington		Lt. Greenly, J.H.M.	Col.-Sgt Bartram
E	Ruardean	Capt. Green, A.L.B.	2/Lt. Sale, R.C.	Col.-Sgt Jones, W.
F	Leominster	Capt. Cowling, C.H.	Lt. Speer, F.A.	Col.-Sgt Herbert, W.
G	Rhayader		Lt. Rogers, E.T.P.	Sgt Evans, J.
	Knighton		2/Lt. Barker, F.G.	Sgt Blakie, A.
H	Hereford		Lt. Bailey, R.E.H.	
			2/Lt. Smith, M.V.	

Twenty bandsmen of the 1st Bn Herefordshire Regiment pose for the photographer in 1912.

*The 1st/1st Bn the Herefordshire Regiment led on horseback by their commanding officer Lt-Col.
G. Drage, march through the streets of Newmarket in Suffolk, August 1915.*

Seconded officers	Capt. Boulton, A.H.
	2/Lt. Giles, P.B. OTC
Chaplains	
Acting sergeant-major	Col.-Sgt Instr Roberts, R.
Quartermaster-sergeant	Qmr Sgt Moore, W.
Bandmaster	Wheeler, W.H.
Regimental call	

The original Territorial Force was intended for home service only, but although the Act of 1907 stipulated that the force should not be ordered to go out of the United Kingdom, it provided that members could offer to serve in any place outside the United Kingdom. Members undertaking to serve abroad or to be called out for military service within the United Kingdom, whether the Territorial Force as a whole was embodied or not, were distinguished at first by the Special Service Section badge and later by the Imperial Service Bar, worn above the right breast pocket of the service dress tunic.

During the First World War, nearly all of the units of the Territorial Force volunteered for service overseas. 1st Battalion the Herefordshire Regiment was among the first to volunteer and was mobilized on 5 August 1914.

The history of the Herefordshire Regiment during the First World War is recorded in chapters 7 to 11, wherein an account is given of the original 1st Battalion, known as 1st/1st Battalion the Herefordshire Regiment, as well as the second and third line territorial battalions, known as 2nd/1st and 3rd/1st Battalions the Herefordshire Regiment.

The four-company reorganization of the infantry introduced in 1915 caused an amalgamation of the eight old companies of 1st Battalion and to a degree marked the end of the parochial rifle corps tradition in the battalion.

CHAPTER 6

1st Battalion the Herefordshire Regiment, 1914–19

The 1st Battalion the Herefordshire Regiment, commanded by Lt-Col. G. Drage, mobilized with 158 Infantry Brigade of 53 (Welsh) Division on 5 August 1914. It proceeded to Pembroke Dock, and after serving in home defence at Oswestry, Northampton, Colchester and Rusden embarked with 53 Division from Devonport on 16 July 1915 to join the Mediterranean Expeditionary Force.

On 9 August 1915 the regiment took part in the landing at Suvla Bay and remained on the Gallipoli Peninsula until 12 December 1915. It was specially mentioned by name in Sir Ian Hamilton's despatches: 'they attacked with impetuosity and courage between Hetman Chair and Kaslar Chair, about Azmak Dere on the extreme right of the line'. This incident is depicted in a painting which for some years hung on the wall of the stairway of the Shirehall in Hereford, and which is now in the possession of the regiment.

The regiment served in Egypt in 1916, where it took a prominent part in the Battle of Rumani. In February 1917 it reached El Arish and prepared for the advance into Palestine. On 26 March 1917 it fought in the First Battle of Gaza and in the assault on Ali Muntar. It served in the Second and Third Battles of Gaza and distinguished itself at Beersheba and Khuweilfeh. It took part in the advance to Jerusalem, and in December 1917 stormed the villages of Anata and Khamlit. In the ensuing Battle of Tell Asur, in March, it greatly distinguished itself at Drage Hill and Chipp Hill (named after the commanding officer and the adjutant respectively).

On 19 June 1918 the battalion left the Egyptian Expeditionary Force and embarked for France, where it joined 102 Brigade of 34 Division. Before leaving for France the officers of 3rd, 6th and 7th Battalions Royal Welch Fusiliers presented the officers of the regiment with a silver statuette, known as the Palestine Soldier, 'in token of esteem and good fellowship after four years active service together during the Great War'. This statuette holds the place of honour among the Officers' Mess silver.

In July 1918 34 Division was engaged in exceptionally heavy fighting in the Soissons–Chateau Thierry area during the great counter-offensive against the Germans. The battalion distinguished itself greatly in these actions. On 14, 15 and 16 October 1918 it took part in the continuous fighting on the outskirts of Menin. The battalion received a special letter from the brigade commander: 'Congratulations to you and all ranks of your splendid Battalion for the excellent work done during the three days fighting.'

From 23 to 25 October the battalion was fighting continuously near Moen. On 11 November, hostilities ceased and the battalion was selected for the army of occupation. In January 1919 it moved to Siegburg near Bonn on the Rhine, where it was reduced to a cadre, and after returning home it was disembodied in Hereford on 24 May 1919.

Casualties

27 officers killed
46 officers wounded

The 1st/1st Bn The Herefordshire Regiment at Suvla Bay, Gallipoli, 9 August 1915. (From the painting by Charles Dixon)

495 other ranks killed
974 other ranks wounded

Battle honours

For services in the First World War the following battle honours were awarded.

Marne 1918	Gallipoli 1915
* Soissonnais-Ourcq	* Rumani
* Ypres 1918	Egypt 1916–17
* Courtrai	* Gaza
* France and Flanders 1918	* El Mughar
Suvla	* Jerusalem
* Landing at Suvla	* Tell Asur
Scimitar Hill	Palestine 1917–18

* Battle honours emblazoned on the Queen's colour

Campaign medals

1914–1915 Star
British War Medal (1914–1920)
Allied Victory Medal (1914–1918)

In addition, members of the battalion who were ineligible for the 1914–1915 Star, but who had belonged to the Territorial Force on 4 August 1914 or had completed four years' service before 4 August 1914 and had rejoined on or prior to 30 September 1914, qualified for the Territorial Force War Medal (1914–1919), provided that they had undertaken on or before 30 September 1914 to serve outside the United Kingdom and served outside the United Kingdom between 4 August 1914 and midnight 11/12 November 1918.

CHAPTER 7

Chronicle of the War Services 1st/1st Battalion the Herefordshire Regiment, 1914–15 – Gallipoli

1914 – April 1915

The battalion mobilized at Hereford on 5 August 1914 and the next day proceeded by train to Pembroke Dock. After a few days it moved, together with the rest of the brigade, to Oswestry, where war training began.

When mobilized, the battalion was somewhat short of its establishment, and Capt. F.T. Carver, who had been appointed adjutant of the depot prior to the formation of 2nd Battalion, was instructed to try to get some recruits. After seeing the battalion off, Carver returned to the drill hall at about 9.00 p.m. Not a soul was about other than John Bethall, the caretaker. Half an hour later there was a loud hammering on the door and, on going to investigate, Carver found more splendid youngsters outside, all clamouring to enlist. Such was the enthusiasm throughout the town.

There was nothing in the drill hall – no forms, and not even a pen or ink – but after a hectic rush round to the barracks and his office, Carver obtained these, and with the help of a couple of men who had been clerks, nominal rolls were made out. By midnight all had been enlisted. Thus it went on from day to day, so that in the next fortnight four hundred men had been enlisted and fitted out for 1st Battalion the Herefordshire Regiment.

On 31 August the battalion moved to Northampton, where 53 Division was concentrated, and training continued till 1 November, when it moved to Suffolk and was put to work entrenching the east coast. Four days later it returned to Northampton with the remainder of the brigade, with a view to being clothed and equipped for service in India, but this order was cancelled on the 30th and the battalion instead went to Bury St Edmunds with 1st and 3rd Monmouths to continue entrenching.

Numerous changes had been taking place among the battalions of the division, many of which had been sent either to France or to the East, and on 19 April 1915 the division was reorganized and the Herefords were transferred to the North Wales Brigade (158th).

Gallipoli, 1915

By July the division was ready to proceed overseas, and on 3 July orders were received to prepare for service in the Mediterranean. The battalion embarked at Devonport on the S.S. *Euripides* on 16 July. It was then under the command of Lt-Col. Drage, and its embarkation strength was 29 officers and 969 other ranks.

The convoy, which consisted of eight ships, sailed on 16 July, entered the Mediterranean on the night of 21/22 July and proceeded to Alexandria. Here the base details and all of the first line transport were disembarked, and the ship then went on to Port Said, where the battalion was reduced to an establishment of 25 officers and 750 other ranks, Capt. G. Barker, 2/Lt. M.H. Lloyd and 103 other ranks proceeding to Alexandria by rail.

The ultimate destination of the convoy had been kept secret, but there was little doubt as to what it was, as the Dardenelles had been the storm centre of that part of the world for months.

Suvla Bay, 1915

The original landings had taken place at the point of the peninsula and all were now held up. Sir Ian Hamilton's plan was to make a new landing at Suvla Bay and so cut the 'waist' of the peninsula, and this operation was destined to commence on 6 August 1915. On 7 August the convoy conveying the division reached Mudros, but on entering the harbour the SS *Euripides* grounded on the edge of a reef and all personnel on board were transferred to the SS *Snaefell*. This left for Imros on the next day and at once proceeded to 'A' beach, where the battalion was transferred to trawlers, from which it landed on 'C' beach at 7.20 a.m. on the 9th.

It must be remembered that the divisional artillery had been left behind in England, under orders for France. Further, the division had no wheels and no horses, so the supply situation was very difficult. This was further complicated by the fact that the division was scattered in all directions on being landed, no less than seven battalions being sent straight off to support different formations of 10 and 11 Divisions.

The battalion had only been ashore for a few hours when Lt-Col. Drage was sent for by the brigade commander, who told him that Col. Bosanquet of the Sherwood Foresters was anxious about his right flank, near Kaslar Chair, in front of which ran the dry watercourse of Azmak Dere. He said: 'I don't think you will have much to do, or will get a dusting. Get away as quickly as possible.'

Lt-Col. Drage left divisional headquarters knowing nothing of the position of the enemy, and practically nothing of that of the troops he had to get in touch with. He subsequently said:

> I do not know whether I was singularly stupid or unfortunate, but I had never been told anything about the Anzac position, and the troops on the left of that position. This was regrettable, as I now know the Herefords were on the extreme right of the IX Corps, and should have been in touch, if possible, with Anzac. I can say with certainty that, bar the vague position of the Sherwood Foresters, no information as to the operations and plan of action was mentioned, and no information was given as to what our side was trying to do.

The Herefords moved off by half battalions at about 4.30 p.m. Maj. Carless led with B and C Companies, and as soon as they topped the shoulder of Lala Baba they came under artillery fire. The two leading companies extended and ploughed their way across rough ground which, for the most part, was covered with brushwood. After advancing for more than a mile, some wounded men directed them, and they turned half left and eventually got in touch with the Sherwood Foresters who were considerably more to the east than expected. The last part of the journey was completed under hot rifle fire, and by short rushes in the approved 'Newmarket' style.

For their part in the landing at Suvla Bay on 9 August 1915, the battalion was mentioned in despatches by Gen. Sir Ian Hamilton, the Commander-in-Chief, who reported as follows:

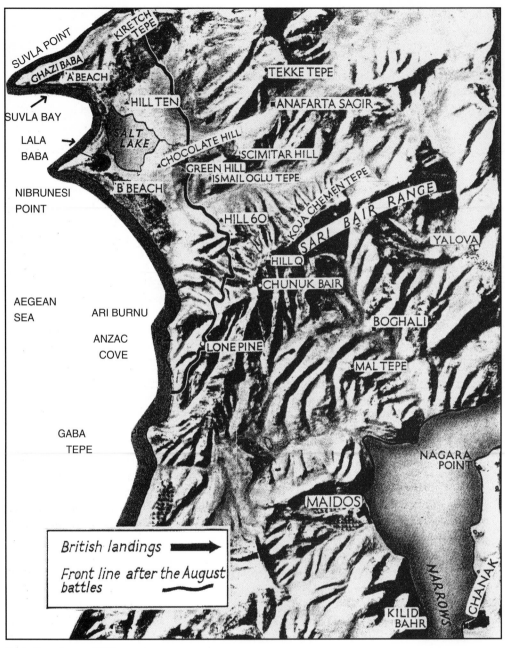

Suvla Bay, August 1915.

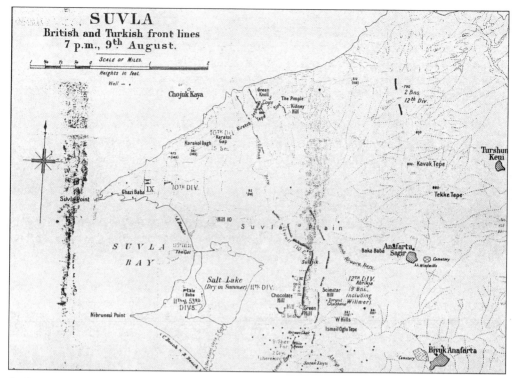

Suvla Bay, August 1915.

Some of the units which took part in this engagement acquitted themselves very bravely. I regret I have not had sufficient detail given me to enable me to mention them by name. The Divisional Commander speaks with appreciation of one freshly landed Battalion of the 53rd (Welsh) Division, a Hereford Battalion, presumably the 1/1st Herefordshire, which attacked with impetuosity and courage between Hetman Chair and Kaslar Chair about Azmak Dere on the extreme right of his line.

Lt-Col. Drage, in the meanwhile, kept on the line given him and lost touch with his second-in-command:

It became increasingly difficult, owing to the dust raised by the enemy's shrapnel, and the nature of the terrain, to see anything to the flank as we approached the Azmak Dere . . . We now came to a dried up water course with steep little banks about two feet high. This was the Azmak Dere, and I think we crossed it exactly between K and D as ordered.

We pushed on and eventually reached a low hill covered with scrub, to our immediate front . . . The position of the two second line Companies was now at the foot of Damakjwlik Bair . . . The Company Commanders, Rogers and Capel, came to me for orders. I was in a quandary and confess I did not know what to do. I had lost touch with my two leading Companies. In front of me was a jungle with, according to the map, an extremely difficult line of country at the back of it. No knowledge of the enemy's position and a very vague idea of our troops on the left. It also seemed to me that I was 1000 yards in front of where I was told I might get in touch with our own side. (I now know that Captain Green had sent a runner back from the leading Companies stating that they had met the Sherwood Foresters, who put them right as to the position of their Battalion). I decided to withdraw the supports to the Azmak Dere, whose left bank afforded two feet of cover in places, and a fairly open field of fire.

While discussing the situation with his officers, a shell burst over their heads and Lt-Col. Drage, Capt. Yates, Capt. Capel, Capt. Nott and Lt. Bourne were all wounded. Nevertheless, Lt-Col. Drage carried on, succeeded in closing up his two companies and commenced to withdraw.

Before he reached the sheltering bank of the Azmak Dere, Drage saw a horseman approaching him at a gallop and waving his hand. 'This was a Staff Officer from the 53rd Division with a paper in his hand. He did not deliver it to me, but told me I was to return to Lala Baba.' The object of this order is wrapped in mystery. Having contacted Maj. Carless, Lt-Col. Drage withdrew his battalion to Lala Baba only to be ordered to report to the Sherwood Foresters again on the following morning. The commanding officer having been taken to hospital, the battalion moved off after an early breakfast and returned to the left flank, where it stayed in support of the Sherwood Foresters till 12 August, when it rejoined its own brigade.

By the evening of 9 August the abortive attempt to cut the 'waist' of the peninsula had failed, due to bad staff work, the lack of enterprise and leadership displayed, and a hopeless inertia which seemed to prevail among all commanders. At the start only 2000 rifles, 3 field guns and 2 mountain batteries opposed Gen. Stopford's two divisions, and at times success was so near that individuals could be named who had it in their grasp, and with nothing to oppose them.

Sir Ian Hamilton issued orders to suspend operations, and on the receipt of these orders the corps commander reorganized his line into three sectors, allotting one to each division, the 53rd being in the centre. There then followed a period of trench warfare which was made wearisome by the heat and flies, while dysentery, which had first made its appearance at Mudros, and jaundice both rapidly spread and became very serious – sick casualties rose in appalling numbers.

From 12 to 20 August the battalion was busily engaged in constructing defences and erecting wire. On the latter date, Lt-Col. Rome arrived and took over command, but he only remained until the 29th.

At the end of the month, Brig.-Gen. Mott paid his first visit to the battalion after assuming command of the brigade. The commanding officer had not yet returned from hospital; Major Holman was in command, and the following story is told about him. The scene was in a cow-house just behind the front line. Everyone was very tired and the news had just come that the new brigadier would visit battalion headquarters after dark. He arrived at 9.00 p.m. The commanding officer was fast asleep, and his adjutant seized him by the shoulder, shook him violently and shouted in his ear that the brigadier had arrived. Lifting his head for a moment, Maj. Holman opened one eye to gaze rudely at the disturber of his slumber and murmured: 'Tell them to go for a row round the bay.' His head fell back and he appeared to be asleep again. Suddenly, however, in response to renewed shaking and pinching, he leapt to his feet and said: 'Good evening, Sir, I am glad to see you here', just as if nothing had happened.

The battalion remained in the same sector until 21 September, and throughout this period work went on unceasingly on the defences. This was very strenuous, as much rock was encountered. The remainder of the brigade had been relieved a few days earlier and it was not until the 25th that the battalion rejoined it at Karakol Dagh. The brigade was fortunate in being

The 1st Hereford Regiment

Imperishable Glory won at Suvla Bay.

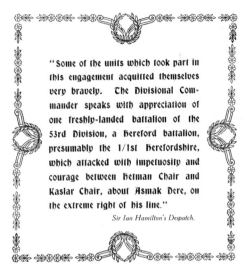

"Some of the units which took part in this engagement acquitted themselves very bravely. The Divisional Commander speaks with appreciation of one freshly-landed battalion of the 53rd Division, a Hereford battalion, presumably the 1/1st Herefordshire, which attacked with impetuosity and courage between Hetman Chair and Kaslar Chair, about Asmak Dere, on the extreme right of his line."

Sir Ian Hamilton's Despatch.

AUGUST, 1915.

For their part in the landings at Suvla Bay opening the ill-fated Gallipoli campaign on 9 August 1915, the 1st/1st Bn The Herefordshire Regiment was mentioned in despatches by the Commander-in-Chief, Sir Ian Hamilton.

allocated to this camp as the remainder of the division was at Lala Baba, a most unpleasant and unsanitary site. The brigade, which was on the seaward slope of Karakol Dagh, was employed in providing fatigues for beach duty.

The actual camping ground was on the North Western slopes of Karakol Dagh. There were no tents or hutments and men lived in the open on the bare hillside. The ground sloped steeply from the crest of the ridge until it fell away into the sea in a precipice which you could only climb down in certain places, and then with great difficulty. On the other side of the crest you got a most excellent view of the Bay, with 'A' beach lying almost beneath you, then 'B' beach with its hospital tents and then Lala Baba, with the Salt Lake on the left, stretching away to Nebrunesi Point. 'C' Beach was hidden from view, but Anzac stood out with its bold heights and beach resting at the foot of the hills; and away in the distance was Achi Baba and Cape Helles. On the left of the panorama we had an excellent view of the plain, Anafarta Ova, as it was called on the maps, and the village of Anafarta Sagir just on the foothills. In the distance was the ring of hills from which the Turks could see you blowing your nose on the beach, and which we longed to climb, but never did. Across the sea to the West, you could see Imbros, looking so peaceful, and which was Army Headquarters ... We had a fairly good rest in this camp, but some of the fatigues were heavy, particularly the water fatigue. Water had to be carried by hand from 'A' beach twice a day in petrol tins, and as it was a long and steep climb up, it was not at all a popular event. The morning party used to leave about 4 a.m. Another unpopular fatigue was the construction party for the new

Corps Headquarters. I never saw them, but heard it was a wonderful place, cut out of the solid rock, with fireplaces etc., and it was about the only place on Suvla Bay that a shell could not hit.

A good description of work on the beaches is given by Revd H.S.F. Williams, who said:

The area is tightly packed with mules, horses and men; streets and lanes of boxes piled 15 to 20 feet high; barges and lighters unloading at roughly thrown-out jetties; pyramids of baggage, mountains of forage; above all the din and noise a faint moaning is heard, growing rapidly louder and deeper – thud – bang – and up goes a column of dust and debris. The air clears, heads bob up, and where there had been a pile of biscuit boxes there remains a shell crater, with a litter of scrap tin, matchwood etc., and the work goes on.

In the middle of October the weather changed: heavy rains with very cold winds set in, and life was generally very unpleasant.

The last phase of the Suvla Bay operation may be said to have commenced on 31 October, when 158 Infantry Brigade was attached to 2 Mounted Brigade. They were on the right of the line, and on 26 November the battalion was holding some trenches which ran into the Azmak Dere, not far from the scene of its first adventures after landing. The bed of the Dere had been barricaded by both the Turks and the British. Rain had set in, but as yet it was not very cold, and there was a thunderstorm. Beyond the misery of being wet, no one expected anything to happen. Suddenly a torrent swept down the dry watercourses, and filled the trenches waist deep with water and slimy black mud. Apparently the Turkish barricade had held up the water that drained from the hills into the Dere until it gave way under the pressure, and the pent-up force burst through everything it met. Some guns, comfortably sited in the stony bed, were immediately submerged, with nothing but the sights to be seen.

The scene is well described by Capt. Peter Ashton in his diary, from which several extracts are given. He served with the battalion on the peninsula, but was at brigade headquarters while in Palestine.

The other diary quoted from belonged to Maj. H.E.P. Pateshall, also an officer of the battalion, but he served the whole time at divisional headquarters. Ashton wrote:

I was in my little dug-out, opening out of the rear line trench, and found the trench getting rather puddly, as I only had a waterproof sheet roof. I remember I had a sort of doorstep to prevent paper and rubbish blowing in, about a foot high, the floor level of the dug-out being the same as the trench. Suddenly, without warning, my doorstep entirely dissolved, and a brown flood poured in. The water rose as you watched, until it was about 3½ feet deep, and then stopped. As I didn't want to drown, I struggled out of the trench, and met the C.O. emerging from next door where the same thing had happened. It was quite obvious what had occurred. The very heavy rain, probably still heavier back in the hills, poured down from the high ground behind the Turks till it got caught up behind their barricade. This, presumably, had held until there was a respectable weight of water behind it, when it collapsed and the whole tearing flood came rushing down at ours. It didn't gather or pause for the twinkling of an eye at ours, it simply swept it away as if it hadn't been there, and swept on to the sea, a solid river, 20 yards broad and 8 or 9 feet deep. All our trenches opened out of the Dere, and though their floor level was higher than the bottom of the stream, they were still deep enough to take in about 4 feet of water. As the ground sloped slightly upwards towards the front line, the rear lines were the worst.

Our first consideration being the front line, I at once started off to see if it were still there . . . I went on till I got to the support line, about half way up it. As I couldn't cope with about 3 feet of rapidly flowing water any longer, I got on to the top and reached the front line.

There I found they had only about 18 inches of water, and though the first onrush had washed away a good deal of kit and some rifles, there was nothing much the matter. After talking to Barker for a bit, I determined to get across to the other side, where we had two vital machine guns. It wasn't possible to cross anywhere near the front line, so I went down-stream about 300 yards, to wade at a pebbly place I remembered, and managed to get across. The water was about waist deep and running very strong.

The RE's two wooden bridges had absolutely disappeared. On my way downstream I heard something snorting and blowing in the dark in the water, and I found it came from a little Turkish ammunition pony, which had come downstream and got caught in a bush. I put two men on to get him out, and he continued his career in the British Army.

When I got across I walked overland to the front line, and found our two precious guns intact. It had now stopped raining, and the Dere was running down fast.

It was then about 10 p.m. All the troops had got out of the trenches and were wandering about 'on top', but the Turks were doing the same and not a shot was fired. The night passed and it was not too bad as regards cold. A general drop in temperature had occurred some days before, with occasional cold winds, but this night was not so cold. About 6, however, the wind changed, and it began to freeze, and continued all through the next day. The rations were got up somehow during the night with the loss of one cart stuck in the mud, and all were distributed early the next morning.

At about 9 p.m. The Fife and Forfar Regiment came up to relieve the Battalion, and received the distressing intelligence that they would have to bivouac among the open sand dunes about Lala Baba. It was blowing hard, and snowing – a regular blizzard.

Ashton continued:

Men were pretty badly knocked about by now, as we hadn't had much food all day, on top of the previous night, and they slept and fell all over the place. We even had some casualties from this. We arrived some time and were directed to a resting place, a bleak stretch of snow-covered sand dunes, with sundry clumps of a sort of gorse. When I had shepherded in the last straggler, I felt like lying down and dying . . .

Dawn, Sunday 28th November, found it still snowing. We rose with considerable difficulty and started a little circulation back into our frozen limbs. A great many people were unable to get up at all; Holman for one, was practically unconscious, and we thought he was dead. But worse was to follow. Overnight, our rations had been sent to us in a lorry. The folk who sent them out, presumably sorry for those unfortunates in the snow, sent with them a double ration of rum. The wagon drivers who brought the stuff – apparently before we arrived – finding no-one to hand it over to, had simply dumped the things by the side of the road and gone home. When morning broke, men began wandering about, as men will, and unhappily found the dump. Instead of telling somebody, or even eating the food, which would have been sensible, they broke open the rum jars and started in. The effect on empty stomachs and in that cold was simply devastating. Filled with a spurious warmth, they lay on the ground, and in many cases took off their coats, boots, and even tunics!

Those in the immediate vicinity of the dump were quickly put in the 'bag', but unfortunately the majority had filled their mess tins, and water bottles, and crawled into the bushes to enjoy themselves. We fairly combed those bushes all the morning, but by the time we found them all a certain number were dead. I remember finding one man in particular in only his shirt and trousers, holding an empty mug in a perfectly stiff arm, quite dead. Coming on top of everything else, it was heart-rending. Luckily there were ambulances quite close, and we evacuated Officers and men in a steady stream. When it was all over and the M.O. had gone too, there were left, Rogers, 77 Other Ranks, and myself!

Lt-Col. Drage was in hospital when this disaster befell the battalion. Ashton said: 'In the afternoon who should come staggering in, to my great joy, but the Colonel, wearing his uniform on top of his hospital pyjamas.' This, however, was denied by the CO:

I don't think there were any available in the Field Ambulance. I do remember my anxiety about my 'breeks'; I took them off to have the flood and mud removed by a RAMC cook – he took my remarks as to the honesty of his noble Corps in good part.

By 7 December, in spite of a large number of men having returned from hospital, the battalion was reduced to a strength of 130 in the line, where it was employed in digging trenches on Lala Baba.

Ever since the division had been taken out of the line the construction of winter quarters had been the order of the day, and all expected to stay on the peninsula till the spring. However, evacuation had been under consideration since 11 October, and Sir Charles Munro, who had replaced Sir Ian Hamilton, had quietly been laying his plans for withdrawing the army. The division began to embark on 11 December, the battalion leaving the following evening. Ashton wrote:

We packed up, not having much to pack, and embarked about 8 p.m. on a single 'beetle', which is a barge with a paddle wheel in the stern. By a strange co-incidence we left from identically the same bit of beach, 103 U, as we had landed on just eighteen weeks before. As I had been the first ashore I was the last to leave. It was impossible to help noticing the contrast – that brilliant August morning, the Battalion full of fight and high endeavour, 750 strong – this dark December night, slinking away, under 100 strong, weary, dirty, blase, disillusioned. And yet, I was sorry to go.

On 12 December what was left of the battalion then embarked on the SS *Elkahira*, a very dirty Greek ship, for Lemnos, where it arrived on 13 December. It marched out to a camping ground about 2 miles away in the direction of Kastro, and there pitched camp. As it turned out, the battalion only stayed there for two days, as on 15 December it again embarked, this time on the SS *Tunisian*, but the ship did not sail till the 18th, Alexandria being reached on the 22nd.

KINGTON SERGEANT'S LETTER
ENEMY MACHINE-GUNS AS PLENTIFUL AS FLOWERS
The following are extracts from a letter received from Company Sergt.-Major Chipp, 1st Herefordshire Regiment, who has been wounded.

Writing from St. David's Hospital, Malta, under date 21st August, to Quartermaster-Sergt. Bore, of Kington, Sergt. Chipp gives an interesting account of the Regiment's voyage in the troopship. As to the landing in which the 1st Herefords took part, Sergt. Chipp says that the division went to the Island of Lemnos, and when all were there they were conveyed in small steamers to make the new landing and taken to the beach in boats. It was just daybreak, and they took the Turks by surprise. 'But they soon began to pour shells on us. As soon as we had formed up we attacked and drove them inland. They shelled us heavily all the time with shrapnel. The Colonel and Adjutant and a great many went down, including poor Bill Faulkner, shot through the heart. The naval guns shelled the enemy heavily, but their artillery is so cleverly concealed that it is nearly impossible to silence it. When they were driven into the hills we entrenched ourselves and held them there. During the attack a shell burst at my feet and a piece of rock hit me on the ankle and lamed me for a bit. We held that position until Thursday night, when we were relieved and retired to the beach, being shelled all the time. Friday night our Brigade attacked another position and drove them back and held them. They have machine-guns as plentiful as flowers. They keep up a terrific fire all night in case we should attack. They gave us a heavy shelling on Saturday night, blowing up everything, and just after dark I had a bullet in the arm. It was daylight when I got to the R.A.M.C. on the beach, and as they were shelling the hospital I was sent right out to the hospital ship. I may say they shell the hospital the same as anything else. When we left the troopship on Sunday we had two days rations of bully and biscuits and our water-bottles full. We did not get any more rations until 3 a.m. on Friday morning. On Tuesday our water was gone, and we had six men killed in my company trying to get more. At last we got some, and it was one pint between seven men. The same on Wednesday and on Thursday we had a quarter of a pint each. The bully is so salt men cannot eat it. The heat is very great during the day, but it is cold at night. We had driven them about three miles inland when I went down. I told you we had lost all our officers wounded in my company; the total of men it is very difficult to give, as we were under fire the whole time I was there. When you can get near enough they won't stand the bayonet, but they are in splendid positions. Their snipers paint themselves green, and also women snipe as well. One woman caught had 60 identification discs on her, and a man had over £70 in money.

THE DEAN AT MALTA
VISITS TO THE HEREFORD WOUNDED

To the Editor of the Hereford Times
Dear Sir, – I have just received a most welcome letter from the Dean of Hereford, whose kind visit to those in hospital will have been a great comfort to the wounded, and I venture to think that their relatives may be glad of this news of them, so I enclose the letter in case you like to publish it. – Faithfully yours,
A.B. WOOD
Byletts, Pembridge, Herefordshire,
August 30th, 1915.

THE DEAN'S LETTER
Dear Lady Wood, – Going through the Hospital of the Blue Sisters this morning, I came across half a dozen Hereford officers, among them your nephew, Lieut. R.C. Bourne, who had just returned from the Dardanelles wounded. He seemed very cheerful and, as far as I could make out, not badly wounded.

The Herefords had a terribly hot time of it the same day as they arrived. Those I saw were Captains Lewis, Yates, and Capel, Lieut. Nott, and I found Sergeant Treherne at Pembroke Convalescent Camp, about six miles from here. At present I do not know of any more Herefordians in Malta. They were all very pleased to see me, and I told your nephew I would write to you.
(Signed) J.W. Leigh.
Malta, Friday, August 20th, 1915.

LETTER FROM CAPTAIN CAPEL
Captain E. Amphlett Capel, of the 1st Herefords, in a letter to his father, the Rev. A.J. Capel, Vicar of St. John's, Hereford, states that he has been wounded in the left arm, and also in the

thigh, by bullets (probably shrapnel shot). The bullets have happily been extracted in hospital at Malta, and the gallant officer hopes that he 'will soon be able to get back (to the front) again'. He is progressing comfortably, but by this time has no doubt left for a period of convalescence in the Old Country.

Captain Capel says the Dean of Hereford has visited the hospital two or three times. He says how pleased he was to see Dr. Leigh, a feeling which is no doubt shared by other officers and men of the Herefords whom our worthy Dean has brightened by his genial presence. Captain Capel was wounded soon after the Herefords landed.

LETTER TO MRS. FOSTER

The Dean of Hereford writing from Malta on August 20th to Mrs. Foster, of Brockhampton Court, states that he has visited the hospital of the Blue Sisters, and seen five or six of the Hereford officers who were wounded at the Dardanelles immediately on their arrival, and returned to Malta on August 19th. Among them was Captain F.C. Nott, who was very cheery and smiling, Captain Yates, and Captain Capel; Captain Lewis was in another ward. He had also found Sergeant Treherne in a convalescent camp 12 miles from there. All of them, the Dean adds, were very pleased to see him. He was not aware of any other Hereford officer on the island then. The medical officers who were staying at the same hotel were very good in letting him know. There were 20 hospitals there, and he had visited about 12. The hospitals were very light and airy and very well organised.

CAPTAIN ROGERS

Captain Rogers, one of the officers of the 1st Herefordshire Regiment reported wounded in the recent fighting in the Dardanelles, has cabled to his wife at Hereford to the following effect:–
No time for writing; very busy, noisy life; no letters received.

This message was sent to Alexandria and cabled from there to Hereford. The assumption is that Captain Rogers quickly recovered from his wound and is again in the fighting line with his regiment. Captain Rogers says nothing about his wound, and it is conjectured that the wound was only slight and enabled him to rejoin the Battalion almost at once.

CO.-SERGT.-MAJOR W. FAULKNER

Confirmation of the death of Sergt. W. Faulkner is given in a letter which has been received by Mr. Taylor, 20, Millbrook Street, Hereford, from his son, Sergt. Taylor, of the 1st Herefords, now at the Dardanelles, in which he states that Company-Sergt.-Major W.H. Faulkner, of 51, Chandos Street, Hereford, and of the 1st Herefords, has been killed in action.

Mr. 'Bill' Faulkner, as he was familiarly called, is well known in the city, having been associated with the old Volunteers and the present Territorials for many years past. A brother, Mr. Christopher A. Faulkner, is a sergeant in the 3rd Herefords, now at Abergavenny. Mrs. Faulkner and family will, we are certain, have the deepest sympathy of their fellow-townspeople in this sad intelligence.

A letter from his son, Sergt. C. Faulkner, with the 1st Herefords, also bears the same news. His father was quite near Capt. Capel when he fell. The deceased was an ardent Territorial and old Volunteer, and a first-rate shot.

MAJOR CARLESS MISSING

We understand that Mrs. Carless, Hampton Park, Hereford, received official notification on

Thursday stating that her husband, Major W.T. Carless, of the 1st Herefordshire Regiment, is missing. It will be remembered that Major Carless was formerly announced as having been wounded in the first engagement in which the Herefords took part in the Dardanelles, and since then no authentic news of any sort reached Mrs. Carless until Thursday. The sympathy of all the citizens, we are sure, will go out to Mrs. Carless in such a time of anxiety.

THE 1ST HEREFORDS

At the time of writing the list of casualties in the 1st Herefordshire Regiment, officially and unofficially reported, amounts to more than 150. This figure represents about half of the full total of killed, wounded, and missing as the result of the fighting in the Gallipoli Peninsula in August soon after the 1st Herefords had landed at Suvla Bay. It is therefore quite clear now that the baptism of fire was a very severe ordeal, depriving the Battalion of nearly a third of its effectives as soon as it landed on the Peninsula. Few regiments have been as unfortunate as that within so short a time, and more especially in the loss of officers. In that connection we regret to announce that Major Carless is now officially reported missing. There has been much uncertainty as to the whereabouts of this gallant officer, and everybody will sympathise deeply with Mrs. Carless in her great anxiety, and hope for speedy news of his safety. Major Carless and Captain Sir Archer Croft. Bt., are the only missing officers of the regiment, and the public interest in their fate is universal. From the latest reports it seems that heavy fighting has taken place recently in the Anafarta region, where the 1st Herefords are believed to be operating. Wherever they are we know they will uphold the traditions of Herefordshire and of Radnorshire, and fight as only Britishers can fight. We regret to hear that the recruiting for the Herefordshire Regiment this week has shown a remarkable decrease. One cannot understand this at a time when the needs of the country are so great and the bravery of the Herefords in the Dardanelles so inspiring.

MEN AND MATTERS

Captain Sir H. Archer Croft, to whose reported death we referred yesterday, was a member of an ancient family. He was the tenth baronet (the title was created in 1671), and was at the head of one of the few families in England able to trace a direct male descent from before the Conquest. The family descends from one Bernard de Croft, who lived in the reign of Edward the Confessor, and is mentioned in Domesday Book as holding the lands which his descendants retained until the property was sold at the end of the eighteenth century.

Ever since the Crusades, the Crofts have continually fought for King and Country. Godfrey of Boulogne created Sir Jasper Croft a Knight of the Holy Sepulchre on the taking of Jerusalem in 1100, and later members of the family fought at Agincourt, in the Wars of the Roses, and in the Civil Wars. In the last, they staunchly espoused the Royalist cause. At a later date, there were Crofts fighting in Flanders, where our troops learned to swear so terribly, and it is interesting to recall that a Croft was wounded at Quatre Bras a century ago. Two of the late baronet's brothers are now in the Army.

CHAPTER 8
Egypt and Palestine, 1916–17

On disembarking at Alexandria, the battalion immediately entrained for Wardan, about 40 miles north of Cairo. This was destined to be its home for the next six months. It was a thoroughly uninteresting place, with a small native village on the far, east bank of the Nile, the railway line, the usual canal crawling with bilharzia germs, and nothing else but desert rising up to a ridge in front of the camp some 3 to 4 miles distant.

We found that two of our most cherished illusions as to deserts were wrong; we had thought the desert would be flat, whereas it is generally an everlasting tumbled mass of sand dunes and hillocks. We had thought it always soft sand, whereas it varies and is generally fairly hard . . . Wardan was a mixture. We found places hard enough to make possible football grounds, and others as soft as treading in flour.

Some, however, found an aesthetic charm about the place.

You know the paintings you see of sunrise in the desert? – they are not half so gorgeous as the real thing. We crossed the canal at Wardan Station, secured some donkeys, and set off across the strip of desert that separated us from cultivation. We jogged along for about a mile, when we came to a rise in the sand followed by a sharp dip, and from there we were in as pretty a spot as you could wish to see. On both sides lay green crops of maize, and bersin (clover), groves of date palms and oranges, scattered sycamore, tamarisks and lebbek trees. Away on the left, amongst the trees, a white tomb. As we jogged along a narrow path, we passed between crops of broad beans. On the fields were goats, camels, donkeys and water buffaloes innumerable. We soon came to a village (Beni Salameh), a mass of mud huts, with a big insanitary looking pond in front of it. All the women fled, but the children swarmed round demanding backsheesh.

The battalion did not stay in the same camp for the whole period, as during the latter part 158 Infantry Brigade was moved on 25 March up into the desert to Wadi Natrun, where there was a salt and soda factory which was threatened by the Senussi. The battalion occupied various outposts around the oasis and the heat was intense, the wadi being about 30 metres below sea level, and on one occasion the temperature rose to 130 degrees in the shade.

On 25 May the battalion returned to Wardan, and on 30 May it moved to Zeitoun near Cairo. From Zeitoun, on 3 June, the battalion took part in a parade and review of troops at Abdin Palace, Cairo, on the occasion of the birthday of HM King George V. The battalion then commenced a full course of training, starting with musketry and elementary training, and finishing with divisional exercises. This continued till the middle of June.

On 21 June the battalion, together with the rest of the brigade, moved by rail to Moascar, where it rejoined the division. On 28 June A Company was sent on detachment to Ismailia. Training continued until 19 July, but at 2.30 a.m. on the 20th, A Company having rejoined, the whole battalion entrained for Kantara, which was reached at 5.30 a.m. The day was spent resting in camp, and in the evening the brigade marched to Hill 40, and the next day to Hill 70, to further harden the men.

On 19 July the RFC had discovered that a large body of the enemy had moved from El Arish, and on the 20th the cavalry reported that Oghratina was held by strong forces of the enemy, who were entrenching, and it was soon obvious that the Turks meant to fight. However, it was not till 2 August, when von Kressenstein made a strong reconnaissance towards Rabat-Quatia-Bir el Hamisah, that it became evident that he had taken the initiative.

For several months the slow penetration of the desert had been going on and all preparations were being made to assume the offensive when everything was ready, but that date was still a long way off.

Rumani, July 1916

Early on 22 July the brigade entrained for Rumani, where the battalion was met on arrival by the general staff officer 2 of 52 Division, and split up into garrisons for five posts, numbers 6, 7, 7a, 8 and 9. Each of these accommodated about 150 men, and the battalion remained in occupation of them until 4 August, being kept busy in strengthening and improving them.

On that date the Battle of Rumani opened. Von Kressenstein's object was to attack and envelop the extreme right (southern) end of the British line. No. 6 post, the most southerly one held by the battalion, and which had a garrison of about 175 men, was on the left of this attack.

At about 3.30 a.m., rifle fire was heard to the south-west, and at 5.30 a.m. four or five enemy planes flew over and dropped about 160 bombs on the post, but no British personnel were hit. The Turks then proceeded to shell the camps, railway station and no. 6 post, as well as those to the south of it. Turks were also seen in the desert to the south-west and were fired on by no. 6 post, the only one of these held by the battalion to be engaged. No direct attacks were made on the post, but later in the morning it was repeatedly subjected a a heavy bombardment by six-inch guns, which caused a number of casualties, 13 men being killed and 26 wounded. In addition, 2/Lt. G.L. Wallis and 3 men attached to the machine-gun company were wounded. Eighty-nine shell craters were counted inside the wire surrounding the post, which was sandbagged and stood up to the bombardment unexpectedly well.

At midday, Capt. Capel was able to direct artillery fire onto the Turks seen massing in the distant desert. A little later an attempt was made by the enemy to advance against posts 4, 5 and 6, but there was not much behind the Turkish attack, which threatened for about three hours and then melted away. Isolated bodies tried to advance against no. 6, but never got very close. This state of affairs lasted all the afternoon, the men firing on any Turk within range.

Midday marked the high point of the Turkish advance, but at 4.00 p.m. a counter-attack swept them away from their position on the right flank of the British. By 3.00 a.m. on the 5th, shelling had ceased. At dawn the British counter-attack was resumed, the Turks near the position surrendered and the remainder rapidly retreated to the positions prepared during their advance, but heavy casualties were inflicted during the retreat and some four thousand prisoners were taken.

The battalion remained in the line holding the posts till 14 August, when it was withdrawn to Kantara, where it was employed finding the guards on the depots, etc. Here it stayed till the 24th, when it was sent up to take over the posts at Rail Head. Lt-Col. Drage was OC troops.

The battalion was relieved on 12 August by 175th Welch and moved via Ferry Post Staging Camp and Moascar to El Ferdan, where it camped on the east side of the canal and was employed in training, fatigues and work on the defences. In the beginning of November a new routine was introduced, *viz* three days' training and three days on defences.

On the 11th a welcome reinforcement of 114 other ranks, including 5 old first line sergeants under 2/Lt. F.G. Burgess, joined from England.

El Ferdan was destined to be the home of the battalion for three months, and the battalion was fortunate in being located on the banks of the canal, where it was possible to sit in the cool of the evening and watch large steamers making their way up and down, with all their lights on, orchestras playing and ladies singing. All ranks bathed daily. The weather generally was cooler and consistent. In the morning a slight breeze blew from the south-west, then dropped at about 7.00 a.m. From then to 9.00 a.m. seemed to be the hottest part of the day. Then the breeze came from the north, and continued steadily until 9.00 p.m. The nights were absolutely calm.

The whole of the division was now concentrated on the canal, including the divisional artillery, which had begun to arrive from France at the end of February. Preparations were commenced for the advance across the desert and the division was reorganized on a camel transport basis. The end of the month of August, therefore, found the battalion busy organizing and training its new transport, which consisted of 12 riding horses, 29 pack mules and 110 camels. The camels had 36 native drivers and were allotted 102 fanatis, a sort of receptacle for water, two to each camel.

While the division was on the canal in reserve to the Eastern Force, Sir Archibald Murray, the Commander-in-Chief, had by 20 December been ready to strike, but the enemy withdrew from El Arish to the Wadi el Arish, and by the end of the month the province of Sinai was free. Continuous pressure by the mounted troops caused him to withdraw still further, and by the end of February the field was ready for the first battle of Gaza.

The award of the DSO to Lt-Col. Drage was published in the *London Gazette* on 1 January 1917.

Gaza, I March 1917

The battalion began its march across the desert on 4 January, and moving via Gilbran and Pelusium it reached Mahemdia on the shore of the Mediterranean and due north of Rumani at 3.00 p.m. on the 8th.

As there was an acute water shortage there, all animals had to remain at Rumani. The battalion stayed there training, which was relieved by excellent bathing, till 21 January, when it marched to Khirba, and the next day to Bir el Abd, where another five days were spent on training and fatigues. On 29 January the march was resumed and El Arish reached on 3 February. The next day the battalion took over the southern section of the outpost line with two companies on outposts and two in support.

Tours of duty in and out of the outpost line were carried out till 23 January, when the battalion moved on to El Burj where it had to take up a line of defensive positions, south-west, south and east of the column's bivouacs. On the 25th it marched to Sheik Zowaiid, where all were employed on well-sinking, a good and plentiful supply of water being found at 30 feet.

The advance now became slower as the force was covering the construction of the railway line along the coast to Rafah. It was not till 8 March that the battalion moved to El Rasum, where it took over the right sector of the outposts, and here it remained till the 21st, when the opening move of the first battle of Gaza took place.

The march across the desert was an interesting experience, but there was nothing to relieve the monotony, so much in keeping with the surroundings; yet for some of us the desert grew to have a certain charm – the feeling of wide open space, a horizon beyond which lay mystery, the amazing quiet and stillness around. It was not without a kind of wild beauty, especially at dawn and eventide, when the changing light caught the bollowing [*sic*] sandhills

Trading camels at Sheik Zowaiid, Palestine, in the opening months of 1917, before the advance on Gaza.

and shadows break up the burning waste. Then, when you come in from a ride which had taken you out of sight and hearing of human beings, there is something so homelike in the camp, something comforting in the twinkle of a fire and the snugness of tent or bivouac.

The scene is also well described by both Maj. H.E.P. Pateshall and Capt. Peter Ashton. The former said:

It was not always possible to see the scarce and welcome group of palm trees and wells, only about 200 yards square, and all completely hidden below the surface of the country. All the sand hereabouts is in ridges, all sloping the same way, north-west to south-east, and one sees a huge sand dune and just below it, stuck away under the steep bank, the trees or Hod, as it is called.

Ashton wrote:

The crossing of the Wadi el Arish, the old river of Egypt and nature's boundary, was an experience few will forget. The change was magical! From waste to growth, from sand to green grass again. For the first time, practically, since leaving England we were moving on grass again. The same main features of country persist right up to Gaza. Next to the sea there stretches a continuous band of high, soft sand hills, varying in width from one to five miles; next to the sand dunes comes a green valley, again varying in width, a corridor, as it were, on

55

which runs the so-called road, trodden by innumerable soldiers from back in the dim past to Napoleon. Further inland high ground rises, passing to rolling downland mostly cultivated, with patches of scrub and sand, gradually relapsing into desert again to the south east. On the 25th February we marched on 9 miles to Sheik Zawaiid, and found the grass much better and the flowers brighter at every step. It really was like going on holiday to have such surroundings to live in after the everlasting sand.

It must be remembered that this was the best time of year, after the rains, when grass and flowers grew strongly until they were scorched by the sun and parched by the drought.

At the beginning of 1917 the order was for pressure on all fronts. In Palestine the Turkish position extended from the sea across the front of Gaza, while its left was at Beersheba, away east, at the foot of the central range and on the edge of the desert. The British force was collected at the railhead, on the coast, with its communications running back along the coastal route. To attack in the direction of Beersheba would have meant extending the lines of communications across the enemy's front, so Sir Archibald Murray decided to attack at Gaza. He therefore reorganized the desert column, which now consisted of the Imperial Mounted Division, less one brigade, the Australian and New Zealand Mounted Division and 53 Welsh Division. With this and 52 and 5 Divisions he intended to strike at Gaza.

The cavalry screen was spread out far towards Gaza and reconnaissances were carried out without molestation, brigadiers, commanding officers and regimental officers all riding out with it, reconnoitring the country. Ashton said that they were rather jolly outings:

One would make one's way slowly and steadily out all morning, till one reached the desired spot, when one would have a real good look with glasses and a map. A picnic lunch followed, an hour's ease, and one would start off home again, and everything was so green and fresh with the ground fairly covered with little scarlet tulips. These were generally about forty mile rides, and the Turks adopted the policy of watching rather than strafing, which added to the attraction.

Reconnoitring parties found no difficulty in getting up to and across the Wadi Ghuzze, one of the great features of the country. The soil in these parts is a sandy loam, and the volume of water brought by the heavy winter rains, seeking its natural course from the inland heights of the Judaean Hills, has cut deep into this light soil.

The Wadi Ghuzze is the most important of these great draining ditches – dry, of course, for the greater part of the year. It is wide and has steep mud cliffs. From the coast it runs down in a south-easterly direction, and it receives, mostly from the rolling, down-like country on its northern bank, a great number of minor tributaries. The longer tributaries have, in their turn, feeding slots all well defined, biting deep into the soil which, through centuries, has been unable to resist the wash of the gathering water. So in the vicinity of the Wadi Ghuzze there are innumerable nullahs cutting across the country up to the watershed to the north of it. One great branch, the Wadi Sheria, strikes to the east then forks towards Sheria and Beersheba; further inland a second branch, the Wadi Saba, leads to Beersheba itself.

In the plan for the first battle of Gaza, 53 Division was to cross the Wadi Ghuzze and seize the necessary bridgehead. The Cavalry Division and 54 Division were to seize and occupy the Sheik Abbas position, then 53 Division would move forward for the attack on Gaza, its objective being first the Ali Muntar–El Sire ridge as far as El Shelur. From there, visual reconnaissance could be made for the attack on the final objective: the enemy's position about Ali Muntar. The mounted divisions were detailed to cover the flank of this advance.

On 21 March the battalion moved to Rafah, crossing the Palestine boundary at noon, and at night it was on outposts.

On the morning of the 24th a mixed cavalcade cantered through the streets of Khan Unis; it was an advanced party of British Officers seeking out for their units hiding places in the shady fruit groves surrounding the town. It was our first real glimpse of the 'promised land'. On all sides were groves of fig trees, mish-mish, olives and oranges, protected by high impenetrable hedges of prickly pear. On the north this green gem ends abruptly in a golden setting of sand hills, beyond which lies the deep blue of the Mediterranean. An old crusader's fort raises its tower above the surrounding squalor of mud huts. As we clattered through the lane, for it was scarcely a road, running through the centre of the town, savage looking but stately Bedouins gazed at us with curious eyes, and no doubt spies on the roof tops took a more technical interest in our passage.

That evening the battalion bivouaced in the groves north-east of Khan Yunis, being again on outposts. Late the following evening it moved out of its cover, and crossing the Wadi Ghuzze at dawn worked its way up the spur leading to Mansura. By 11.30 a.m. the whole brigade was concentrated in a covering position north of the village and about 4,500 yards from the enemy's position. It had been a beautiful starlight night, but at daybreak a rolling fog came in from the sea, which delayed the advance so that the force was two hours behind its scheduled time, the brigade being caught by the fog just as it was going to make the difficult crossing of the wadi.

In the attack on Ali Muntar, 158 Infantry Brigade was in the centre, with 159 on its right, but this brigade had been behind them and though they strained every nerve to catch up, their leading units were echeloned well to the right rear of 158's. 160 Infantry Brigade was on the left, attacking up the El Sire Ridge, and there was a considerable gap between it and 158, which had been increased by the fact that the leading battalions of the latter had gone too far to the north.

The battalion was in reserve at first, but 5th RWF on the left was soon held up by fire from Green Hill on its left, this flank being exposed. The battalion was consequently ordered up and at 1.12 p.m. it was deployed, C being on the right and D on the left, with A and B in support. The advance was carried out with the regularity and coolness of a manoeuvre. Almost at once the battalion found that its own left flank was not strong enough and a platoon of B was sent up to prolong the line, while two platoons of A were moved across further to support the left flank. The very gallant advance of the leading companies managed to establish the firing line about 500 yards from Ali Muntar. There, however, all progress was stopped by hostile machine-guns and rifle fire, and by the fact that the Green Hill trenches were as yet unassailed. By 2.00 p.m. the brigade was definitely held up all along its front. 161 Infantry Brigade had been brought up and was put in late in the afternoon, but before this reinforcement could make itself felt a very gallant charge was made by Capt. Walker of 7th RWF with about forty men. This took the Turks by surprise, penetrated their position and with 161 Brigade attacking Green Hill in a most determined manner the whole line was able to go forward at a little before sunset. When the advance was first held up the cavalry were despatched round the enemy's left to attack Gaza from the rear, and as there was thought to be no water for them they had to be withdrawn by 6.00 p.m.

It was now that a tragedy occurred due to the fog of war. Neither Gen. Chetwode nor Gen. Dobell knew of the successful effort of the division and 161 Brigade, which were in occupation of the whole of the El Sire ridge, and that the Turks had retired. A withdrawal to the original concentration position was ordered. After dark there was considerable confusion on the top of the ridge and units were much disorganized and mixed up, but there is no doubt that the position could have been held. However, it was not to be.

At about midnight, while it was still consolidating and reorganizing, the battalion, to its stupefaction, received the order to withdraw, and by 3.30 a.m. the whole brigade was back in its new position.

To illustrate the greatness of the tragedy, some of the troops, including Capt. Latham of the 7th RWF, never received the order to withdraw, and it was only at dawn that they did so when they found that no one else, not even the enemy, was there. Also, a party of British troops met some Anzac Cavalry, who had come right through Gaza from north to south. The remnant of the garrison and Gaza itself was simply waiting to be taken.

In the early hours of the morning of 27 March, Gen. Chetwode realized what had happened and ordered the divisional commander to re-occupy Green Hill and Ali Muntar. Although the troops had had no rest, they responded at once. After a hasty breakfast the battalion moved off at 7.00 a.m. and the leading company actually got on to Ali Muntar, which was found to be held by some of the Essex, but at that moment the Essex were being forced to retire in face of a strong enemy counter-attack from the east, and they and the battalion were forced to fall back along the ridge in a south-westerly direction until a consolidated position occupied by the Essex was reached. This was the second attack that the enemy had made, the first having been repulsed by the Essex.

The battalion then withdrew to the original concentration position north of Mansura, after suffering heavy casualties – 17 out of 22 officers were killed, wounded or missing:

	Killed	Wounded	Missing		
Officers:	4	11	2	total	17
Other ranks:	13	181	24	total	218

As the enemy had succeeded in recapturing Green Hill and Ali Muntar, Gen. Dobell considered that the position then held was not a good one for further operations, and decided to withdraw behind Wadi Ghuzze. So the battalion fell back to a bivouac 1 mile north of Dir el Belah, which was reached at 3.00 a.m. on 28 March, and there it remained till 17 April.

The division was holding the line of the Wadi Ghuzze from the Gaza road to the sea, and was left in peace by the Turks, who made no move. The battalion was employed in digging trenches until 17 April, when it marched to Tel el Ajjul and, on the 19th, was put under command of 160 Infantry Brigade.

Preparations had begun immediately for a second attempt on the Gaza positions. This was finally planned as a direct attack on Gaza, and was to be carried out in two phases. The first was carried out on the 17th with practically no opposition when 54 and 52 Divisions occupied the Sheik Abbas–Mansura position. The 18th was spent reconnoitring for the second phase.

Gaza II, April–May 1917

The division had dug a new line well forward on the coast and running back to Kurd Hill, and the attack, as far as it was concerned, opened at 5.30 a.m. on 19 April, 160 and 159 Brigades attacking on the right and left respectively with 158 in reserve, holding the new line.

By midday 160 had succeeded in capturing Samson Ridge, but this was only a very useful forward observation position and did not embarrass the enemy's main line. Further, the line held was very sketchy, with several gaps in it, and more troops were required to carry on the attack, so the battalion was ordered up. At 2.00 p.m. it began to advance with A and B Companies leading, and with a ridge running south-east from Samson Ridge as the objective. The enemy's fire was not heavy but was very accurate, and the position was occupied after a certain amount of resistance had been overcome. The companies had become a good deal mixed, and the right flank was in the air and had to be thrown back. This was done, the position consolidated and the battalion reorganized, and there the battalion stayed for the rest of the day.

Along the whole front the attack had been going none too well, and by the end of the afternoon it had been brought to a standstill everywhere. As it had not as yet drawn any of the enemy's reserves, Gen. Dobell decided not to throw in his general reserve, and during the night further decided not to resume the attack the next day, but to consolidate the position gained.

At 1.00 a.m. on 20 April the battalion was ordered to concentrate and hold the extreme right of the line. By then both Green and Crossley had been severely wounded, so the acting adjutant was sent up to take over command of the two companies on the right. This he did, and soon reported that they were consolidating in their position. The battalion stayed on what was now officially known as Hereford Ridge, consolidating, improving its position and making trenches to link up with the Queen's, who were on the right on Sniper's Ridge.

On 24 April the battalion was relieved and returned to a position in reserve where it dug shell trenches. On the night of 2/3 May it moved still further back to a bivouac site, and on the 7th it was finally withdrawn from reserve, going to Dorset House, the division having been taken out of the line and moved into the back area.

This 'rest area' behind the Mansura line was very dusty, the light soil being churned up by traffic, and was infested with fleas and flies – mostly the latter. 'Rest' meant innumerable fatigue parties, a certain amount of training, and reorganization on the new platoon system, with rifle, Lewis gun, bomb and rifle grenade sections. The battalion was also employed on working parties on the Mansura Ridge, and in constructing dugouts, while the opportunity was taken to fumigate all blankets. The heat was very trying, but this was slightly alleviated by heavy thunderstorms on 15 May.

On the 26th the division took over the right sector of the British line. That day the battalion moved out to the new area and took over posts 10 to 17 from the Buffs and the Sussex Yeomanry. These it held till 18 June, working on the defences and doing a certain amount of specialist training. On 19 June it was relieved by 5th RWF and moved back into reserve, bivouacing in a healthy open site that had not previously been occupied and where there was plenty of room.

The battalion remained out of the line till the end of July. In spite of the extreme heat, training was carried on persistently. Gen. Mott, who was now divisional commander, was addicted to night operations. The procedure was a wire at about 6.00 p.m. – 'Stand by to move at a moment's notice' – followed by another – 'March out and take up a certain position and dig in after dark.' The men generally got back to camp in the middle of the night. This long period of routine became very boring and monotonous, and it was with great joy that the news was received that leave to Cairo was to be granted.

On 1 August the division was relieved by 60 Division and moved back to the sand dunes near the coast, where it took over from 54 Division. The battalion moved to Belah on the 1st and the next day went into the line on Hereford Ridge. Trench warfare was more active here: the enemy's snipers were very much on the alert, a heavy desultory fire was kept up at night and there was also occasional light shelling. The enemy was busy improving his positions, and working parties were heard on several occasions to the rear of Umbrella Hill, but a few bursts of machine-gun fire soon stopped the noise. It was found that the enemy was now using much larger parties to patrol no man's land at night. On 10 August a patrol consisting of Lt. Linzell,

Men of the battalion construct dug-outs in the rest area behind the Mansura line in May 1917.

2/Lt. Fraser and 6 men encountered and stalked an enemy patrol of 6 men and got behind it. Then 14 more came along followed by a further 15 or 16. Linzell ordered one round to be fired and then charged through them, making for the post. Two men were seen to fall, but the others got through. He later took out a party to find these men, but encountered the enemy in strength and was forced to withdraw.

7th RWF relieved the battalion on the 18th and it moved back into brigade reserve, then went to Belah on the 26th. The division had been relieved by 54 Division and withdrawn to the back area for training in open warfare.

While this period of trench warfare had been going on, great changes had taken place. Sir Archibald Murray had been recalled and replaced by Gen. Sir Edmund Allenby, while the whole of the rear communications had been improved and reorganized so that the striking range of the Army was no longer confined to a short radius from the railhead on the coast. The Eastern Force was also doubled in strength, having received 10, 60 and 75 Divisions. The Army was reorganized and now consisted of the Desert Mounted Corps, plus the XX and XXI Corps.

The enemy front remained the same, that is from the sea and Gaza to Beersheba; but every week it got stronger and stronger, while Gaza had been converted into a veritable fortress. The line was continuous except for a big gap of about 4 miles between the Abu Hareira–Arab el Teiaha trench system and Beersheba, which stood by itself, though covered by strong works.

Gaza III, October 1917

The new plan in the third battle of Gaza was to capture Beersheba, deploy a force on the high ground to the north and north-west of the town, and then attack the Hureira–Sheria line. The first move of any unit was made by 158 Infantry Brigade. On 20 October, at the close of a beautiful autumn day, it crossed the railway below Belah, where Gen. Mott took the salute, and marched east towards the concentration area.

The greatest secrecy was preserved and every device utilized to mislead the enemy's airmen. All bivouacs and camps were left standing and occupied by a few personnel detailed to move about and simulate proper occupation, while when on the move across, the force only used old camping sites and concealed itself as much as possible.

After a 15 mile march the brigade took over the Kent Fort and Shellal defences from 60 Division, the battalion being in the former, and there it remained till 25 October, carrying out ordinary trench routine and preparing for the coming offensive. On that day the brigade moved forward into no man's land and took up an outpost position stretching in a curve from Goz el Basal to El Imara, the battalion being in support. This position covered the concentration of the other brigades and also the construction of the railway to Karm.

A further advance to another outpost position occurred on 27 October, and this resulted in a little action known as the Backsheesh Stunt, presumably because it was so unnecessary. The position to be taken up had already been occupied by 8 Mounted Brigade and no opposition was expected. The two main points in the outpost line were Hills 720 and 630, and 5th RWF and a battery were sent off to the latter some 8 miles distant. At dawn the sounds of battle were heard, and at 6.50 a.m., there being no signs of improvement, the battalion was despatched to assist. It followed up the RWF, then was itself followed at 9.00 a.m. by the whole of the brigade, which was ordered to march on Hill 720.

The air was very clear and visibility perfect when at 10.15 a.m., while about 4 miles away, Hills 720 and 630 were seen to fall and the Turkish Infantry and Cavalry swarm over the positions. Both defences were entirely wiped out, except for a small party which managed to hold on to a little trench to the rear of Hill 630. At that time the RWF and the battalion, though moving up as quickly as possible, were too far away to assist.

The situation then became distinctly unpleasant as the force was operating in a large 'saucer', of which the Turks, through the capture of these posts, held the eastern edge and so had a perfect view of every movement. From air reports their strength was about two thousand rifles, and it was obvious that the RWF, which were now in touch, could not attack a position of such strength alone, the battalion still being some distance behind, followed by the rest of the brigade.

By noon the battalion got up on the right of the RWF, came under a good deal of light shell and rifle fire, and there it remained. By about 3.00 p.m. the situation was perfectly ludicrous. The whole plain was covered with troops, as 160 Infantry Brigade was moving across the rear of 158 to take up a position on its right, and there were batteries, camel convoys, ambulances and the divisional commander in his car. The enemy artillery observer must have lost his head on being presented with such a target and nearly missed the lot. Finally, at 4.00 p.m. the attack went in and the Turks at once slipped away, and the position was reoccupied without difficulty.

The battalion occupied its position by 5.30 p.m., encountering no opposition. It at once started to dig in and consolidate, being assisted in this by two companies of 6th RWF.

At 4.30 a.m. on 28 October the battalion withdrew to daylight positions leaving only observation posts out, and at 11.30 a.m. it was relieved by 5th Welsh and came into brigade

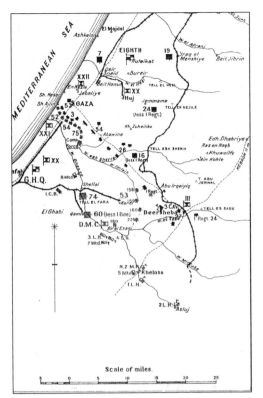

Gaza, 28 October 1917.

Gaza, 1 November 1917.

British trench, Gaza, 1917.

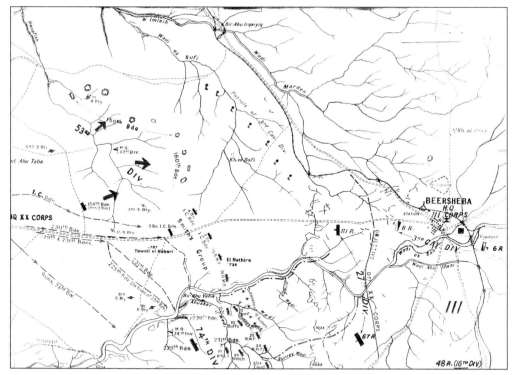

Operations towards Beersheba, 30 October 1917.

reserve. The occupation of this outpost line masked all movement to the west of it from the Beersheba lines, and the final concentration of the forces now took place, while the Sappers worked feverishly on the construction of the railway towards Karm. As the forthcoming operations were expected to lead to a considerable advance, the division was reorganized into brigade groups.

The main attack was to be made by 60 and 74 Divisions, the role of the division being merely to cover the left flank, but 158 Brigade Group was more concerned in the battle than either of the others. The group had been split into two parts, one being under the command of Lt-Col. Drage, and the battalion being under Capt. A.R.G. Whitehouse.

At 5.30 p.m. on 30 October, these two columns moved forward via El Buggar, crossed the Wadi Hanafish, and took up position on the high ground to the east, the occupation being completed by daylight on the 31st. At the same time the other two divisions were deployed on their right for the attack.

The offensive on the 31st was completely successful and Beersheba was captured. The 5th RWF, who were in the other column, advanced in touch with 229 Infantry Brigade on their right, but were hardly in the picture, being only able to bring long-range Lewis gun fire onto the enemy. Lt-Col. Drage's group, which was lightly shelled during the day, merely sent forward patrols towards the barricade, a nasty looking heavily wired place which was held by the enemy. Late in the evening the enemy evacuated it and 5th and 6th RWF took up an outpost position through it and along the road to Beersheba to link up with 225, which was holding the town.

To get elbow room for the next phase, the division was ordered to relieve the cavalry pickets on the hills to the north of the town and occupy the line Towal Abu Jerwal–Muweileh, the Camel Corps to operate on its right.

At 5.30 a.m., Drage's column moved forward to the Saba Triangle where it joined the remainder of the division. It was a long march of about 16 miles over a terribly mountainous and trackless country, particularly for the last few miles. The men, who suffered considerably after living so long on soft sand and soft going, had in many cases to go in single file. The position was reached by 3.15 p.m., the enemy being only just forestalled, and the brigade group, now concentrated again, took over the outpost line, the battalion being one of those on outpost duty.

Water difficulties were serious, the nearest source being in Beersheba, several miles away, and all horses had to be sent back there. Prior to the operations, two water bottles were issued to each man and this eased the situation. This, however, was none too good as the ration convoy lost its way, so no rations or water came up during the night.

Subsequent events involving the division had a decisive effect on the whole operation. In 1920 Col. Garsia, who at a later date became general staff officer of the division, visited Berlin. There he saw Gen. Kress von Kressenstein, who good-naturedly answered certain questions. He was asked the following: 'When you realized that Allenby's main attack was against your left flank (he had already told me that right up to the last minute he had expected it via Gaza), what did you do!' His reply was that 'he moved his general reserves to strike the outer flank of the turning movement, his object being to get outside it'. However, the whole of his plan failed through the occupation by British troops of some hills, from which he was unable to dislodge them. The troops, of course, were 53 Division and the Imperial Camel Corps, which was attached to them and operated on their right, or outer, flank.

The outposts were withdrawn shortly before dawn, and at 10.00 a.m. Gen. Chetwode visited Gen. Mott and ordered the division to remain on the defensive and dig in. Later in the morning the commanding officer and company commanders proceeded to reconnoitre a line just north of Towal Abu Jerwal, and at 3.30 p.m. the battalion moved out and occupied this line, 7th RWF being on their right, 159 Infantry Brigade on their left.

From dawn to 9.30 a.m. on 3 November, several hostile columns were seen moving across the front in an easterly direction, and at a distance of between 4 and 5 miles.

For the Gaza operations Maj. A.L. Green was awarded the DSO for conspicuous gallantry and devotion to duty, and L/Sgt J. Symonds and L/Cpl James were awarded DCMs; all published in the *London Gazette* on 16 August 1917.

CHAPTER 9

Palestine Campaign, 1917–18

Khuweilfeh, November 1917

The division again moved forward, its objective being two main features in the Turkish position: the dominating hill of Khuweilfeh and the key to the whole position, and a flat-topped hill called the Tell, on the Turkish left.

The brigade was in reserve and the battalion did not move until 8.30 p.m., when it went out in the direction of the Lekiyeh Caves to a starting point indicated by brigade. It took some time for the battalion to extricate itself from its position in the dark, owing to the rough and steep nature of the ground, companies having to move in single file on a narrow track. Shortly before dawn on 4 November it reached its rendezvous – the fork roads 1 mile north of Kh el Ras.

The division had been pushing forward steadily against increasing enemy resistance and 160 Brigade had had an arduous day, so the divisional commander decided to attack the Khuweilfeh Heights with a fresh brigade, 158, but this was cancelled as a result of 160 protesting.

Capt. Chipp, who was commissioned in the field after Suvla Bay, was decorated for a key patrol at Khuweilfeh. His citation was as follows:

Citation for the Military Cross for Lt (A/Capt.) Wilkins Fitzwilliam Chipp, Hereford Regiment

For conspicuous gallantry and devotion to duty. He carried out a valuable reconnaissance and cleared up an obscure situation. He readjusted parts of the line with great skill, and showed complete disregard of danger.

Place and date of deed: Khuweilfeh, 4 November 1917

The brigade again advanced at 5.00 a.m. on the 4th, but the artillery ammunition had not come up, so it was stopped and dug in, so the battalion, together with the brigade, remained in the concentration area all day. The weather now took charge. It had been terribly hot and the khamsin, which had been blowing, became worse and put a stop to all operations, the corps commander ordering the division not to attack on the 5th as had previously been ordered. The commanding officer and company commanders, however, carried out a reconnaissance of the enemy's left flank in readiness for a further attack. The lull caused by the khamsin came to an end that evening and the attack was ordered for the 6th. In this the division was finally instructed to assault and capture the Khuweilfeh Heights, and the task was allotted to the brigade, supported by the whole of the divisional artillery.

At 8.00 a.m. the battalion moved out to the brigade position of assembly, where the whole battalion formed up in platoon waves, each company with one platoon in the front line. D (Capt. H. Carver) was on the right, then C (Capt. C. Evelyn), B (Capt. C. Bernay) and A (Capt. C. Russel) on the left. The frontage was supposed to be 500 yards, but owing to errors on the map and the necessity of being astride the ridge leading to Table Topped Hill it was increased to

65

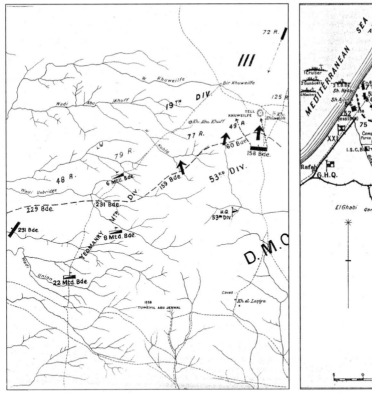

Khuweilfeh, November 1917.

Gaza, 6 November 1917.

well over 1000 yards, and this in spite of the fact that a battalion of the Imperial Camel Corps was ordered to operate on the right flank of the battalion.

At 4.00 p.m. the battalion moved steadily forward on a compass bearing, covered by heavy artillery and machine-gun barrage. Owing to the configuration of the ground the tendency was for the battalion to converge to its left. It is not quite clear whether D on the right moved over Flat Topped Hill, but some of its men became mixed there with the Imperial Camel Corps, which afterwards came up on this flank. The battalion pushed steadily on and reached the reverse slopes of Tell el Khuweilfeh, shooting and bayonetting many Turks on the way.

It was here that Capt. G.N. Berney, with a company of Herefords, found nine Turkish guns limbered up in a ravine ready to move back, as well as the transport of a machine-gun company. He at once charged, bayonetted the personnel, captured the guns and decimated the transport. Just at that moment a thick mist came down and there was a certain amount of mixing of units. This caused a good deal of confusion and resulted in 7th RWF mistaking the advanced units of the battalion and 6th RWF for Turks, and resulted in their calling for artillery fire. The gallant Capt. Berney was killed, but whether from his own artillery fire or not is uncertain, and a general retirement took place, with the guns having to be abandoned. The result of this was that the battalion was just short of its objective and there were several minor features from which the right of the line was swept by machine-gun fire. The enemy's snipers also took full advantage of the mist and caused severe casualties.

The battalion consolidated the position won and during the day the enemy made five separate attacks on the position held by the brigade, but these were all repulsed. In this the battalion was ably supported by the divisional artillery and the machine-guns. The whole day was spent under galling fire. The officer casualties were particularly heavy, 6 being killed while gallantly leading their men and five wounded. During the day the battalion captured 5 officers and 39 other ranks, and then took another 10 the next day.

For his valour on 6 November, Capt. John Fox Russell MC RAMC, attached to 6th RWF, was awarded a posthumous VC. He served with the Herefords as medical officer for most of the day. His citation, which appeared in the *London Gazette* on 11 January 1918, read:

> For most conspicuous bravery displayed in action until he was killed. Captain Russell repeatedly went out to attend the wounded under murderous fire from snipers and machine guns, and, in many cases where no other means were at hand, carried them in himself, although almost exhausted. He showed the highest possible degree of valour.

Shortly after dusk the battalion was relieved by 5th RWF and moved back to a position to the rear of brigade battle headquarters, where it remained all day on the 7th. That day saw the commencement of the general withdrawal of the Turks, and as far as the division was concerned the third battle of Gaza was at an end. On 8 November the battalion was sent to guard the Khuweilfeh Wells, where it remained till the 10th, being employed in clearing up the battlefield.

These operations had involved great hardships:

> There was very little water, never enough for a wash; bully beef and biscuits unvaried; no mails; Officers kits only 30 pounds and often miles behind; dust and heat. Tin hats were worn and the intense heat of the sun on them made one's head feel like a poached egg. The Battle of Khuweilfeh has been described in many narratives and despatches, but I have never seen mentioned the appalling shortage of water from which we suffered. We had about three pints for every 48 hours, which included a long march up the stifling, winding ravines of the Judaean foothills, followed by incessant fighting, the temperature, thanks to the Khamsin, which prevailed, being that of August. It was real hell. A lot of men nearly went mad with thirst.

The brigade was moved back to Sakaty to ease the supply difficulty, and at 4.00 p.m. on that day the battalion withdrew to Bir Saba. Here it remained till the middle of December, resting, refitting and working under the Engineers.

While the remainder of the Army was in full pursuit of the Turks on the Maritime Plain, the division had remained in isolation on the right flank. One part of the Turkish Army retreated to form a line north of Jaffa, and the remainder turned east to defend Jerusalem.

Jerusalem, December 1917

By the end of November the Turkish left flank was covering Bethlehem, and on 4 December the division was ordered to move forward and operate on the right flank of the Army. As all available transport had been given to the remainder of the Army for the pursuit, this was no easy task, and transport had to be improvised and dumps formed well forward. On receiving warning on 24 November to be prepared to move, the divisional commander ordered all horses and wheels not essential to units to be sent back to a railhead at Karm, thus saving the carriage of forage. Artillery teams and all camels were used to form an additional train, and by this method two days' supplies for the whole division were moved daily to Beersheba. To ease the transport situation further, only two brigade groups were to move forward, 158 being left in position. The latter was eventually ordered to concentrate in the Jerusalem area by 21 December.

The battalion started its march at 5.00 p.m. on the evening of 16 December, and after bivouacing at Bir el Makrune and Bir el Alaska it reached Hebron on the 18th. Here it was fortunate enough to be billeted in the Russian monastery, as there was very heavy rain that night.

A very good description of the road to Hebron, which was made by the Turks, was given by Maj. H.E.P. Pateshall, who wrote:

The views were simply gorgeous. Huge gorges, and more green scrub and cultivation in terraces. The road had very many hair-pin turns and twists, and had been barricaded by stones in several places. Our camp (it was at Divisional HQ at the time) was in a lovely site, plenty of running water, up a gorge, with daisies, dwarf cyclamen, crocuses, buttercups, marigolds, marrows, radishes, turnips and birds-eye periwinkles; it was a real treat. Oranges too, were on sale. At Hebron it was really lovely to see the vine leaves turning a beautiful autumn colour, all in terraces, vines, figs and olive trees. What struck me was the whiteness of the people, lots of Russian Jews about.

We trekked at 6 a.m. to the hill country beyond; you would then see a glimpse of a place called Hulhul, where Jonah was supposed to have been buried. Past an old ruined square tower of Roman origin, with a Roman milestone lying alongside the road called Beit Ummar, and Beit Fejjar, which was a very fine upstanding place perched on the top of a hill with very long views. We came to running water in the valley below, and camped around it. The advanced guard could see Bethlehem and Jerusalem and we went up and could plainly see it in glorious sunlight.

After three days of continuous rain and very cold weather, the battalion eventually bivouaced north-west of Jerusalem, which had been captured on 9 December. Capt. Peter Ashton gave an attractive account of the doings of the brigade during this period, when it was employed on the lines of communication:

As the Division moved up the road to Jerusalem, General Mott's HQ got further and further away, till by the beginning of December the Brigade HQ was practically detached and on its own . . . As the Division got further away, and our sphere of road mending enlarged, we had to send first Detachments, and then whole Battalions after them . . . Hebron proved to be most beautiful, a city of gardens, with the great square tomb of Abraham in the middle. On the 10th we went up to see Bethlehem, where the Division was installed in the Mar Elias Convent. We got our first view of Jerusalem, a mile or two further on, and saw heavy fighting going on on the Mount of Olives . . . On the 16th we were ordered to concentrate the whole Brigade forward at a place called the Wadi el Arab, about half-way to Bethlehem, by the 19th. The Herefords, R.A.M.C. and sundries, were still at Beersheba, and had 39 miles to go, so we got them as far as Bir el Makrune the first evening . . . On the 18th we moved Brigade HQ forward to the Wadi el Arab, sitting down in a big bare Russian Hospice on the top of a hill. By the night of the 19th the whole Brigade was concentrated there, less one Company of the Herefords, temporarily dropped at Hebron for the Military Governor, till some Indian troops should arrive. After a day's rest we moved on again to join the rest of the Division, through Bethlehem, and finally bivouaced in the north west quarter of Jerusalem, with troops in the Valley of Jehosaphat, and Brigade HQ at St. George's School, opposite the Church of England Cathedral.

Pateshall wrote:

Sunday the 9th of December will be a day to store up in my memory, because I came through Bethlehem and entered Jerusalem! We went through the outskirts of Bethlehem, where, being a Christian town, everyone was out to welcome us, Sisters, Nuns, and the very picturesque Bethlehem women in their high white head-gear and magyar blouses and skirts beautifully worked. Priests of all Christian Sects welcomed us. I rode on with the troops to the Monastery of Mar Elias, where I went on to the roof, where the Signals and Staff were given white wine and pork brawn by the monks. Very fine, lovely day, but cold wind. Glorious view looking back at Bethlehem, and you could see the Dead Sea and overlook Jerusalem to a certain extent. Got into touch with the other forces coming up by helio, which gave one a very happy feeling that at last the fruit of our labour was within our grasp. I was ordered on with the A.P.M. and police to the head of the column close outside the station at Jerusalem; then was sent out to the Jaffa Gate – past the Jaffa Gate and on to the Turkish Post Office, where our first troops had met the first troops of other Divisions. It was a glorious feeling, having at last joined up again. That night guards were mounted on all the Gates by the 7th Cheshires, guided by the Turkish Police, who had surrendered. I was then sent to the Governor of Jerusalem, Borton Pasha, as a Staff Officer.

This was the period of winter rains, and it poured incessantly up to 26 December. Half of the battalion were granted passes into the city on Christmas Day, and 16 officers and 66 other ranks attended service in the cathedral. At 4.00 p.m. that day the battalion moved into the Dominican monastery, where it was billeted in corridors and cellars. By this time all ranks were wet through and were only too thankful to get indoors under cover. On the following day the battalion went into the line in relief of 5th RWF.

On the night of 26/27 December the Turks made their great counter-attack to recapture Jerusalem, and drove in the outpost line of 60 Division. By dawn the attack had spread to 160, which was on the right of 158, but the enemy was repulsed after heavy fighting which lasted all day. One party attempted to advance up a nullah between C and D Companies, but was cut off by a party from D. Of the Turks, 12 were captured, of whom 5 were wounded. The battalion had only one man wounded.

As soon as he realized that the Turks were committed to an attack on this front, Gen. Chetwode ordered 10 and 74 Divisions on the left to advance. This they did, capturing nearly all of the objectives allotted them. The result of the day's fighting was that the British offensive had been successful, while the Turks had been held: thirteen costly attacks on 60 Division's front had only gained them one or two minor features. On the 160 Infantry Brigade front they were repulsed everywhere. The fighting had all been on the front of these two formations and the brigade, which was in the centre, was hardly engaged.

As soon as Gen. Chetwode was assured of the success of the day's operations, he ordered the advance to be resumed and the division to move forward and protect the flank of 60 Division.

The morning of 28 December was quiet, and in the afternoon the brigade launched its attack, 7th RWF being on the right and the battalion on the left. After assembling behind the hill of Ras el Kharrubeh, the battalion deployed in two waves, and at 3.45 p.m. it advanced round the sides of the hill. It was well supported by the gunners and passed straight through the village of Anata, leaving parties to bomb the cellars and clear up, and it pushed on to Welsh Hill, the high ground beyond.

The RWF had not succeeded in taking Ras Arkub es Suffa on the right, so B and C, the assaulting companies, consolidated on the crest. They were somewhat exposed, but managed to establish contact with the RWF. At 10.00 p.m., however, the latter succeeded in capturing its objective and so came up into line.

During the fighting, 5 prisoners were captured, while 15 dead were counted on the battalion's front. A patrol under Lt. Rooks pushed forward into Khirbet Amit and found it unoccupied, so, as the battalion had been freed by the advance of the RWF, a company was at once sent forward to occupy a hill near the village, which it did without opposition.

At 7.00 a.m. on 29 December the battalion moved forward in support of 4th Cheshires and took over Hizmeh from them. The general advance caused a rapid withdrawal by the enemy and by the evening of the 30th all organized resistance on the divisional front had ceased and only a few snipers remained. Eight deserters came in on the morning of 1 January 1918, and during the rest of that and the whole of the next day the battalion was hard at work, making roads and improving communications.

On 4 January the division took over the line in the Beitin area, the brigade being in the right sector. The battalion was relieved by 2/20th London Regiment and moved off on a narrow track through Jeba and Er Ram, where it joined the main road and proceeded to Bir el Sultan in brigade reserve. Capt. Peter Ashton recalled:

> The country around Beitin was like that we had come through south of Jerusalem – very steep and precipitous, planted where there was enough soil to plant anything, with here and there terraced hillsides to save the precious soil all being washed away to the bottom in the rains. As soon as one got off the Jerusalem–Nablus road the country was impossible for wheeled transport. The natives don't use wheels, using donkeys or camels in single file; their tracks are merely narrow lanes, about three feet wide, with stone walls on either side. A further trouble lay in the fact that the only map was one made by Lord Kitchener in 1878, and it was rather sketchy.

Just behind the line of the brigade was a deep wadi, and all units in turn had to find many tiring fatigues constructing a road in and out of it. Indeed, road-making was the principal occupation of all troops for some months, and as at that time the winter rains had not ceased, it was a far from pleasant one.

On the brigade front the enemy had no settled line, and merely occupied a succession of positions, sangars, rocks, edges of villages, and so on.

From 4 to 10 January the battalion was on road-making, and right up to the evening of the 8th this had to be done in high wind and driving rain, but at last it turned fine on the 9th. On the 11th the battalion went into the line in relief of 6th RWF, and, on the 18th, D advanced and occupied Garden Hill and B occupied Hog's Back. This was carried out without opposition, but there was heavy and accurate sniping during the day from an orchard about 800 yards distant.

From then until the end of the first week in March, the battalion carried out ordinary tours in and out of the line, with, as before, plenty of road-making in the rain. In the line, meanwhile, considerable trouble was experienced with numerous small parties of natives who had been expelled from Abukush by the Turks.

On 19 January an enemy plane was brought down in front of the battalion's line near Surdah Hill. D Company captured the observer, a German, who was unhurt, and the pilot, who was badly wounded.

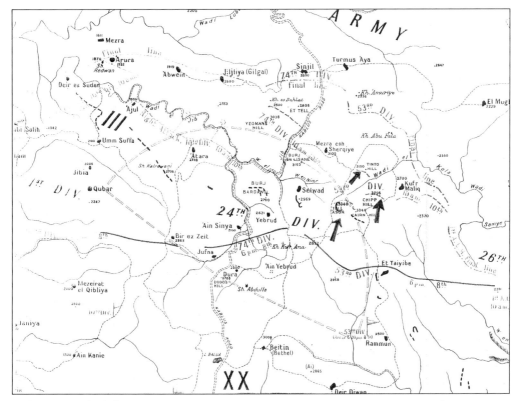

Tell Asur, March 1918.

Tell Asur, March 1918

A further advance was about to take place and the Battle of Tell Asur opened on 9 March. In this the division was really on the right flank of the Army as although 60 Division was on its right again, it was down in the valley of the Jordan and so far away as to be out of touch. The division was confronted with the most forbidding country: a succession of high, rocky ridges and deep valleys, with many places where men had to hoist themselves up or lower themselves down. As was discovered afterwards, the conformation of the ground frequently confined troops to one ledge on which the enemy could concentrate his fire.

The operations of the brigade were of great importance as Tell Asur was the highest hill in Judaea, and so a position to which the enemy could cling tenaciously. Chipp, Cairn and Drage Hills were also important features. Cairn Hill was a kind of hump between Drage Hill and Tell Asur. Ashton said:

We could see Tell Asur as a high steep rocky hill going straight up out of the valley at its foot, and we somehow assumed that the country would fall on the other side in the same way; most hills do. Actually Tell Asur was the edge of a high plateau.

71

For the attack, 159 Division was on the right and the brigade was on the left, with the Herefords as right battalion, 5th RWF to the left and slightly in front. The objectives of the battalion were Drage Hill and then Chipp Hill, while the RWF were to take Cairn Hill and then assault Tell Asur from the east. A considerable space separated the position of assembly from the objectives, but the Turks held no intermediary ground and the artillery was therefore silent at first. The advance across that rough country, in the dark, was difficult and, of necessity, slow.

Between 1 and 6 March the battalion was in the line at Medway Wadi, and on the 7th it moved to a position in the Wadi el Ain, companies being scattered along the west side of the Wadi for concealment. A patrol of 15 men under 2/Lt. Ward was sent out to examine a sangar reported by natives as unoccupied, but found it held by the enemy and withdrew unobserved. It went out again the next day and found it still held, but this time was fired on.

At 2.00 a.m. on the 9th the battalion moved to the head of the wadi, but at 2.30 a.m. a fog unfortunately developed and this slowed down the advance still more. The advanced screen bumped the Turkish listening post, but after a short grenade fight the enemy withdrew and the advance continued. By 6.30 a.m. the RWF had taken Cairn Hill and the battalion advanced across the eastern spurs, crossed the Dar Jebir Wadi and attacked Drage Hill. This was taken by 7.15 a.m., having already been partly occupied by 4th RWF. A and C Companies then pressed on to Chipp Hill, which was taken by 8.00 a.m., but the advance was checked, after the crest had been taken, by machine-gun fire which enfiladed the forward slopes. The situation at 8.30 a.m. was that A and C were on Chipp Hill and B in support of D on Drage Hill. The fighting on Chipp Hill had been severe: the Turks launched a counter-attack almost at once and shortly before 10.00 a.m. the two companies were driven off the hill. It was just at this time that 5th RWF which had failed to take Tell Asur at the first attempt, succeeded in doing so at their second.

There followed a long pause during which both forward battalions were relieved, 7th RWF taking over from the battalion on Drage Hill. This had only just been achieved when the Turks launched a heavy counter-attack, which was repulsed.

At 3.30 p.m. a combined attack was made by the battalion and 4th RWF on Chipp Hill, but though the Welch managed to take the ridge on the north-east of the hill, the battalion, which encountered severe opposition, failed to get the hill. Soon after it became dark, A and C Companies, under Lt. Parker, again assaulted, without artillery preparation, and this time they succeeded in capturing a position on the crest, where they were immediately relieved by 7th RWF. This relief was completed by 10.00 p.m., and the whole battalion moved back to Drage Hill, where rations and grenades were issued.

Equally heavy fighting had gone on on the left of the brigade front. Here 6th RWF were also attacked immediately after it had taken over. They were driven off Tell Asur, and the enemy held the hill for some time, but a counter-charge eventually drove them off again.

Orders were issued for a further advance on 10 March, and at 3.00 a.m. the battalion went forward to relieve 7th RWF so that they could carry out the advance. During the relief the enemy counter-attacked, and hard hand-to-hand fighting ensued, which resulted in the enemy being driven off everywhere. This took some time, as the enemy were in considerable strength, and as a result the RWF found that they were unable to advance, so they were left in occupation of the hill and the battalion concentrated on and behind Drage Hill.

6th RWF on Tell Asur met with no better success, and after attempting to advance were driven back to their original positions. In the early hours of the morning of the 10th, 6th RWF started to move forward in the centre. By dawn they found that the enemy had withdrawn, and two companies were pushed forward across the Wadi el Kola and occupied a ridge to the north of it.

This ended the fighting as far as the battalion was concerned, as it remained in its position in brigade reserve till noon on the 14th, when 160 Infantry Brigade took over the front, and it moved back to Medway Wadi in corps reserve. During the next three days it rained heavily, and the battalion merely rested, but it cleared up on the 18 March and the battalion was able to carry out some administrative work.

On the 19th, Lt-Col. Drage proceeded on leave to Egypt and Maj. A.G.R. Whitehouse took over command, which he held till 1st April, when Lt-Col. E.M. Lawrence of the Cameronians joined.

The battalion moved to Shafat, near Jerusalem, where it carried out training till 29 March. The division now moved down into the Valley of the Jordan and on the 29th the battalion reached Talaat ed Dumm after a hot and trying march, only to go in to a very bad old bivouac area. The next day it moved to Kh Kakua, where it stayed till 2 April.

The march to Talaat was far from being a pleasant one: besides being very hot and stiflingly dusty, it was very unsavoury, as there were quantities of dead camels which no one had buried. At Talaat there were the ruins of another Crusader Castle, a famous stronghold, and also the remains of a building said to be the inn to which the Good Samaritan took the wounded unfortunate who fell among thieves.

Operations in the valley, however, were soon cancelled and the division was ordered to relieve 74 Division, which, with 52, had been put under orders for France. The battalion consequently retraced its steps back to its old area, and on 7 April went into the line in relief of 12th (Norfolk Yeomanry) Battalion the Norfolk Regiment. From then till the end of the month it carried out ordinary tours of trench warfare.

The left sub-sector was described by Capt. Peter Ashton as very strong,

though not so strong as the right, where we were to go to later, on our right we were on the Tell Asur plateau, the northern end of which was a prominent height called Mount Harry, which sloped down and onwards to a final feature known as Beachy Head, which, like its name-sake, stuck out like a cape into a flat green valley to the north, which formed No-Man's-Land. Up the west side of the cape ran the main road, and so down into the green valley, a mile or so wide, and disappeared into the hills beyond on its way to Nablus. Just across the valley were the ruins of Shiloh. Immediately west of the road and about level with the end of Beachy Head there arose, running east and west, a ridge which took its name from the village of Sinjil on its northern slope. Behind this ridge was a little open valley with a funny little sugar-loaf Tell in the middle. Further along the Sinjil ridge we joined with the 10th Division. Behind the line there were numerous hills of various size which were made into defended localities.

Trenches were practically impossible, as the rock cropped through everywhere; breast-works and sangars were the usual order of things, defended with barbed wire and held only at night. By day the garrisons retired behind Beachy Head or the crest of Sinjil ridge as necessary.

Far down on the right was Nejmeh as a detached locality, under Divisional Command. Then, after a gap of 4000 yards along the Wadi Samieh, Rock Park, Round Hill and Ide Hill, all in line.

The position faced north-east and at the left end of it nearly north, and was really the far end of the Tell Asur plateau. On the right our line ran on the near side of the Wadi Samieh, a tremendous ravine with steep sides; in the centre the ground was more open and the main positions were beyond the Wadi. On the high ground of the plateau we had all the guns and the most wonderful observation imaginable.

On 1 May, while in the line, the enemy heavily bombarded the battalion's area and at 1.20 a.m. on the 2nd they attacked on the right of the left centre post held by the battalion but were repulsed.

At 1.45 p.m. they again attacked at the same place and succeeded in reaching the sangars. Hand-to-hand fighting ensued, but they were driven off and pursued for 100 yards in front of the British line. Two patrols sent out at 3.30 p.m. to clear up the situation reported all clear on the front. Lt. Lewis and Lt. R. Timmings did some excellent work during this action.

On 5 May the battalion moved back into brigade reserve and was kept busy on road-making. It then went back into the line for what was to be the last time in Palestine, as on 30 May, while in brigade reserve, it was finally relieved by 2/22nd London Regiment at 2.30 p.m.

The division was to be reorganized on an Indian basis, three Indian battalions replacing three British ones in each brigade so that they could return to France. The battalion was one of those selected and was destined to sever its connection with the division. That evening the divisional band gave a concert and the divisional and brigade commanders, as well as representatives of other units, came to say farewell and wish the battalion the best of luck and *bon voyage*.

On 1 June the battalion marched off, being played out by the divisional band and, after bivouacing at Hawk Hill, Enab and Latron, reached Sura on the 4th. There it rested for one day and handed in surplus stores. At 10.00 a.m. on the 6th the battalion entrained for Kantara, which was reached at 11.00 a.m. the next day. Here it camped till the 15th, when it entrained for Alexandria, and the following day embarked and sailed on H.M.T. *Kaiser-I-Hind*. The voyage was uneventful, except for the fact that an enemy submarine fired a torpedo at the ship at 11.30 a.m. on the 21st, but the ship fortunately avoided it and it passed harmlessly astern. The ship arrived at Taranto at 3.00 a.m. and that afternoon the battalion disembarked and spent the night in hutments.

So ended the second episode of the Herefords in the First World War, the battalion ceasing to belong to the EEF on 19 June 1918.

CHAPTER 10

France, Belgium and the Rhine, 1918–19

When the Herefords landed in France, the great German onslaughts of 1918 were still continuing, and in July they launched an offensive on either side of Rheims. This had been expected by Marshal Foch, and at his request XXII Corps, under Lt-Gen. Sir A. Godley, was sent down to the French front.

After a long and tiring train journey from Taranto, the battalion arrived at Proven on 30 June and marched to Cost Cappel, Les Cinq Chemains, where it was billeted in barns and hutments. Transport and equipment were drawn the next day, and till 7 July the battalion was busy reorganizing. On the 7th it marched to Schools Camp, St Jan ter Biesan, where training started in earnest. Gen. Plumer, the army commander, and Gen. Godley both inspected the battalion and complimented it on its turnout and smartness.

The battalion formed part of 102 Infantry Brigade of 34 Division. This division had previously been reduced to a cadre and employed in training American troops. It was now re-formed and all five battalions from 53 Division were posted to it.

Detraining at Sur Villiers, the battalion reached Berest, in its new area behind the French front, on 17 June, after a march of nearly 15 miles. On the 20th it proceeded to a brigade rendezvous at Vez, where a violent thunderstorm broke and soaked everyone to the skin. Posieux was reached that evening. The following day the battalion moved up through the woods and reached the front line at 11.00 p.m., where it took over from the French 58 Division.

Bois de Reugny, July 1918

On 18 July Marshal Foch launched his great counter-offensive between Chateau Thierry and Soissons, supporting it with vigorous attacks on other parts of the German salient. It was in this fighting that the division was to be involved. Its role was to link up two attacks being made by the French XX Corps and the French XXX Corps.

The brigade attacked on a two battalion front, 7th Cheshires on the right and the Herefords on the left. B and C Companies were the forward companies, with D in support and A in reserve. The advance commenced at 7.40 a.m. under a heavy barrage, but high standing corn made control difficult and from the very start severe casualties were inflicted on both battalions by the enemy's machine-gunners. They succeeded, however, in advancing about 1,200 yards, when they were finally stopped by the intensity of the machine-gun fire from the west edge of the Bois de Reugny.

Owing to an error in timing, neither 101 Infantry Brigade nor the French advanced at the right time, and when they tried to do so later on without the help of the barrage they were unable to get forward. As a result, the brigade was finally held up at about noon and dug in, with both flanks exposed. Continuous and heavy shelling throughout the afternoon made the search for and evacuation of casualties difficult, especially as the battalion was experiencing gas shells for the first time. That night the battalion was relieved by 4th Cheshires and moved back to the old front line.

Casualties had been heavy, the battalion losing 8 officers and 230 other ranks. At dawn on 24 July it was withdrawn into brigade reserve, where it proceeded to reorganize into two companies. It was also visited by the brigadier, who congratulated it on its fine performance.

The Herefords did not get much rest, as the reserve area was shelled all that morning, as well as on the next two days, so that on the evening of the 26th it was moved to a new area a little further back. It was eventually relieved by a French battalion on the night of 27/28 and bivouaced in a field. The following night it moved back to a reserve position, but the French guide detailed to lead the battalion lost himself completely. Traffic on the roads was very bad, carts and motors being all double-banked, and in this confusion the battalion had to look for the place themselves. Luckily it found the right one. The battalion eventually got in at 00.30 a.m. on the 29th, but had to go forward at 10.30 a.m. to occupy the 'Paris trench system' so as to be near the front line.

The division again attacked on the 29 July, the brigade being in reserve. The two assaulting brigades captured their first and second objectives, but were then held up by machine-gun fire. The brigade was now ordered up, but before this fresh impetus could be given to the attack, the enemy counter-attacked and all troops were driven back to their original line, where reorganization took some time, as they were all considerably mixed up. The enemy shelled the whole area vigorously on the 30th.

Bucy le Bras Ferme, August 1918

The next night the brigade moved back a little into a support position in readiness for a new attack to be launched on 1 August. This was preceded by an intense bombardment by both the British and the French artillery. The battalion, which had advanced in rear of 10 Infantry Brigade, was now given Bucy le Bras Ferme as an objective. During the preliminary advance, Maj. A.G.R. Whitehouse was most unfortunately killed by a party of Germans who suddenly appeared from a dugout 120 yards in front of the battalion headquarters party. This was a complete surprise, as half of the brigade had already passed over this area. By 11.25 a.m. the battalion was finally held up by machine-gun fire from the area of the crossroads west of Bucy le Bras Ferme. Here it dug in and remained till 7.00 p.m., when, on relief by 103 Infantry Brigade, it moved back into a support position. That night a French division passed through to continue the offensive, and on the 3rd the battalion was withdrawn into brigade reserve, and the next day it moved back to billets in Sill le Long.

Marshall Foch's counter-offensive had been a success and had changed the whole situation. As a result, the division was to return to the British front where Haig was preparing his counter-stroke at Amiens. After resting on the 5th, the battalion entrained at Plessis Belleville on the evening of the 7th and arrived at Bergues at 7.00 p.m. the next day, from where it marched to billets 1 mile south of Ziggers Capel in the 2nd Army area. The division for the time being stayed in headquarters reserve.

Here the battalion received a welcome reinforcement of 3 officers and 157 other ranks, and it remained reorganizing and training till the 13th, on which day it moved to Hezeel. There, training was continued and at the Brigade Sports the battalion won the Transport Cup, which was presented by the brigade commander.

The division went into the line again and, after moving up via Proven and Siege Camp, the battalion took over from 4th KOYLI and came into divisional reserve, where it was employed on defence and in carrying out reconnaissance of the adjacent area.

At the end of the month the division was withdrawn from the line and ordered to take over the Scherpenberg sector. After being relieved by 14th York and Lancs on 27 August, the battalion proceeded by two trains on the light railway to Lancaster Siding, and then marched to Road Camp at St Jan ter Biesan. The next day it entrained at Proven for Cormette Camp, St Omer, where it carried out musketry till the end of the month. At the same time the commanding officer and company commanders carried out a reconnaissance of the Kemmel area.

On 1 September, after going by train to Abelle and then marching to Scherpenberg, it took over from 26th Royal Fusiliers in brigade reserve, and the next day the battalion went into the line in relief of 4th Royal Sussex.

Kemmel, September 1918

The withdrawal of the enemy extended to the new front held by the division. Kemmel Hill was occupied early on the morning of 31 August and by the evening 101 Infantry Brigade was in occupation of the trench line known as the Vierstraat Switch. 101 Brigade continued its advance on 1 September, gaining all of its objectives, but it was so far ahead of 103 on its right that it had to fall back slightly so as to link up with them. It was from this position that it was relieved on the evening of the 2nd by the brigade, which was due to continue the advance.

On 4 September the battalion attacked at 5.34 a.m. under cover of a barrage, but it met with no success. By 7.00 a.m. the right company was held up by uncut wire and the left company also failed to get to its objective. By 8.00 a.m. both had been driven back to Farmer Trench, less one platoon under 2/Lt. Learmouth, which held on all day to the edge of a crater and did not fall back until after dark. The battalion stayed in its original position in the line from the 5th to the 7th, and on the 8th was relieved by 7th Cheshires and moved back to a reserve position at Willebeck. This was a very uncomfortable patch with no accommodation other than dilapidated French and German trenches. It also rained all the time they were there between the 9th and the 12th, but on 13 September the battalion moved to French Bank, a much better area.

On 15 September the battalion relieved 2nd Loyal North Lancs in the left sector of the front line, where it stayed till the 20th. During this tour the battalion kept pushing outposts steadily forward, and occupying old trenches and craters all along its front. On relief it went back into support at Vierstraat, and on the 22nd to French Bank, where it was again in divisional reserve.

During this lull in the fighting, preparations for a further advance were made, and on the 28th, 101 and 103 Infantry Brigades attacked in conjunction with the troops on their right and left. The result exceeded all expectations, and by the evening of the 30th the whole of the left bank of the Lys from Comines southwards had been cleared. This naturally meant that the whole of the Wytschaete Ridge had fallen.

On 28 September the battalion had moved up to Vierstraat and on the 29th it moved forward in rear of 103, under whose command it had been placed, and occupied some trenches. On 1 October it moved to Wytschaete.

Menin, October 1918

The division was ordered to take over the Wervicq–Menin line, so on 2 October the battalion moved to near Houtem as support battalion, the brigade having been detailed to take over from 124 Infantry Brigade. As it happened, the latter had no support battalion to relieve, so the

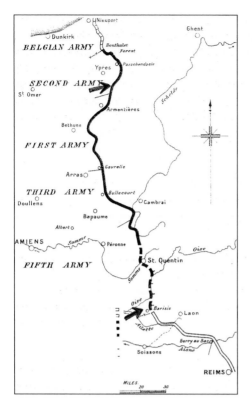

Western Front, 1918.

battalion had to dig in. It was a very dark night, no guides were available and there was no one who knew the ground. When light came it was found that the battalion was in dead ground, so a new support position had to be found and dug on the 3rd. On 7 October the battalion was relieved by the North Lancs and moved back into divisional reserve in a new area. Here again there was no accommodation, save for a few pillboxes, and everyone was out in the open. After working on roads and communications until the 12th, the battalion moved up into the support line.

The attack on Menin opened on 14 October, the battalion being in support. It moved forward at 9.15 a.m., occupying different positions in turn. The line on the left flank had been considerably extended and a counter-attack drove 4th Cheshires back a little, so one company was sent up to reinforce them. During the night the remainder of the battalion was moved up behind the Cheshires, and at 5.50 a.m. on the 15th it passed through them and pushed on to the eastern outskirts of Menin.

Battle patrol pushed forward and was met by slight opposition. It was followed by C Company, which took up a position in touch with 103 on its left, and with A covering the river. At 6.00 p.m the line was readjusted, and the Cheshires, which had also sent patrols forward, were withdrawn into support.

At 1.00 a.m. on 16 October a patrol was sent out to the outskirts of Halluin. It succeeded in crossing the Lys by the remains of the Marathon Bridge and advanced 1,200 yards towards the church. In doing so it surprised an enemy machine-gun post, capturing the gun and returning with it to the river bank. Here the patrol discovered a pontoon bridge lying alongside the enemy's bank, and this they swung across the river and thus returned to the British side.

At 7.30 a.m., B Company was ordered to cross by means of this bridge and reinforce 8th Royal Scots, which had succeeded in pushing a platoon over to the Halluin side. The latter were unable to clear the bridgehead and machine-gun fire also stopped B from crossing. The battalion was now busy trying to find a means of getting across, and at midday A Company succeeded in doing so under cover of artillery and machine-gun fire. It made a small raft of duckboards, capable of carrying two men at a time. The Cheshires worked this for them, and as platoons crossed they advanced and cleared the enemy from some buildings called Rascals Retreat. The company then dug in to hold the crossing.

Citation for Distinguished Service Order for Lt. (A/Maj.) Wilkins Fitzwilliam Chipp MC 1/1st Battalion, Hereford Regiment

During the operations near Menin, on 14th, 15th and 16th October 1918, he commanded his battalion with great skill and gallantry. With only part of his command he was ordered to take over the whole front and push on – an extremely difficult operation, which he carried out at once under heavy shelling and machine gun and minenwerfer fire. It was entirely due to his own personal reconnaissance of the country under fire and his perfect control that enabled his men to overcome every obstacle.

D Company worked for five hours trying to repair the lock and make a bridge of timber, etc. All of the material had to be obtained from houses in Menin, and during the whole time the lock was shelled and sniped by the enemy.

At 4.00 p.m., just as it was nearly completed, the enemy opened up a heavy artillery bombardment and destroyed the whole of their work in a quarter of an hour. At 6.00 p.m. the battalion was relieved by 2/16th London Regiment and moved back to rest in brigade reserve, north of Gheluwe. After being there for two days it marched up through Lauwe, where the civil population were greatly excited to see British troops. It proceeded to Aelbeke, and then to St Anne, where all ranks were accommodated in a monastery for the next three days, before finally going into the line on 23 October in relief of 23rd Royal Fusiliers.

Moen, October 1918

The battalion had been detailed to carry out an attack on 24 October to clear the Courtrai–Bossuyt Tunnel and canal crossing, but this was contingent on the advance of 41 Division on the left. As the latter did not make sufficient progress, companies were ordered to dig in where they were, without attacking, and a fresh plan of attack was made for the next day.

Early on the 25th the brigade formed up in depth on the west bank of the canal, minus the Cheshires, who were on the east bank. As soon as it had cleared the crossing, which was at about 9.15 a.m., A Company crossed by platoons and moved on in support of the Cheshires. The three other companies followed in quick succession, and by 10.15 a.m. were all clear of the canal. The advance of the Cheshires was hindered by machine-gun fire from the right flank, but in each case A Company was able to deal with it effectively and enable the advance to continue. B also assisted when a strongpoint in a building held up the Cheshires. This they assaulted and captured, taking 30 prisoners and a machine-gun. At 11.00 a.m. C Company was detailed to

Major W.F. Chipp's medals.

clear Moen, where the enemy had a couple of machine-guns on the eastern outskirts. This they did, the place being cleared just before 1.00 p.m. By 4.30 p.m the brigade had reached its final objective and the battalion dug in during the night, during which time the enemy shelled the whole area. The battalion remained in the same position during the 26th, but in the early hours of the 27th it was relieved and returned to billets at St Anne. On 29 October it moved to Harlebeke in divisional reserve, and there it still was when hostilities ceased on 11 November 1918. This was celebrated by a day of rest, and a programme of games was carried out on the 12th, followed by Brigade Sports on the 13th. In these the battalion won the Transport Turn-out Cup, tug of war, 220 yards and long jump.

The division had originally been selected as one of the first to march to the Rhine, but this was soon cancelled and instead it moved to the area about Lessines, the battalion being billeted at Floebecq, which it reached on 17 November. Here, light and recreational training were carried out, while a divisional education scheme was drawn up, but a lack of books and material greatly hindered its progress.

1st Bn the Herefordshire Regiment: NCO survivors of the First World War, photographed in Bonn, early in 1919, when part of the Allied forces of occupation in the Rhineland.

On 12 December the battalion was on the move again when the division moved to the angle of the Meuse and Sambre near Namur. Moving by easy stages via Silly, Seignies, Le Restre and Monceau, Chatalet was reached on the 18th. Here the colours arrived, having been brought out from England by Capt. O.B. Wallis and 2/Lt. J. Jones. The next day the battalion moved on to Fosse and there it stayed till the middle of January. Training and education went on as before, varied by joy rides to Brussels, for which one lorry per brigade was allowed. Demobilization, which had begun on 22 December, also proceeded steadily.

The move up to the Rhine eventually started on 17 January, when the division was ordered to relieve 2nd Canadian Mounted Division in the right sector of the Cologne bridgehead. This move was carried out by rail, the battalion being stationed at Sieburg, near Bonn. During February, demobilization made great inroads into the strength of the battalion, and at the end of the month it was allowed to run down. By 18 March only the cadre remained, and this eventually returned to Catterick in Yorkshire.

The final scenes occurred on Friday 23 May, when the cadre, with the colours, returned to its county, under command of Lt-Col. E.H. Evans MC. Owing to the early hour at which it would arrive, it was decided to detrain and breakfast in Leominster before proceeding on to Hereford. Although the news was only received the evening before, the mayor, in spite of the early hour (5.00 a.m.), immediately organized a civic reception, which met the cadre at the station. From there the men were marched by the recently reconstituted town band, which was mainly composed of former 1st Herefords, to the square, where they were officially welcomed. Afterwards the party proceeded to the Royal Oak Hotel for breakfast.

The cadre then re-entrained for Hereford, where a great welcome awaited them, the town being gaily beflagged. The official welcome took place in the square, where they were received by the Lord Lieutenant, Sir John Cotterell Bt and the mayor. After the colours had had laurel wreaths placed on them by Lady Evelyn Cotterell and the mayoress, a procession was formed and the entire party marched to the Town Hall, where a banquet took place. In conclusion the cadre proceeded to the barracks, where the colours were deposited. The following day the men dispersed and proceeded to their homes.

In the war the battalion had done well and had established a tradition and reputation for itself, one which was not only nobly upheld but also further enhanced in the Second World War, twenty years later.

CHAPTER 11

2nd/1st and 3rd/1st Battalions the Herefordshire Regiment, 1914–19

At the outbreak of the First World War in August 1914 the Territorial Force was mobilized, and in addition the Regular Army was augmented by the enlistment of men 'for the duration of the war', and these volunteers formed the famous 'Kitchener's new armies'. In 1915 the National Registration Act (5 & 6 Geo V C60) provided for compulsory registration of all persons between the ages of 15 and 65 years who were not members of the forces, and subsequently all men between the ages of 18 and 40 were canvassed with a view to their voluntary enlistment. Lord Derby, the Director General of Recruiting, introduced a scheme under which men were attested, classified into groups and transferred to Class 'B' Army Reserve until their group was mobilized.

These measures proved inadequate, and conscription was introduced in 1916 under the Military Service Acts (5 & 6 Geo V C104 *et seq*), which provided that all male British subjects between the ages of 18 and 51 were liable for compulsory military service and were deemed to have been enlisted into His Majesty's Regular Forces for the duration of the war. Unless they were excepted under the terms of the Acts they were called up in classes in a similar manner to recruits under the 'Derby Scheme'.

Conscription was suspended in November 1918 and the Acts expired on 31 August 1921, but to provide against a possible outbreak of hostilities in the period between the Armistice in November 1918 and the ratification of the Peace Treaty in 1920, all men released from service with the colours were transferred to Class Z of the Army Reserve. This class was abolished in March 1920 and the men were automatically discharged from the Army.

In 1914 Col. A.H.J. Doyle was recalled to command the depot of the KSLI at Copthorne Barracks, Shrewsbury, and 53rd Regimental Area with competent military authority over the counties of Shropshire, Herefordshire and Radnorshire. He held command until 1917, when he was succeeded by Maj. A.T.C. Rundle.

From 1 November 1917 recruiting was in the hands of the newly formed Ministry of National Service, but between 6 August 1914 and 26 February 1917 the number of men recruited by his staff in the area was as follows:

	Shropshire	*Herefordshire*	*Radnorshire*
Men enlisted	12,679	5,471	721
Mobilized from groups	6,527	2,957	481
Mobilized from classes	1,636	619	264
Total	20,842	9,047	1,466
Population	246,307	113,088	22,590

Percentage 8.08

The Territorial Force, comprising fourteen infantry divisions and fourteen mounted brigades, each with its complement of artillery, engineers and supporting arms, was constituted for home defence, but the possibility of its use abroad in a national emergency had always been considered, and in this respect a precedent had been set by the employment of the Imperial Yeomanry and Infantry VSCs in the South African War.

On 5 August 1914 the Territorial Force was mobilized and, although nearly all units volunteered for overseas service, the force was not used as an expeditionary force, neither were the Territorial associations used to the full advantage. The county associations were allowed to raise 2nd, 3rd and Reserve Territorial Battalions, but the great mass of the nation that volunteered was swept into the 'New armies' raised by Lord Kitchener, Secretary of State of War.

53 Division was the original Welsh Territorial Division, but the wartime expansion soon caused the formation of 68 (Welsh) Territorial Division, a home service division, in which 2nd/1st Battalion the Herefordshire Regiment served.

It was recorded in Chapter 7 that 1st Battalion the Herefordshire Regiment was mobilized on 5 August 1914 and that it proceeded immediately to its home defence stations. The vast majority of the battalion having accepted the Imperial Service obligation, it volunteered for overseas service, and on 16 July 1915 it embarked with 53 (Welsh) Division to join the Mediterranean Expeditionary Force at Gallipoli.

2nd/1st Battalion the Herefordshire Regiment

The Herefordshires, being a single battalion Territorial 'county' regiment, had no draft-finding organization of its own, and in consequence the War Office ordered a second line battalion to be raised on 22 August 1914. Lt-Col. J.H. Gilbert-Harris from 1st Battalion was appointed to command and Capt. F.T. Carver was his adjutant.

Capt. Carver had been appointed adjutant of the depot in Hereford prior to the formation of the 2nd Battalion, and he did tremendous work in the first vital days of the war. Merely to say that the battalion was raised fails to give a true picture of the situation as it existed at that time. Carver was absolutely alone at the depot until joined on the afternoon of 7 August 1914 by Capt. J.H.M. Greenly, who had been delayed en route to join. These two officers had to do, and improvise, everything on their own: buy food and clothing; select NCOs; and organize the men. The few old NCOs remaining were invaluable, and with their aid order was created out of chaos.

For the first few weeks the battalion was accommodated at the drill hall and at Scudamore Schools. During this time more than 1,200 men were enlisted, while 400 were received from 1st Battalion, having been found unfit for overseas service or not having accepted the Imperial Service obligation. About 400 replacements were readily found and posted to the 1st Battalion. It will be appreciated that at this time members of the Territorial Force were under no obligation to serve overseas, but later, under the Military Service Acts of 1916, any individual member of the Territorial Force who had not accepted the Imperial Service obligation automatically became an army reservist and subject to the provisions of those Acts.

Towards the end of September, Lt-Col. Gilbert-Harris vacated the command, being replaced by Maj. W.B. Wood-Roe. The battalion proceeded to Aberystwyth, where it joined 68 Division, being brigaded with battalions of the Monmouthshire Regiment. Here it stayed until April 1915, when it moved to Northampton and formed part of the central force. It subsequently moved to Billericay on the Thames estuary in the summer, and to Bedford in the autumn.

Numerous drafts were sent out to 1st Battalion, and eventually, in the spring of 1916, it was reorganized. All unfit and Home Service men were transferred to a home service battalion under the command of Lt-Col. A.D. Bacon.

During the earlier stages of the existence of the battalion, great credit was due to Capt. Carver, who organized central messing for the battalion. This was a great success in more ways than one, and by the time he handed over the messing fund it had a credit of no less than £3,300.

By 1 April 2nd/1st Battalion the Herefordshire Regiment was part of 205 Brigade of 68 (Welsh) Division. On or about 20 June 1916 Lt-Col. J.H. Addie took command of the battalion. On 5 December 1916 205 Brigade was stationed at Lowestoft, and it was there on 24 July 1917 that 2nd/1st Battalion the Herefordshire Regiment, under the command of Lt-Col. D. Bates, was ordered to 'be absorbed'. By November 1917 it had joined 205 Brigade at Herringfleet, Suffolk, which in January 1918 was located at Oulton Broad. In April 1918 the remaining details were absorbed by 4th (Reserve) Battalion KSLI, then forming part of the Welsh Reserve Brigade attached to the Milford Haven defences and stationed at Pembroke Dock.

3rd/1st Battalion the Herefordshire Regiment, later 1st Reserve Battalion the Herefordshire Regiment

The third line battalion of the Herefordshire Regiment, known as 3rd/1st Herefordshire Regiment, was raised in Hereford in the autumn of 1915. Lt-Col. R.H.T. Symonds-Taylor was the commanding officer and Capt. G. Barlow-Ascroft was the adjutant. This was more in the nature of a composite battalion, as it contained personnel of the Herefordshire and Monmouthshire Regiments. In 1916 it served at Abergavenny and Oswestry.

On 20 June 1916 the battalion is shown as belonging to A Group 3rd Line Welsh Division, and on 1 July 1916 it was termed 1st Reserve Battalion of the Welsh Reserve Brigade. On 20 September 1916 3rd/1st Battalion the Herefordshire Regiment became 1st Reserve Battalion the Herefordshire Regiment, and on 5 December 1916 it was stationed with the Welsh Reserve Brigade at Oswestry.

On 24 July 1917 1st Reserve Battalion the Herefordshire Regiment was located at Swansea, where it was linked with 4th Reserve Battalion KSLI, which prior to 1916 had been 3rd/4th Battalion KSLI. The two units were to amalgamate as 4th (Reserve) Battalion KSLI under the command of Lt-Col. R.H.T. Symonds-Taylor.

The amalgamation was complete by November 1917 and by January 1918, 4th (Reserve) Battalion KSLI had moved to Pembroke Dock to join the Milford Haven defences, but it continued to belong to the Welsh Reserve Brigade. Presumably this move was necessary to replace 3rd (Special Reserve) Battalion KSLI (late the Shropshire Militia), which in December 1917 was moved to Queenstown, Ireland, after having been stationed at Pembroke Dock since mobilization.

In April 1918 the commanding officer was Lt-Col. R.E. Cheyse, and during this month the Battalion absorbed the details of 2nd/1st Battalion the Herefordshire Regiment as mentioned above. In January 1919 4th (Reserve) Battalion KSLI was commanded by Brevet Lt-Col. J. Fane DSO, and it continued to serve at Pembroke Dock until it was disbanded after the Armistice.

PART III: THE HEREFORDSHIRE REGIMENT (TA), 1921–39

CHAPTER 12

1st Battalion the Herefordshire Regiment, 1920–39

In 1919 the Territorial Force was disbanded, but the force was reconstructed in 1920 and in 1921 the designation was changed to Territorial Army. Only members who would accept the liability to serve overseas were accepted, but it was laid down that an Act of Parliament was necessary before the TA could be despatched overseas.

In the original proposals the Herefordshire Regiment was to re-form as a heavy artillery unit, but after vigorous protest throughout the county it reformed as an Infantry Corps of the Kings Shropshire Light infantry. This post-war reorganization led to the severance of the association with Radnorshire, which had existed since 1860. In Radnorshire, the TA were re-formed as a Field Artillery Battery, part of 83 (Welsh) Brigade RFA with 53 (Welsh) Infantry Division.

The 1st Battalion the Herefordshire Regiment was under the command of Lt-Col. H.E.P. Patteshall DSO who had a distinguished military record, and formed part of 159 (Welsh) Border Infantry Division. The remaining battalions of the brigade were 1st, 2nd and 3rd Battalions of the Monmouthshire Regiment.

The Defence Force 1921

At the time of the railway strike in 1921, feelings were running high and there was fear of civil disturbances. The TA as such was not called out but a Defence Force was formed of volunteers from the TA. The Herefordshire Regiment assisted with this force by forming a Herefordshire Company of 5 Officers and 57 other ranks under Lt-Col. A.M. Boulton DSO; it was officially designated responsible for guarding vital points and safeguarding essential supplies. There were no serious disturbances.

1st Battalion the Herefordshire Regiment, 1921–1939

There is little of historical interest to record relating to the interwar period; it is sufficient to say that the battalion carried out its normal training and attended camp regularly. In these activities it fully maintained its reputation, both for military efficiency and sport, and it secured many trophies.

Army Order 470 of December 1922 stipulated that a maximum of 10 of the battle honours awarded to commemorate services in the First World War would be borne on the King's colour, and in consequence the following 10 honours were emblazoned on the horizontal arm of the Cross of St George of the King's colour of the Herefordshire Regiment:

Soissonnais-Ourcq
Ypres 1918
Courtrai
France and Flanders 1918
Landing at Suvla
Rumani
Gaza
El Mughar
Jerusalem
Tell Asur

It will be remembered that colours of the Territorial Force were not provided from public funds, and it was expressly stipulated that 'None of the devices, mottoes and distinctions authorised for Regular Regiments will be borne on the Colours of an Infantry Battalion of the Territorial Force, which though affiliated to it, does not bear its title'. Such a regulation prevented the complete unification of all parts of a regiment – Regular, Special Reserve (Militia) and Territorial Force – but during the First World War, Army Order 298 of 1917 stated that

> In consideration of the services of the Territorial Force during the War His Majesty the King has been pleased to approve of units of the Territorial Force being permitted to bear on the badges the mottoes and honours worn on the badges of the Corps, Regiment or Department of which they form part.

This foreshadowed the complete unification of all parts of a regiment or corps, and Army Order 338 of 1922 stated that there would be one honour list only for each regiment. The same unification was authorized in the 1924 TA Regulations in respect of colours; since when, for example, the colours of 4th Battalion KSLI have borne the full regimental battle honours and not merely those of the battalion.

The Herefordshire Regiment maintained its separate status and did not adopt any of the honours of the parent corps, nor did it become light infantry. However, it is recorded in Chapter 20 that the honour of becoming light infantry was conferred on the regiment on 28 May 1947. The status of the Herefordshire Regiment within the Corps of the KSLI was a peculiar one in that it was not only a territorial 'county regiment', but also a heavy infantry regiment, whereas its parent corps was not only a light infantry regiment but also a royal regiment, having the distinction of wearing the blue facings. These differences were further accentuated by the fact that the title of the parent corps did not include reference to Herefordshire.

This omission was the subject of periodic comment, and on various occasions during the years 1911–12 and 1919–20 consideration had been given to the suggestion of altering the title of the regular regiment to either the King's Light Infantry (Shropshire and Herefordshire Regiment) or The King's Shropshire and Herefordshire Light Infantry, but no decision had been reached.

In 1926 on the occasion of the visit of 2nd Battalion KSLI to Hereford, Sir John Cotterell Bt, Lord Lieutenant of Herefordshire, proposed that the KSLI should become the King's Shropshire and Herefordshire Light Infantry in recognition of the fact that the regiment recruited from Shropshire and Herefordshire and had a TA battalion in each county. This proposal was backed by Brig Gen R.J. Bridgford CB, CMG, DSO. On 26 July 1933 with the approval of the Earl of Powys, Lord Lieutenant of Shropshire, submission was made to the Under Secretary of State for War that the title of the Regiment be changed to 'The King's Light Infantry (Shropshire and Herefordshire) Regiment' with the change in TA titles.

After further consideration of all the circumstances of the case the adjutant general recommended that the proposition should not proceed. This recommendation being accepted, the colonel of the regiment notified the lords lieutenant of the counties of Shropshire and Herefordshire of the decision in April 1934. In doing so he made specific mention of the fact that the Herefordshire Regiment (TA) did not desire any change to be made in its status or title.

The Herefordshire Regiment was well supported during the interwar years and in 1927 the members of the band were issued with full dress for the first time since 1914. The scarlet tunics with green facings added a welcome splash of colour to the battalion parades. In 1929 recruiting was greatly assisted by the use of a film depicting the history of the regiment, which was produced by the commanding officer, Lt-Col. J.L. Sleeman CMG CBE MVO, who had taken over command from Lt-Col. H.E.P. Pateshall DSO in 1926. In 1929 the first reunion of the Herefordshire Regiment Old Comrades Association was held. This has since become an annual event. On 30 January 1930 Col. M.J.G. Scobie CB VD TD DL died, aged 78 years. He was the first commanding officer of the regiment and, at the time of his death, the honorary colonel of the regiment. Lord Somers CMG DSO MC of Eastnor Castle succeeded as honorary colonel in 1932.

The 1st Battalion the Herefordshire Regiment comprised four rifle companies and a headquarters wing. B Company was the heavy weapons company, being at first designated (MG) and later, in 1934, support company (S). The order of battle in 1934 was as under-noted, Lt-Col. S.C. Tomlinson having taken over command in 1931 on the appointment of Col. J.L. Sleeman CMG CBE MVO to the command of 160 (South Wales) Infantry Brigade.

Commanding officer	Lt-Col. Tomlinson, S.C.
Second in command	Maj. Taylor, B.S.W. DFC
Quartermaster	Capt. Millington, G. DCM
Adjutant	Capt. Hallowes, J.W. MC KSLI
Medical officer	Capt. Wood-Power, R. RAMC (T)
Padre	Revd Bradley, H.H.
Transport officer	Lt. Davies, D.T.W.

Headquarters Wing, Hereford
Commanding officer	Capt. Challenger, L.H.
6 officers and 142 other ranks	

A Coy, Hereford (with a detachment at Weobley)
Commanding officer	Lt. Roberts, J.N.
4 officers and 109 other ranks	

B (S) Company, Ross
Commanding officer	Capt. Blake, N.G.
3 officers and 92 other ranks	

C Company, Ledbury
Commanding officer   Capt. Parr, H.C.
4 officers and 73 other ranks

D Company, Leominster
Commanding officer   Capt. Carless, T.A.
3 officers and 108 other ranks

The Leominster Company was organized as follows:

13 and 14 Platoons	Leominster
15 Platoon	Bromyard
16 Platoon	Kington

On 2 May 1935, 2nd Battalion KSLI laid up its old colours in Hereford Cathedral, new colours having been presented to the battalion by HRH The Duke of York in Shrewsbury on 25 April 1935. The guard of honour furnished by 1st Battalion the Herefordshire Regiment was commanded by Capt. J.H. Roberts. Lt. C.F. Wegg-Prosser and Lt. T. Holloway were on parade, the latter carrying the regimental colour.

On the occasion of the Coronation of HM King George VI on 12 May 1937, the regiment was represented by Col. S.C. Tomlinson, and a detachment including a street-lining platoon under Maj. B.S.W. Taylor DFC, and the colour party under Lt. F.W. Juckes.

The Coronation year will be remembered in the Territorial Army as that in which preparations for the Second World War commenced. 1937 saw the first serious attempt to mechanize the infantry battalions of the Territorial Army, and in that eventful year Lt-Col. L.F. Sloane-Stanley succeeded to the command of 1st Battalion the Herefordshire Regiment.

By 1938 the likelihood of war had greatly increased, and urgent steps were taken to increase the mobility of the infantry divisions. As a result the infantry brigades were reduced from four to three battalions, and in consequence 159 (Welsh Border) Brigade of 53 (Welsh) Division was reorganized as follows:

4th Battalion the King's Shropshire Light Infantry
3rd Battalion the Monmouthshire Regiment
1st Battalion the Herefordshire Regiment

4th Battalion KSLI transferred from 160 (South Wales) Infantry Brigade in which it had served since 1920. 160 Brigade under the command of Col. J.L. Sleeman CMG CBE MVO had been chosen to take part in regular army manoeuvres in 1935, and as a result of the success of this experiment it had been decided to utilize the Territorial Army as a means of expansion in the event of a major war. This decision was in keeping with the true spirit of the Haldane Reforms and in complete contrast with the method adopted in 1914 when, it will be remembered, the Territorial Force was misused and in its place was raised the 'new armies'.

The experience of mobilization gained in the First World War was invaluable at the outbreak of the Second World War in September 1939. In March 1939 Mr Hore-Belisha, Secretary of State for War, called for volunteers to double the strength of the Territorial Army and to form the 'second line'. Each first line unit of the Territorial Army provided a nucleus of officers and NCOs from which was raised a duplicate. 53 (Welsh) Division thus raised 38 (Welsh) Division and the Territorial Army as a whole formed the basis for the expansion of the land forces in the Second World War.

The Herefordshire Regiment responded magnificently to this appeal and the manner in which it prepared itself for war reflected great credit on those officers who had so patiently trained 1st Battalion during the interwar years. Deserving of special mention are the commanding officers Lt-Col. H.E.P. Pateshall DSO, Lt-Col. J.L. Sleeman CMG CBE MVO, Lt-Col. S.C. Tomlinson and Lt-Col. L.F. Sloane-Stanley; and the adjutants Capt. Sloane-Stanley of the Middlesex Regiment (who later returned to command the battalion), and Captains Green, Shears, Hallowes and Thompson, all from the KSLI.

The reorganization was gradual, and the first change was perhaps the most unpopular, when on 1 November 1938 B Company reverted to its role of Rifle Company and parted with its Vickers machine-guns. Headquarters Company was then reorganized early in 1939 when the establishment provided for six platoons:

1 Platoon	Signallers
2 Platoon	AALA
3 Platoon	Mortars
4 Platoon	Carriers
5 Platoon	Pioneers
6 Platoon	Administration

Recruiting was brisk and a special staff was necessary to attend to the volunteers. The Mayor of Hereford made an appeal for recruits, and National Service demonstrations were staged throughout the county.

In April 1939, 1st Battalion the Herefordshire Regiment was divided to form 2nd Battalion, and the Regimental organization was as follows:

1st Battalion		*2nd Battalion*	
Lt-Col. Sloane-Stanley, L.F.		Lt-Col. Blake, N.G. MBE	
New Company	*Old Company*	*New Company*	*Old Company*
Headquarters Hereford	Headquarters Hereford (Part)	Headquarters Hereford	Headquarters Hereford (Part)
A Hereford	A Hereford (Part)	W Hereford	A Hereford (Part)
B Kington (one platoon at Eardisley)	D Leominster (Kington Platoon)	X Ross	B Ross
C Leominster (one platoon at Weobley)	D Leominster	Y Ledbury (one platoon at Colwall)	C Ledbury
D Leominster (one platoon at Leintwardine)	D Leominster	Z Bromyard	D Leominster (Bromyard platoon)

Lt-Col. N.G. Blake MBE was appointed to command 2nd Battalion. He formerly commanded B Company (Ross) of the original 1st Battalion, and he received his decoration in the 1939 New Year's Honours List.

On 18 May 1939 conscription was introduced in peace time for the first time in our history, and under the provisions of the Militia Act (the Military Training Act 1939) (2 and 3 Geo VI C23), every man reaching the age of 20 was liable for two years' compulsory service: six months with the colours and eighteen months with the Territorial Army. The first 'Militiamen', so known, joined the Colours on 15 July 1939 and received their primary training at regimental depots. (This militia is not to be confused with the old Constitutional Force referred to in Chapter 2.) The National Service (Armed Forces) Act (2–3 Geo VI C81) followed on 2 September 1939 and provided that all able-bodied men between the ages of 18 and 41 were liable for military service for the duration of the war.

The Regular Army, Territorial Army, Reserves and 'Militia' became thenceforth the British Army, and equipment, training and conditions were standardized. The Territorial Army, as such, was suspended, and members were required to remove from their uniforms the small metal T which they had so proudly worn on their lapels or shoulder straps to denote their non-regular status.

In 1939 the United Kingdom was divided into regions for civil defence, each under a regional commissioner. The Welsh Region with headquarters at Cardiff, consisted of the whole of Wales, while the counties of Shropshire and Herefordshire were part of the Midland Region, with headquarters at Birmingham. Militarily, Wales, Shropshire and Herefordshire came under Western Command, with headquarters at Chester, and formed Welsh Area with headquarters at Shrewsbury. This area was divided into four zones, each under a zone commander with powers to assist the civil defence authorities in an emergency.

Certain vulnerable points laid down by the War Office were to be guarded by troops of the recently formed National Defence Companies (Territorial Army Reserve). In 1939 ex-servicemen between the ages of 45 and 55 were encouraged to enlist in a Reserve Company of their local Territorial battalion, which was to be formed for home defence. It was proposed to form a platoon in each large town in the county and enlistment was for four years, and the rates of pay and allowances were as laid down for the Territorial Army. On being called up for service in one of the groups of the National Defence Companies, men, if passed fit, received a bounty of £5. They were clothed, armed and equipped as in the Territorial Army, and British Legion Headquarters were asked by the War Office to assist in raising a force of 25,000 men. However, as it transpired, events moved too quickly and it was found impracticable to deploy the National Defence Companies, and initially most of the vulnerable points were guarded by Militiamen from the depots in Welsh Area.

Until the end of July 1939, Maj.-Gen. B.T. Wilson DSO, commander of 53 (Welsh) Division with headquarters in Shrewsbury, was also area commander of Welsh Area, but on 1 August 1939 a separate area commander was appointed. By 29 August the headquarters of the brigades of 53 Division were ready for war – 158 (North Wales) Infantry Brigade at Wrexham, 159 (Welsh Border) Infantry Brigade at Hereford and 160 (South Wales) Infantry Brigade at Cardiff.

It was decided that, in the event of mobilization, operational control of Welsh Area would be in the hands of the commander of 53 (Welsh) Division. On embodiment of all troops in the area, including 53 (Welsh) Division and 38 (Welsh) Division they were to move as quickly as possible to their civil defence areas.

1st and 2nd Battalions the Herefordshire Regiment formed part of 53 and 38 Welsh Divisions respectively, when on 1 September 1939 the order to embody was received at divisional headquarters. 1st Battalion had just returned from annual camp at Weston-Super-Mare when it was embodied on 2 September 1939, and it concentrated in Hereford on the following day. 2nd Battalion was still attending the annual camp at Weston-Super-Mare on 1 September 1939, and it embodied on 3 September as part of 114 Infantry Brigade. The first week of September was a period of intense activity throughout the division, but by 6 September all units had moved to their civil defence areas, the first move in their long march to victory.

CHAPTER 13

Mobilization and Training for War – 1st Battalion the Herefordshire Regiment 1939–46

The Early Days

The battalion, under the command of Lt-Col. L.F. Sloane-Stanley, was embodied on 2 September 1939 and concentrated in Hereford on the 3rd. At 11.15 a.m. on that eventful day the Prime Minister, Mr Neville Chamberlain, announced that a state of war existed with Germany. At Hereford the battalion commenced a long and varied period of training, which was to continue until the battalion was committed to action in Normandy on 13 June 1944. The battalion started with a strong nucleus of territorials and was quickly brought up to war establishment by drafts of militiamen and recruits.

Although there were many changes in personnel, location and organization during this period, the battalion gradually increased in battle efficiency and developed a fine *esprit de corps*. Initially the headquarters of 53 (Welsh) Division moved from Shrewsbury to Saundersfoot, Pembrokeshire, and 159 Brigade was located at Tenby, where the battalion was stationed in home defence from 8 November 1939 until 10 April 1940.

The German invasion of Norway and Denmark in April 1940 made raids against Northern Ireland, if not a full-scale invasion, possible, and it became essential that the troops in Northern Ireland should speedily be reinforced. The threat of invasion was further increased when the British Expeditionary Force was withdrawn from Dunkirk in June 1940 and the German occupation of France and the Low Countries was completed.

In addition to this primary anti-invasion role, the troops in Northern Ireland were actively engaged in internal security duties necessitated by the activities of the Irish Republican Army. This underground movement, based and recruited in neutral Eire, consisted of partisans opposed to the partition of Ireland. They were not pro-German, but were prepared to take advantage of the war conditions to further their cause, which was the unification of Ireland.

As early as October 1939, elements of 53 (Welsh) Division were moved to Northern Ireland, and in April 1940 they were reinforced with the remainder of the division. On the arrival of 53 Division, Northern Ireland District was divided into three areas. The divisional headquarters was in Belfast, and 159 Brigade, with headquarters at Londonderry, was responsible for the northern area. In June 1940 61 Division was sent to reinforce Northern Ireland further, and Ulster was then divided into two areas. 53 Division became responsible for the southern area, which included the frontier with Eire, and the headquarters of 159 Brigade were then located at Newcastle.

In March 1940 Lt-Col. A.D. Bryant succeeded to the command of 1st Battalion the Herefordshire Regiment, which on 10 April 1940 left Tenby, arriving at Portrush, Northern

Ireland, the next day. The battalion remained there until 7 June, when it moved to Larne, remaining there until 19 June. It was stationed at Castlewellan from 19 June until 9 May 1941, where it spent a most uncomfortable time under canvas, and then moved to Newcastle, where it remained until 16 November 1941, when it returned to England, arriving at Crewe on 18 November 1941, much to the joy of all ranks of the battalion.

The headquarters of 159 Brigade were at Comberbach, and, after training in the Mountains of Mourne, it was a welcome relief to exercise in the Potteries, and later on the Downs of Kent. The battalion left Crewe on 7 April 1942 and arrived at Linton, Kent, on 9 April, remaining there until 11 May 1942, when it moved to the splendid Militia camp at Maresfield, Sussex. In Kent the headquarters of 159 Brigade had been at Bearsted, and while there, in May 1942, 53 Division was selected to be reorganized as one of the 'new model divisions'. These were designed to meet the anti-invasion role in which the main requirement was quick offensive action by a powerful force in order to dislodge any invasion troops while they were off balance, and before they could become firmly established. This was achieved by replacing one infantry brigade by a tank brigade, and in consequence 159 Infantry Brigade – to the regret of the whole Welsh division – was transferred to 11 Armoured Division, then reorganizing in the East Grinstead–Crowborough area of Sussex.

11 Armoured Division

Its conversion in May 1942 to the Lorryborne Infantry Brigade of 11 Armoured Division had a revitalizing effect on 159 Brigade, and while everybody was sorry to leave 53 (Welsh) Division, the idea of training as part of an armoured division captured the imagination and gave a fillip to all. On leaving 53 Division the divisional sign of the red W was replaced by the black bull on a yellow rectangle, which was to become famous as the sign of 11 Armoured Division.

159 Infantry Brigade, with 29 Armoured Brigade, formed 11 Armoured Division under the command of Maj.-Gen. P.C.S. Hobart (later Sir Percy Hobart). Training in close cooperation with infantry and tanks was the order of the day. This relationship soon became firmly cemented, and out of it grew the divisional *esprit de corps*.

The North African False Alarm

The battalion left Maresfield camp, Sussex, on 15 August 1942, having been there since 11 May, and moved to Weeting Hall camp, Brandon, in Suffolk. On 16 August 1942 the division was ordered to mobilize for North Africa to join the 1st Army. Everyone was highly elated by this prospect of active service after months of training, and there was much activity in preparing and re-equipping for the campaign.

In September 1942 Maj.-Gen. M. Brocas Burrows succeeded to the command of the division, and in the same month the command of 1st Battalion the Herefordshire Regiment passed to Lt-Col. J.B. Churcher DSO. Training continued, and by Christmas the division was all but ready. While awaiting embarkation orders, 1st Battalion the Herefordshire Regiment was inspected by HRH the Duke of Gloucester on 7 January 1943, but the occasion was spoiled by pouring rain. On 20 January the battalion left Weeting Hall camp and moved to West Tofts camp, Brandon, and here on 26 January 1943 the brigade was inspected by HM King George VI.

Shortly afterwards, the battalion transport was despatched for loading on the ships in the various western ports, but on 30 January 1943 they were returned to base as the embarkation was suddenly cancelled. The decision not to send 11 Armoured Division to North Africa was made at the Casablanca Conference in view of the fact that the military situation in Tunisia required infantry not armour, and in consequence 1 Infantry Division was embarked instead. This was a severe test of morale: there was great disappointment and the prospect of more training was not viewed with enthusiasm. However, leave was granted, and the Division resigned itself to the situation.

Training was resumed with a series of night exercises, and with assault courses in the Stanford Battle Training area in Norfolk. Special hardening exercises were carried out in the form of six-day route marches by companies.

On 16 March 1943 the battalion left West Tofts camp for Newmarket, where it was stationed in stables until 10 June 1943 on the transfer of the division to the East Riding of Yorkshire. Divisional headquarters were at South Dalton, a village 7 miles north of Beverley, and 1st Battalion the Herefordshire Regiment was stationed at Hornsea on the Yorkshire coast, moving to Leven, a few miles inland, on 3 September 1943.

Training continued at Leven until 23 September 1943, when the battalion returned to Hornsea, where it spent Christmas. In December 1943 Maj.-Gen. G.P.B. Roberts took command of the division, and it was in his experienced and capable hands that it served with such distinction in the North West European Campaign.

In Yorkshire the infantry and armour were finally welded together into a team that worked with perfect understanding and trust. The combined camps at Butterwick and Burrow House were the forging grounds of 11 Armoured Division, and members of the battalion will long remember the strenuous battle exercises which stood them in such good stead in the days which followed. Notable were exercises Eagle and Rum. Exercise Eagle was of twelve days duration and took place in the neighbourhood of the Octon crossroads on about 13 February 1944. Exercise Rum terminated on 25 February 1944.

The battalion spent eight days training at the Combined Operations School at Inverary and also attended the street-fighting school at West Ham. At Inverary was practised embarkation and disembarkation drill in infantry landing ships and tank landing craft, assault landings across beaches, the use of scrambling nets and boat drill. The MT drivers were instructed in waterproofing their vehicles, and they practised driving down ramps and through water obstacles.

The same enthusiasm was to be seen on the sports fields. The battalion football team was the pride of the unit, and in every sporting activity the battalion was well to the fore. The climax was on 1 January 1944, when the soccer team won the East Riding District Services Cup, having won the Divisional League and Knock-out Competition earlier in the same season.

On 2 April 1944 the battalion left Hornsea and arrived in Aldershot on the following Tuesday, and there the division concentrated as part of the Allied Expeditionary Force awaiting D-Day – 6 June 1944.

The following is the order of battle of the 1st Battalion the Herefordshire Regiment, June 1944:

Battalion Headquarters

Commanding officer	Lt-Col. Churcher, J.B.
Second in command	Maj. Turner-Cain, G.R.
Adjutant	Capt. Knyvett-Hoff, G.A.
Quartermaster	Capt. Bryant, T.C.R.
Intelligence Officer	Lt. Woolcott, C.W.P.
Regimental Sergeant-Major	WO1 Wells, P.D.
Regimental Quartermaster-Sergeant	WO2 Rollings, H.H.

Headquarters Company

Commanding officer	Capt. Lloyd, G.H.
	Lt. Hesketh, R.B.
	Lt. Powley, N.A.
Military Transport Officer	Lt. Symonds, F.W.
Regimental Medical Officer	Capt. Hole, E.K. (RAMC)
CSM	WO2 Williams, E.J.
CQMS	WO2 Muirhead, A.

Support Company

Commanding officer	Capt. Fripp, R.C.
Anti-tank platoon	Capt. Lench, R.W.
Mortar platoon	Lt. Gooderidge, D.M.
	Lt. Withey, S.J.
Carrier platoon	Capt. Barneby, R.P.
	Lt. Wardman, A.R.
Pioneer platoon	Lt. Grady, J.
CSM	Col.-Sgt Benfield, E.J.
CQMS	Col.-Sgt Meredith, P.G.J.

A Company

Commanding officer	Maj. Croome, J.F.
	Capt. Mason, C.M.
	Lt. Glyde, S.J.
	Lt. Forques, L.
	Lt. Martin, E.A.
CSM	WO2 Toner, N.J.
CQMS	Col.-Sgt French, J.

B Company

Commanding officer	Maj. Crofts, W.A.P.
	Capt. Lowe, C.T.G.
	Lt. Spittal, A.J.
	Lt. Hopkinson, G.
	2/Lt. Hancox, T.E.
CSM	WO2 Mason
CQMS	Col.-Sgt Grice, R.R.

C Company

Commanding officer	Maj. Phillips, A.J.W.
	Capt. Cowan, R.C.
	Lt. Mills, E.L.
	2/Lt. Kotchapaw, W.J.
	2/Lt. Pickering, R.L.
CSM	WO2 Biddlecombe, D.
CQMS	Col.-Sgt Coghill, D.

D Company

Commanding officer	Maj. Barneby, H.H.
	Capt. Northey, L.
	Lt. Criddle, C.W.
	Lt. Creamer, F.B.
	Lt. Boddy, S.H.
CSM	WO2 Greenhouse, A.J.
CQMS	Col.-Sgt Shanley, J.F.

Above. The officers, 1st Bn Herefordshire Regiment, 1944. In the front row, centre, are Maj. H.H. Barneby, Maj. G.R. Turner-Cain, Lt-Col. J.B. Churcher, Capt. G. Knyvett-Hoff and Maj. W.A.P. Crofts.

Below. D Coy, 1st Bn Herefordshire Regiment, pictured at Aldershot prior to Operation Overlord. In the front row, centre, are Maj. H.H. Barneby, commanding officer, and CSM WO2 Jack Greenhouse.

CHAPTER 14

1st Battalion the Herefordshire Regiment, 1939–46 – Summary

On 2 September 1939, 1st Battalion was embodied, and the following day was concentrated in Hereford. After a few weeks of basic training the battalion moved to Tenby, South Wales, on 8 November 1939, where 159 Infantry Brigade was concentrated.

In April 1940 the whole of 53 (Welsh) Infantry Division was concentrated in Northern Ireland as a precaution against a German invasion, and also to provide internal security necessitated by the activities of the IRA. In May 1942 159 Infantry Brigade, after moving to the Crewe area and then to Kent, was selected to become a lorryborne brigade in 11 Armoured Division, and continued training with that formation in Sussex and Suffolk.

In August 1942 the battalion was fully mobilized for overseas, and was ordered to embark with the division for North Africa in January 1943. After all the stores and transport had been despatched to the various ports for loading, the move was cancelled at the last minute, and 1 Infantry Division was embarked instead. Further training continued in Yorkshire until the division concentrated in Aldershot in April 1944.

1st Battalion landed in Normandy with 11 Armoured Division on D-Day plus 7, and concentrated near Lantheuil. After taking part in the Odon Bridgehead action (25 June–2 July 1944) and the attacks east of Caen (18–22 July 1944), the division broke out of the beach-head at Caumont on 30 July 1944. It took part in the advance from the River Seine to Antwerp and eventually crossed the Rhine on 28 March 1945. At the end of hostilities it had reached Bad Segeberg near Lubeck on the Baltic.

On 23 May the battalion, having moved to Flensburg with 159 Infantry Brigade, took part in the last operation with 1st Cheshire Regiment and 15th/19th Hussars. At 10.00 a.m. Doenitz's Puppet Government was arrested at Flensburg and at the Schloss at Glucksburg. The battalion captured its last trophy in the form of two pennants, flown on Doenitz's car. The pennants have been mounted in a wooden frame with the caption: 'These pennants flew on the car of Grand Admiral Doenitz, Second and Last Fuhrer of the Third and Last Reich; on the 23rd May 1945 they were removed by the 1st Bn The Herefordshire Regiment for safe custody.' They are now displayed in the Officers' Mess.

On 29 September 1945 the battalion, on behalf of the Herefordshire Regiment, received the Freedom of the City of Hereford. A detachment commanded by Maj. W.A.P. Crofts MC and 159 Infantry Brigade band were sent home for this ceremony. On the same day the Mayor and Corporation of Hereford granted the regiment the use of the Militia silver on ceremonial occasions. This silver had been handed to the corporation on the disbandment of the Herefordshire Militia in 1908, as recorded in Chapter 3.

Five months later 11 Armoured Division was disbanded, and 159 Infantry Brigade – consisting of 4th Battalion KSLI and 1st Battalion the Herefordshire Regiment – rejoined 53 (Welsh) Infantry Division in the Ruhr. The battalion moved to Krefeld, where it was employed on internal security duties. In the middle of June it was ordered into suspended animation by 15 July 1946. A final ceremonial parade of 1st Battalion the Herefordshire Regiment was held on 17 June 1946, when it was inspected by the honorary colonel, Maj.-Gen. J.B. Churcher DSO.

Locations of the 1st Bn the Herefordshire Regiment, 1939–46.

Casualties

Officers   8
Other ranks   210

Battle Honours

For services in the Second World War the following battle honours were awarded.

*Odon	*Hechtel
Defence of Rauray	*Venraij
*Bourguebus Ridge	Venlo Pocket
Cagny	Rhineland
Mont Pinçon	*Hochwald
*Souleuvre	Ibbenburen
*Falaise	*Aller
*Antwerp	*North West Europe 1944–5

Campaign Medals

1939–1945 Star
France and Germany Star (1944–5)
Defence Medal (1939–45)
War Medal (1939–45)

*Emblazoned on the Queen's colour

CHAPTER 15

The Normandy Battle, June 1944 – Operation Overlord

D-Day came and preparations reached their final stage. 11 Armoured Division, as part of 8th Corps, was to be committed as a follow-up division, when 1st Corps and 30th Corps had established a bridgehead. At last, on 8 June, orders were received to move to the marshalling area. The following day the battalion moved in two parts, the main body under the commanding officer, Lt-Col. J.B. Churcher, by rail, and the vehicle party under the second in command, by road.

The commanding officer's party was marshalled at Camp J9, Hayward's Heath, and embarked from Newhaven at 1.00 p.m. on 13 June, sailing at 11.00 p.m. on the same day. It landed from its landing craft infantry (LCI) on Mike Beach in Normandy without incident, to be greeted by the smiling faces of the advance party, which had gone across the previous day. By 2.00 p.m. on the 14th, disembarkation was complete, and the main body left by march route for the divisional concentration area at Lentheuil via the transit area at Le Valette.

In the meantime the vehicle party had moved to another transit camp, where it duly embarked in a motor transport ship (MTS) and, after being towed into the Thames estuary, sailed on Sunday 10 June. After a delay off Southend, it proceeded and landed on Queen Beach on 13 June. The vehicles were transshipped onto Rhine ferries, which grounded about 50 yards out, and then driven down the ramps and ashore through quite deep water, avoiding underwater shell holes en route.

The vehicle party, which included most of S Company, landed at the extreme eastern edge of the beach-head and had a long journey across country to accomplish before reaching the battalion assembly area. By 16 June the complete battalion had arrived in the area of Cainet and it was fortunate in having ten days to prepare for action, and to become acclimatized to the Continent and the noises of war before being committed to battle.

Odon Bridgehead: Operation Epsom

On 25 June, orders were received for Operation Epsom. The object of this operation was to break out of the bridgehead, cross the rivers Odon and Orne, and to isolate Caen. Opposing the 2nd British Army on this particular sector of the bridgehead were known to be 1st, 2nd, 9th and 12th SS Panzer Divisions, and somewhere on the front the famous Panzer Lehr Divison. 11 Armoured Division was to be committed in accordance with the progress of 15 Scottish Division and the reactions of the enemy.

On the morning of 27 June the earth trembled and the battalion first witnessed at close quarters a full-scale barrage. At 12.15 p.m. the battalion moved up to an assembly area at Norrey-en-Bessin in the centre of the supporting gun area and dug in. Although no enemy shells were landing at the time, amid all the noise and movement the men needed no encouragement to dig, and soon everyone was 3 or 4 feet underground.

Later in the afternoon the battalion moved by march route to occupy Le Haut de Bosq, about

Anti-Tank Platoon, S Coy, 1st Bn the Herefordshire Regiment, pictured at Aldershot prior to Operation Overlord in June 1944.

2 miles short of the River Odon. Everywhere lay evidence of the stiff fight 15(S) Division had had during their attack, and the unit gradually became accustomed to the sights, sounds and smells of the battlefield. The battalion advanced to Cheux, which was completely devastated, and cluttered with refugees. While in the midst of this pathetic village, fresh orders were received to occupy Tourmauville. The unit regrouped at Colleville and advanced as darkness fell. As it crossed the bridge over the Odon, to take over a narrow bridgehead gained by a brigade of the Scottish Division and elements of 29 Armoured Brigade, it came under spasmodic mortar fire. By now it was dark and the battalion took up its position across the river with 4th KSLI adjoining it on the left. It was no easy task for company commanders to recce their positions and deploy their companies in darkness, but with mutual cooperation all companies were on the ground and had started to dig in by 2.00 a.m.

In front of the battalion the ground folded away and rose to a long, continuous ridge parallel to the front. Point 112, the highest part of this ridge, and east of it the village of Esquay were features which were to be bitterly contested by another formation later on. 29 Armoured Brigade tried to advance, but without success, and the day after the battalion had taken up its position the armour was withdrawn back across the river, leaving the two battalions with two troops of SP tank guns only.

The enemy had infiltrated between the two battalion positions, and snipers were established in a wood and causing casualties. The Herefords were ordered to clear the wood and re-establish contact with 4 KSLI. This task was carried out by D Company, then the reserve and counter-attack company, which gained its first prisoner and inflicted its first

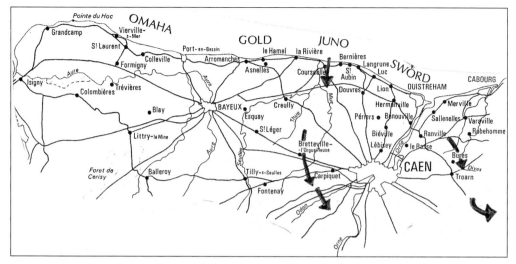

Normandy Beaches and operations round Caen, June–July 1944.

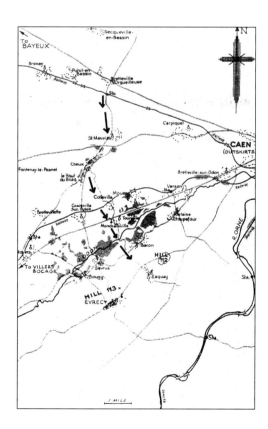

Odon Bridgehead and Hill 112, June–July 1944.

Return to Normandy. Old comrades make a pilgrimage to the battlefields of Normandy to remember their fallen comrades.

Reg Robins (second from right) and old comrades at St Charles-de-Percy War Cemetery.

casualties. Eventually, contact with 4 KSLI was re-established and D Company returned to its own lines.

The brigade was destined to hold this miserable but important bridgehead from 28 June to 6 July. It was a severe blooding to battle, which in itself seemed a campaign. On the left was 4 KSLI, while the enemy was in front and on the right flank. The right flank of the Herefords ran along the wooded valley of the river and was vulnerable to enemy infiltration. The battalion had no contact with a brigade of 15 Scottish Division, known to be somewhere along this valley, and it was alarming, after four days, to receive some stragglers from this brigade who had been badly mauled by a superior enemy force supported by artillery and tanks.

On several occasions, defensive fire tasks were brought down on the battalion front to forestall suspected enemy attacks. Three in particular became well known, and were codenamed Dorothy, Dainty and Duchess.

The night of 30 June/1 July was one which will be remembered by all who were on the bridgehead at the time. The listening patrols heard the enemy moving up to the attack. A considerable fire fight developed and the British artillery D.F. succeeded in keeping the enemy behind his start line. Between half-past midnight and 4.30 a.m., 35,000 shells were put down in front of the battalion.

By 5 July the battalion was very tired and had stood up to severe enemy mortaring and shelling. In the afternoon an advance party of 4th Dorsets arrived to take over. By 2.00 a.m. on

St Charles-de-Percy War Cemetery, the final resting place for many British soldiers who were killed in the battle to break out from the Normandy beachhead.

Pte George Snowzell of HQ Coy died of wounds suffered at La Vacquerie, in the action west of Caumont on 30 July 1944 when the battalion suffered 22 men killed and a further 104 injured. No wonder it was referred to thereafter as Black Sunday. Snowzell is buried in the Bayeux War Cemetery.

Three private soldiers, who died serving with the Herefords in August 1944 during the battle of the Falaise Pocket, are buried side by side in the village cemetery at Sevrai, near Ecouche.

6 July the relief was completed without interference and the battalion was on its way back to a rest area at Fresny-le-Crotteur.

The scale and importance of this action on the River Odon is best illustrated by quoting the citation for the DSO awarded to Lt-Col. J. Churcher, commanding officer of 1st Herefords at the time.

Citation for Distinguished Service Order for Lt-Col. J.B. Churcher, 1 Herefords

During the operations over River Odon from 27 June to 07 July 1944, 1 Hereford and 4 KSLI were occupying an isolated bridgehead position across the river. It was the first battle experience of these Regiments who were mortared heavily for the whole of this period. During the first four days they were subjected to several counter attacks. Lt-Col. Churcher Commander 1 Hereford organised his position most skilfully and during a period of considerable strain was an outstanding example of coolness and efficiency to his whole Bn. The successful defence of the whole bridgehead position was in fact largely due to this officer's personal efforts, as in addition to leading his own Bn, he was of great assistance in supporting the Bn on his left. Later he took Command of the Bde and brought the operation to a successful conclusion.

On the second day of the Odon battle, Lt-Col. J.B. Churcher DSO relinquished command of 1st Battalion the Herefordshire Regiment and was promoted to brigadier commanding 159 Brigade. Lt-Col. G.R. Turner-Cain DSO succeeded to the command of the battalion.

Caen: Operation Goodwood

After the failure of the 2nd Army to break out of the Normandy bridgehead, it was decided to concentrate a powerful armoured force in the area north-east of Caen and force a way out along the rolling country south-east of the town in the direction of Falaise. 11 Armoured, the Guards Armoured and 7 Armoured Divisions were selected for this task, together with 3 British and 3 Canadian Infantry Divisions. The infantry divisions were to work on the left and right flanks of the spearhead.

On 16 July the battalion moved up to a concentration area in Ranville, about 10 km north of Caen. Concealment and security were essential if surprise was to be achieved, and the British move was therefore made by night. By day, movement in the concentration area was kept to a minimum. Whether the enemy had observed movement or not, their aircraft were active, and the night that the battalion crossed 6 Airborne's bridge over the Orne the enemy bombed it, but without success, although a number of echelon vehicles of the Guards were destroyed.

On 17 July, orders were received for the attack, and at 7.00 a.m. on the 18th the battalion moved into the FUP. It was a wonderful summer morning, and the air armada which carried out the preliminary bombardment was a sight never to be forgotten – the sky appeared to be full of aircraft. The bombing was terrific, and morale that morning was extremely high. About 1000 heavy and 500 medium bombers took part in the attack.

As far as the battalion was concerned, the first phase was to secure a firm base. This was carried out by D Company and a squadron of 2nd Northamptonshire Yeomanry. They attacked and captured a feature of high ground east of Cuverville. Then, with A Company right, C Company left, and B in reserve, together with machine-gun support from the carriers and smoke and HE from the mortars, the next attack was launched. This was to capture a wooded area east of Demouville and exploit forward. Helped by S Company and artillery support, the leading companies eventually fought their way on to their objectives, despite considerable enemy opposition. British casualties were slight, most of them due to enemy shelling or mortaring. About 80 prisoners were taken, and most of these were completely 'bomb shocked'. It was apparent that the aerial bombardment, followed by the artillery barrage, had effectively unbalanced the enemy.

It soon became clear that all wooded areas and likely forming-up places for further attack had been registered by the enemy as D.F. tasks. All companies were, in consequence, subjected to intense and accurate mortar and shell fire. Later that same evening the battalion was ordered to take over an area of high ground at Grentheville, which had been captured at considerable cost to the armoured brigade during the day. It was the misfortune of the infantry in an armoured division to be required to fight all day, and then either to fight, patrol or guard by night, with little time for sleep, as the armour could not contain itself by night nor replenish its petrol and ammunition while in close contact with the enemy without a protective screen.

Throughout the 19th, shelling and mortaring continued, and casualties increased. From intense heat the weather changed to drenching rain, and the battlefield was transformed into a sea of mud. The enemy's anti-tank defences had checked the British armoured thrust, and the division was therefore concentrated in a pivot area just north of Grentheville, and remained there a further forty-eight hours, still under shell fire.

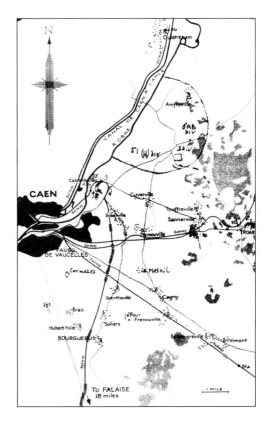

Bluecoat Phase I.

On 22 July the division was withdrawn to a concentration area at Bitot. The rest was badly needed to reorganize and refit for battle, as 29 Armoured Brigade had suffered severely and needed replacement tanks. The return journey of 21 miles from the Caen sector to Bitot, over bulldozed tracks covered in Sommerfeld tracking and thick with mud, took seventeen hours and was a gruelling experience.

It was during this rest period that the regimental band played for the last time as such. Out of the original 30 players, only 14 were left. The stretcher-bearers had done great work in the field but, like the rest of the battalion, had suffered casualties. At a later date in the campaign a 159 Brigade band was formed, incorporating the remnants of the battalion band and using its instruments.

Caumont – Black Sunday: Operation Bluecoat – the Break-out

The third attempt to break out of the Normandy bridgehead, in which the battalion again took part, was successful. It was part of the higher plan for the British 2nd Army to contain the German armour on its front, in order to give the American forces greater freedom of action in the west. This objective was achieved, the German armour was contained on the British front and the American breakthrough on the west of the bridgehead around Avranches had succeeded and was being exploited towards Rennes and Nantes.

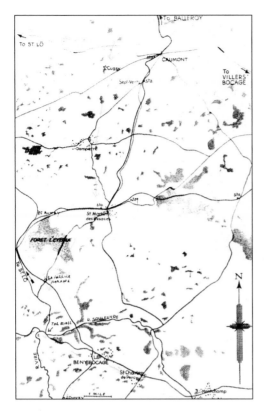

Bluecoat Phase II.

On 29 July 1944 11 Armoured Division was switched across to the extreme right flank of the British sector and concentrated for action just west of Caumont. Orders were given out late on the evening of the 29th, and the battalion set out for the FUP at 2.00 a.m. on the 30th.

The country there was very much closer, and the battalion was entering the bocage. This necessitated very close cooperation between the infantry and armour, and for this purpose the division was reorganized into two brigade groups, each with two armoured regiments and two infantry battalions. 159 Brigade Group on the right consisted of 2nd Fife and Forfar Yeomanry, 2nd Northumberland Yeomanry, KSLI and 1st Herefords.

The close country and enemy mines made progress slow, and the battalion had to fight a stiff battle to clear Cussy, La Vacquerie and the surrounding woods. The battalion's casualties for this day's fighting were Capt. S.H. Boddy and 21 other ranks killed; 2 officers and 102 other ranks wounded, and it was not without reason that it was referred to thereafter as Black Sunday. The day started off badly when one of the battalion's wireless carriers was blown up on a mine. The start line ran through an orchard which contained an Allied minefield, and during the night the engineers had cleared lanes, but some mines were deeper than normal and had not been detected. The tanks had an equally unpleasant start, and it was several hours before a way round the obstruction was found. Once the enemy had observed movement, they opened up with guns and mortars. The orchard was pounded from every direction, the enemy having good observation from the high ground to the front. The ground was hard and digging difficult, and the battalion was hemmed in the orchard area until the route had been cleared. Eventually the

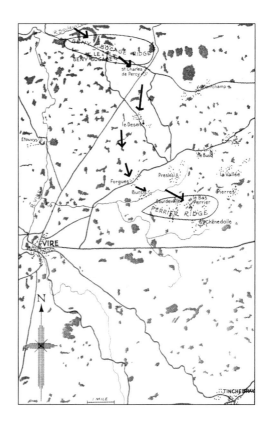

The advance on Burcy and Le Bas Perrier.

advance began and the battalion fought its way forward to clear Cussy, where the enemy resisted strongly and was well concealed in the hedgerows and woods with numerous machine-gun posts.

Citation for Distinguished Conduct Medal for A/CSM A.F. Evans, Herefordshire Regiment

In the break out from Caumont on the morning of 30 July 1944 a depleted 'A' Coy advanced under heavy enemy mortar fire to the first objective, where it had to wait for two hours pending air bombardment of enemy positions Their location was in fact the DF (SOS) task, and this area was mortared and shelled by the enemy consistently for two hours.

During this time the Coy endeavoured to dig in as best they could in the open. About twenty, including all stretcher bearers, became casualties. In the midst of this heavy enemy fire CSM Evans with complete disregard for his personal safety, went round all the casualties, bandaging up their wounds, comforting and cheering them. Whenever there was a short pause in the enemy shell fire he collected men and evacuated the wounded. By his untiring and courageous efforts CSM Evans succeeded in moving all the wounded to a place of safety.

The Reserve Platoon had suffered most casualties losing their Pl Comd and Pl Sgt. After evacuating all the wounded he then re-organised this Platoon so efficiently that when the time came for the advance, they were completely ready to move forward in good heart. He presently led them forward with such determination that they successfully captured the next objective against stiff enemy opposition.

The fearless example and courage of this WO undoubtedly raised the morale of the whole Coy at this critical stage. It can be stated that it was through his personal bravery that the enemy position was overcome; and the successful attack by his Coy enabled the subsequent break through by the British Forces later the same day.

Cussy was cleared by 6.00 p.m. and 4 KSLI, with 2nd Fife and Forfar Yeomanry, passed through to capture La Fouquerie. During the night of 30/31 July 1944, 4 KSLI infiltrated forward and opened the way for the capture by four armoured cars of the Household Cavalry (reinforced by six tanks of 2nd Northamptonshire Yeomanry) of an unprotected bridge over the River Souleuvre on the main road from St Lo to Le Beny Bocage. The capture of this bridge, and the advance southward which it made possible, settled the fate of the German 7th Army. The advance breached the German positions. With the American 1st and 3rd Armies sweeping round to the south and bearing up towards Argentan, and 1st Canadian Army thrusting down east of Caen towards Falaise, the trap was closing on the enemy.

The Falaise Pocket

The battalion was continuously in action from 30 July to 23 August in the battle of the Falaise Pocket. The Germans attempted to cut off the rapidly advancing American forces by an armoured counter-thrust westwards towards Mortain and Avranches, which failed. They then fought a bitter rearguard action in an attempt to extricate their 7th Army from the clutches of the Canadian, British and American forces, which were encircling them and rapidly closing the escape route between Falaise and Argentan. Here the German Army suffered its greatest disaster since Stalingrad: 10,000 dead and 50,000 taken prisoner. Even so, a third of the German 7th Army eluded the trap.

From the battalion's point of view, this period was one of fierce action and rapid movement. Part of the time, companies advanced on foot, clearing up pockets of enemy resistance. Then, when there was little or no opposition, the infantry climbed on the tanks and continued to advance.

The division was operating on two routes with 29 Armoured Brigade left and 159 Brigade right. 1st Herefords were working with 2nd Fife and Forfar Yeomanry. The rate of advance came as a surprise after the heavy slogging and yard by yard progress which had been the form to date. The enemy encountered fought fanatically, and had to be dealt with ruthlessly, but were in scattered pockets fighting a rearguard action. By 2 August the battalion was on a feature of high ground east of Vire, where it remained until 7 August. While in this area, more reinforcements arrived and the grimness of 'Black Sunday' faded.

On 8 August the battalion took over a very unhealthy area from 2nd Battalion Royal Warwickshire Regiment of 3 Division at Le Bas Perrier. Heavy fighting had taken place, knocking out tanks, and the bodies of enemy dead littered the area. The battalion was relieved by 1 Welsh Guards on 10 August and withdrew to a rest area at La Marvindière, about 6 miles behind the line. The relief was carried out without shelling, but the rest turned out to be short lived. Regrouping for further operations was taking place, which necessitated an exchange of positions between 11 Armoured Division and the Guards Armoured Division, which took place

Medals of Sgt A.W. Evans DCM.

without incident on 9 August. By the morning of the 10th, the changeover was complete and the whole of the very narrow front was assigned to 159 Brigade. The front consisted simply of the area of Le Busq. 11 Armoured Division was to provide flank protection to the Guards Armoured Division during its attack on 11 August. This involved merely an advance by 1st Herefords to occupy a spur in front of it. By 1.00 p.m. on the 11th, 32 Guards Brigade had reported the village of Chenedolle clear, whereupon 1st Herefords advanced, and by 4.45 p.m. it was in position and fully organized. At midnight a battalion of the Coldstream Guards took over, and the battalion left Le Bas Perrier for the last time, returning to La Marvindière.

On the evening of 13 August the battalion formed up in the village of Estry and at first light on the 14th advanced on two routes towards Le Thiel to mop up the area, as the enemy were reported to have withdrawn. Le Thiel was reached without opposition, apart from snipers and mortar fire. However, on advancing from Le Thiel, the battalion came under heavy fire, and it was obvious that the enemy intended to resist on the hill feature 212. In the late afternoon an attack was put in on this hill, with B Company right and D left. Despite fierce opposition, the hill feature was carried, but the two assault companies suffered heavily in the action. As darkness fell, the companies dug in, but were harried all night by enemy patrols.

The following morning the enemy withdrew, and the battalion group moved south-east to Vassy to carry on the advance to Flers. On the morning of the 16th the advance continued through Vassy, and in the early afternoon the feature of Mt de Cerisi was reached. Strangely enough, this prominent feature was not held by the enemy, so the battalion pushed on and harboured that night some 20 miles north of Flers. The following day, Flers was entered without opposition, and for the first time the battalion witnessed the joy of a liberated people. The populace climbed all over the vehicles and smothered the troops with flowers and kisses.

The advance continued through Flers, and in the afternoon the leading elements encountered the enemy in Durcet and St Opportune. Company actions cleared these places, and on the morning of 18 August, riding on the tanks, the battalion reached Briouze. It was here that liaison was made with the American forces. The FFI now came into the open and the men wore their Cross of Lorraine armbands for the first time.

In the early afternoon the advance continued eastwards in the direction of Ecouche, the companies being carried in TCVs. The column came under shellfire while on the move, and that night battalion headquarters received a direct hit from three shells, which killed two pioneers. The adjutant and three signallers were wounded.

The battalion advanced northwards the following morning in the direction of Montgaroult on the Putanges–Argentan road. On the next two days, operations were uneventful, the Falaise gap was virtually closed and the remaining enemy were being shot up from the air by fighter aircraft. The battalion passed through Argentan and eventually reached Gace on 21 August. On the 23rd, the battalion was pulled out to a rest area at Laigle, where it re-equipped for the next stage in the campaign.

CHAPTER 16

Taurus Pursuant, Antwerp, September 1944

The divisional flash and the motto of 11 Armoured Division were most appropriate to the next phase of operations, for the division made the most spectacular advance from the Seine to Antwerp in six days – a distance of 260 miles. It was a bold dash which paid good dividends. The enemy were confused and disorganized after the rout of their 7th Army, and every opportunity was taken by the Allied armoured columns to exploit the situation. The enemy resistance was spasmodic and quickly brushed aside – the main delays were caused by damage or administrative problems. Along the whole route, both by day and night, the troops received an enthusiastic welcome.

Having crossed the Seine at Vernon on 29 August, the battalion passed through Amiens on 31 August and Arras on 1 September. The Belgian frontier was crossed south-east of Roubain on 3 September 1944. The 4th found the battalion approaching the outskirts of Antwerp. Pockets of the enemy were holding out and the battalion was detailed to cover the left flank of 29 Armoured Brigade, which, with 4 KSLI, were clearing the town. On the 5th, having spent the night on the southern fringe of the town, they were ordered to clear the east side of the city, including the forts. Antwerp is ringed to the south and east by a series of strongly constructed forts dating back to the eighteenth century, but luckily these proved not to be strongly defended. When C and D Companies cleared them, large stocks of weapons were found, which were handed over to the Belgian White Brigade (underground movement). No serious trouble was encountered apart from that of overjoyed civilians hampering movement. Eventually, by midday, the task was completed, and the battalion was able to concentrate in the Berchem area and relax.

The Germans had withdrawn from the city to the north side of the Albert Canal, but still occupied the Schelde estuary and were spasmodically shelling the city area. During the evening of 5 September the Germans blew the bridge over the Albert Canal, and that night orders were received to cross the canal at Merxem and to liquidate the enemy concentration north-east of the town. 4 KSLI carried out a difficult night crossing, but by the time it was established the enemy had accurately ranged the bridgehead, which became untenable. 4 KSLI fought a determined rearguard action to recross the canal, and the attack was then broken off.

Helchteren and Hechtel, September 1944

While 11 Armoured Division was clearing Antwerp, 30th Corps had advanced from Brussels and forced a crossing of the Albert Canal. 11 Armoured Division was now switched south, to give flank protection to this thrust towards Holland, for the enemy was infiltrating to the right rear of the Guards Armoured Division. On 9 September the division moved south via Louvain and crossed the canal at Beeringen. For this next operation, 1st Herefords were to be grouped with 2nd Fife and Forfar Yeomanry under 29 Armoured Brigade, and they moved forward that evening to join the tanks in a concentration area in the woods just west of the small village of Helchteren.

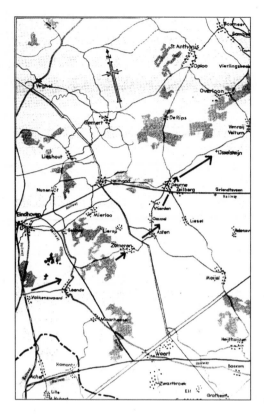

The battlefields of southern Holland, including Zomeren.

During the night, B Company had a sharp action clearing woods in the company area, the company commander and two others being killed. D Company, which went forward to clear the village of Helchteren, also had an unpleasant time, but eventually carried the village in fierce hand-to-hand fighting. Two platoon commanders and four section commanders were lost in this action, and only three prisoners were taken, the majority of the enemy being killed with the bayonet in close-quarter fighting. The company held the village throughout the night in close contact with the enemy. The following day the battalion moved north towards Hechtel, working in close conjunction with the Fife and Forfar Yeomanry. Considerable enemy opposition was encountered, and a tough battle ensued, but by the end of the day the group, having reached Wychmael and taken more than 500 prisoners, concentrated in the darkness in the small village of Heonrik.

Citation for the Distinguished Conduct Medal for L/Cpl I.R. Everall

North of Helchteren, in the wooded area on the morning of 10 Sep 44 an enemy position held by 700 or 800 men was attacked by C Coy 1 Herefords and C Sqn Fife and Forfar, practically all enemy being either killed or captured.

In the early stages of the attack, during very fierce fighting, 15 Pl lost its Pl Comd, Pl Sgt and all Sect Comds. LCpl Everall took command of the platoon and under his guidance they fought their way through innumerable enemy posts to an objective 1000 yards in depth. But for his determined and inspiring leadership the other leading platoon would have had an open flank and been subject to enfilade fire which would have stopped the attack.

When on the objective this young and junior NCO properly organised the consolidation and pushed forward his contact patrols.

There is no doubt that the action of the LCpl is in no small way responsible for the complete defeat of this German Para Bn.

Citation for the Distinguished Conduct Medal for Pte D. Evans

During the evening of 9 Sep 44 at Helchteren 3575 (Map Sheet 47), a Company attack was put in to clear the Eastern end of the village. The enemy held not only the houses on either side of the road with two platoons, but had a third platoon dug in on the NW outskirts around the windmill. These positions were in turn covered by Mortar and Machine gun fire from woods on the left and right, and a sunken lane immediately beyond. It was quite the strongest and most bitterly defended position ever attacked by this unit.

On reaching the end of the houses, Private Evans found his platoon commander and his own section commander were casualties. Without further orders, Evans took charge of his section, reorganised it and prepared to attack the strong Windmill position. He led them in their attack through Machine gun and Mortar fire without fear or hesitation and put his men into the Gun position, clearing them at the point of the bayonet.

He personally captured the Bazooka which a little time previously had put one of our tanks out of action. He then organised his section position in the consolidation.

A number of our own and enemy wounded were left in the windmill area, but these could not be reached by the Stretcher bearers owing to heavy enemy fire which then swept the area. Private Evans himself volunteered to go forward alone and evacuate these wounded. He located the wounded and personally brought back the German Platoon Commander. Undaunted, he organised a small carrying party and went forward again to evacuate the remainder of the wounded. Although the area was under heavy enemy small arms and Mortar fire, he organised the evacuation so successfully that no wounded were left in the position.

On 11 September, Peer was cleared, and here the group reorganized, during which period patrols were sent east towards Bree, near the Meuse–Escaut Canal, from where the Germans had withdrawn. By this time, virtually all enemy opposition had been cleared from the area between the Albert and the Meuse–Escaut Canals, and the division enjoyed a short period of rest and maintenance in this area before continuing the advance.

Zomeren to the Maas

During the period when 11 Armoured Division was at rest in the Peer area, preparations were afoot for the airborne landings at Arnhem. The division had no direct part in this operation, but on 16 September 1944 it was transferred to 8th Corps, which included 3 Infantry

Division. 8th Corps was directed to protect the right flank of the armoured thrust which was to be made by 30th Corps, with the Guards Armoured Division leading, to join up with the airborne divisions in Holland. The airborne assault commenced on 17 September, and on the 19th the battalion moved forward, still grouped with the Fife and Forfar Yeomanry, as part of 29 Armoured Brigade. They crossed the Escaut Canal at De Groot Barrier, and passing through 50 Division continued over the Dutch frontier to Volkenswaard, where they harboured for the night.

At first light the following morning, the advance continued eastwards to Leende against moderate enemy resistance. Orders were then received to seize the bridge over the Bois Le Duc Canal at Zomeren. The bridge was blown at the commencement of the attack, and it was evident that there would be an opposed crossing of the canal. The battalion and the Yeomanry were regrouped under 159 Infantry Brigade with 4 KSLI, and on the night of 21 September 1st Herefords forced a crossing. A and D Companies crossed in assault boats and formed a bridgehead, then C Company crossed by the lock gates which had been left intact, and B Company remained in reserve. Immediately C was in position the enemy counter-attacked, and infiltrated between the leading company positions. There was fierce fighting throughout the night, but by dawn, after a local counter-attack, the situation was restored. The Engineers having completed the bridge by 8.00 a.m. on the 22nd, all was clear for the Fife and Forfar Yeomanry to cross with 4 KSLI on the backs of tanks to secure Asten. Despite heavy small arms fire, by 9.00 a.m. the leading tanks were moving on towards Ommel on the Deurne road, secure in the knowledge that 1st Herefords were holding the bridgehead.

WO 2 A.F. Evans was awarded the DCM for his part in action to the north-west of Roermond on 21 December 1944.

On the morning of 10 September 1944, the 1st Herefords were grouped with tanks of the Fife and Forfar Yeomanry under 29 Armoured Brigade, for the thrust into Holland. C Coy was heavily involved in an attack on enemy Fallschirmjager positions, which resulted in practically all enemy being either killed or captured. L/Cpl. I.R. Everall of C Coy was awarded the DCM for his gallantry in this action.

Citation for the Distinguished Service Order
Lt-Col. G.R. Turner-Cain

Lt-Col. Turner-Cain was appointed to command 1st Herefords on 4 July 44. On the night of 21/22 Sep 44, his Battalion was ordered to make an assault crossing over the Willems Canal at Zomeren. Zero hour for this attack was 1930 hrs.

The enemy were holding defensive positions close to the canal banks. Despite stiff opposition and the heavy enemy artillery and mortar fire which was brought down on the area of the crossing, three Rifle Companys had successfully crossed and were establishing themselves on the far bank by 2100 hrs.

The initial success of this operation was largely due to Lt-Col. Turner-Cain's sound tactical ability and leadership.

Shortly afterwards, before the perimeter of the bridgehead was secured, a strong enemy counter attack developed; it was discovered later that this counter attack was delivered by no less than a Battalion of Infantry of high quality and long battle experience. Some of the enemy succeeded in infiltrating into the perimeter, and in the darkness the fighting was bitter and confused.

Lt-Col. G.R. Turner-Cain was appointed to command the 1st Herefords on 4 July 1944. He was awarded the DSO for his part in making an assault crossing over the Willems Canal at Zomeren on 21/22 September 1944, and then successfully holding the bridgehead against a strong enemy counterattack.

Despite the critical situation Lt-Col. Turner-Cain remained at all times cool and undaunted; he maintained control of his Companies under the most adverse conditions, and committed his fourth Rifle Company at the right moment to restore the situation.

His presence in the crossing area for long periods, without regard for the heavy defensive fire, was a magnificent example and encouragement to his troops.

Throughout the night his Battalion maintained the Bridgehead against all enemy efforts to dislodge them. This enabled a Class 40 Bridge to be built by the Royal Engineers, over which tanks and a further Infantry Battalion of this Brigade were able to advance at first light to exploit the initial success and to capture Asten. Lt-Col. Turner-Cain's sound tactical ability made possible the great success achieved by his Battalion at heavy cost to the enemy; his coolness and personal bravery under fire were an inspiration to all ranks.

29 Armoured Brigade then passed through and cleared the way to Deurne. On 25 September 1944 1st Herefords were involved in further fighting in the town of Helmond and in the surrounding woods, but the enemy were rapidly withdrawing to their next defensive positions and the weather was beginning to slow down operations. It became clear that the war would continue into the next year. The remainder of September and most of October were spent in a series of actions designed to mop up all enemy operating west of the River Mass, and to establish suitable defences for the winter months. The battalion moved from Helmond to St Anthonis on 26 September, from where a company was detached to Beugen to observe enemy

activity east of the Maas. This was the first time that the battalion saw the river. On 30 September regrouping took place, and the unit had moved to Handel where it trained and reorganized for a week.

Winter on the Maas: October 1944–January 1945

The enemy were still operating from a number of outpost positions west of the river, and they retained a bridgehead area around Venlo. A cordon of British troops was drawn around the German bridgehead, and A Company, 1st Herefords, was despatched to Meijel with a troop of tanks and some artillery on 6 October to watch the Deurne Canal to the east. On 7 October the division was relieved by 7th US Armoured Division, and the battalion took over an area of forest north of Overloon. On the 9th D Company carried out a raid on German positions situated in 'Boot' Wood, with the object of securing prisoners for interrogation. This proved to be a very sharp but successful engagement. On 12 October 3rd British Infantry Division passed through the battalion to capture Overloon, and then followed the last offensive act by the battalion from this base, which was a sweep towards Vierlingsbeek.

11th Armoured divisional sappers clear the railway line of mines at Deurne-Amerika, Holland, 1944.

The following day the battalion retired to Deurne, ready to continue operations eastwards, and was ordered to pass through a small American bridgehead over a canal, where the enemy opposition from the direction of Ijsselsteijn was intense. B and D Companies put in a successful attack on that place at 4.00 p.m. on the 17th, and the battalion consolidated for the night. 4 KSLI had passed through and established themselves at Veulen on 18 October, and here 1st Herefords joined them. The period from 20 October to 27 November was one of constant moves and patrolling in the area. On the 20th the battalion was at Ijsselsteijn, moving up to Veulen on the 21st and back to Deurne on 25 October 1944.

On the southern flank, 7th US Armoured Division held a bridgehead over the Deurne Canal at Grientsveem, and from there hoped to advance to Amerika, a small village on the railway 4 miles further east. However, on 27 October the Germans launched a strong attack from their bridgehead, captured Meijel and threatened Asten. On the evening of the 27th, 1st Herefords took over the Grientsveen bridgehead from the Americans, to enable them to concentrate their whole force against the German attack from the south. The battalion returned to Deurne on 3 November, but on the 8th was again committed at Ijsselsteijn, where it remained until returning to Deurne on 19 November 1944.

Operation Nutcracker

The approaches to the port of Antwerp having been secured, the elimination of the Maas pocket once more commanded the attention of High Command. The task was to be completed by 8th and 12th Corps. In view of the swamps of the Peel country, tank warfare was impossible, and the whole operation by 11 Armoured Division devolved on 159 Brigade. The objects were Amerika, and then the area of Meterik and Schadijk to the north-east. On 21 November 1944 1st Herefords assembled at Helenaveen for the attack on Amerika, which was scheduled for 22 November. 4 KSLI began its advance from Grientsveen at 7.00 a.m., but was held up by mines and deep mud, and 1st Herefords, having launched their attack at 7.40 a.m., occupied Amerika without opposition by 12.30 p.m. Never had an army crossed the Heide before, and the Dutch had said it was impossible. 4 KSLI continued the advance to Meterik and Schadijk, and on the 23rd were joined at Schadijk by 1st Herefords. On 25 November 1944 1st Herefords returned to Deurne for a well earned rest in the Helmond rest area.

On 28 November the battalion relieved 7th Seaforths and commenced its vigil on the Maas. The area occupied was Houthuizen and Grubbenvorst, about 2 miles north of the Venlo pocket.

On 17 December a move was made south to the Horn Sector of the river, north-west of Roermond, a much more active area where the enemy were enterprising and frequently crossed the river with fighting patrols.

On 27 December the battalion left Horn, and the next day held its belated Christmas celebrations in the reserve area at Baexem. Part of the period in reserve was spent at Weert, and here on 12 January 1945 the division was visited by FM Montgomery, who conferred on officers and men decorations won up to that stage of the campaign. On returning to the line on 21 January 1945, the Heel sector was occupied just to the south of the previous sector, and here patrols were resumed, and shelling and counter-shelling were the order of the day.

Pol, Heel, Beegden, Panheel, Wessem and Pannenhof were all subjected to patrol activity, and special vigil had to be kept on the lock gates and the 'island' between the Maas and the Juliana Canal. On 16 January 12th Corps had begun operations to clear the area north of its front line between the rivers Roer and Maas. 11 Armoured Division was to provide supporting fire from its side of the river and to operate across the river as opportunity afforded and occupy

Captured German staff officers are questioned by Capt. How, Divisional Intelligence Officer for the 11th Armoured Division, 1945.

the 'island'. No. 3 Commando and 80th Assault Squadron Royal Engineers were allotted the task of crossing the Maas, which they completed successfully at 1.00 p.m. on 19 January. The 'island' was found to be unoccupied, and the commandos rejoined 1 Commando Brigade operating with 7 Armoured Division.

The northward progress of the attack had now reduced 11 Armoured Division's river front to 1,400 yards. This formed the western flank of the small bridgehead over the Roer, which the enemy still retained south of Roermond, and opposite it 1st Herefords continued to hold the front for the remainder of January. The battalion handed over to 46 Royal Marine Commando on 2 February 1945 and withdrew to Weert Barracks.

The Allied forces were now commencing to regroup for the spring offensive and the preliminary operations preparatory to crossing the Rhine. On 17 February 1945 159 Brigade moved to Turnhout in Belgium, where the division came under the command of the 1st Canadian Army, which had been given the task of clearing the west bank of the Rhine.

CHAPTER 17

Hochwald and the Schlieffen Line, Germany, February 1945– 1 June 1946

O n 23 February the battalion left Turnhout to take part in Operation Blockbuster. The object of the operation was to clear the enemy between the rivers Maas and Rhine. The Canadians operated from Nijmegen and Cleve and swept southwards, while the Americans, with British elements, advanced northwards from the Roermond area. At this time 29 Armoured Brigade was still refitting with Comet tanks, and in its place 4 Armoured Brigade, consisting of Scots Greys, 3/4 CLY and 44 Royal Tank Regiment, came under command of 11 Armoured Division.

The operation had already been in progress for a week before the division was called in to take part in the fourth phase – to break through the Hochwald (Schlieffen) line and capture a feature of high ground north of Sonsbeck. Moving up through Tilburg, S'Hertegenbosch and Nijmegen, the battalion crossed the German frontier on the 23rd and concentrated in an area south-east of Cleve on the 24th. Most of the move was carried out in darkness, and the journey through the Reichswald forest was not easy. The Engineers had developed a white-taped track through the trees, and everywhere there was evidence of the crashing barrage put down to assist 53 Division in its earlier wood-clearing operations. After three days in the concentration area the division was committed to battle, and the battalion moved to its FUP.

At 11.00 a.m. on 27 February 1945, a fresh assessment was made and it was decided to pass the battalion with 3/4 CLY, through Udem to capture the Gochfortzberg feature, a ridge of high ground about 4 miles west of the Schlieffen line. The whole area beyond this feature was overlooked by the Hochwald forest, which 3 Canadian Division was dealing with from the north. Udem had been captured the previous night by a Canadian brigade, and the whole village was just a mass of rubble. Odd pockets of enemy were still holding out on the exits from the town, and operations were further hampered by an anti-tank ditch which ringed it. The bridges across the ditch were reported blown, and further movement forward was held up while fascines or some other form of bridging could be brought up to allow the tanks to cross. In the meantime, B Company dealt with isolated enemy posts to the south of the town, and after well executed platoon operations rounded up about 20 prisoners and killed the remainder.

The enemy realized that an attack was about to debouch from the town and brought down heavy mortar and shell fire. A Company moving up through the streets, suffered several casualties, not only from falling shells and shrapnel, but also from collapsing buildings and flying masonry. The streets were alive with bullets and bursting HE. It was essential to get the company through to start the attack on time. At the time, the company was composed of about 50 per cent reinforcements, seeing their first action, and was in danger of going to ground. By exemplary work on the part of the company sergeant-major, unmindful of personal danger, all unwounded men were encouraged, persuaded and forced to go forward, and finally reached their allotted FUP before zero hour. Thus the companies were manoeuvred into position, ready to carry on the advance across open country, at 2.30 p.m., with 3/4 CLY in support. The going

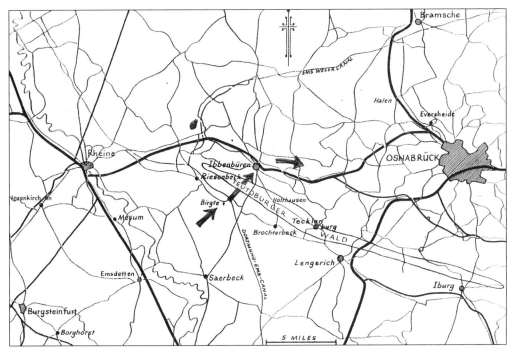

Ibbenburen, April 1945.

was difficult for tanks, and the enemy had ideal observation, both from the Gochfortzberg feature and from the Hochwald beyond. In consequence, the whole operation was severely impeded by well coordinated and heavy artillery fire. Practically all farms between the objective and the start line were held in considerable force, and had to be cleared by platoon and company attacks, but in two hours the battalion had reached the crest and taken 120 prisoners.

By a series of such attacks, in which there were many infantry casualties and several tanks lost, the objective was finally cleared and consolidated against grim and determined opposition. By this time it was dark, and administration, which went on throughout the night, was made doubly difficult. Vehicles moving up behind across open country became bogged down axle-deep in mud, and several more casualties were suffered from shelling. The night's hot meal arrived eventually, but few members of the battalion had much heart left to eat it. Enemy patrols were active and shelling persisted throughout the night. Dawn came to find everybody bedraggled, but with the battalion still in possession of its objective.

Early in the morning, 3rd Mons passed through, with 15th/19th Hussars, in an attempt to establish a bridgehead over a minor stream, constituting an anti-tank obstacle. As soon as they showed themselves over the crest, down came intensive and sustained artillery fire, and their assault was checked before it started. Severe shelling and mortaring persisted throughout the day, and they had only limited success in capturing and holding two wooded positions across the stream. The enemy's artillery and anti-tank defence was flexible and well controlled, and any move by daylight was hotly countered. It was therefore decided to launch an armoured night attack and to try to force a way through the defences of the Schlieffen line. The defences consisted of a continuous and well dug trench system, wired in and covered by mines. The strength of the enemy holding the trenches was not known, but it was certain that they would be well supported by defensive artillery and anti-tank fire.

The attack was to be put in by 1st Herefords and 15th/19th Hussars, supported by artillery fire on previously registered targets. It was to be a case of blasting a way through the enemy. The operation was as distasteful to the tanks as it was to the infantry. They were restricted to one ribbon of a road, leading straight up to the defence line, and because of the very soft going on either side they could not deploy. To add to their distress it was not certain whether the bridge across the stream, improvised by the Engineers, would stand up to their weight. Just after darkness the tanks moved up to the battalion area and the companies entanked, A Company leading. Command post, consisting of the commanding officer and adjutant, was mounted in a tank loaned by 15th/19th Hussars, as it was unlikely that any other vehicle would make the bad going. At 7.55 p.m. the leading squadron/company moved up to the bridge, followed by command post and the remaining companies.

As soon as the leading tanks nosed their way over the bridge, mortar bombs started crashing down. Woods, thought to be held by friends, were in fact infested by the enemy, who opened up with automatic SA fire at close range. The tanks bounded forward, blazing away with their guns and Besas at every copse and building. The leading companies detanked and started dealing with the situation.

D Company took part in an encounter typical of the night's fighting. A small wood, thought to be held by friends, was found to contain about twenty Germans, well supplied with automatics. The leading section all became casualties in the first burst of fire, and, although the remainder of the platoon charged the position, they were beaten off with heavy casualties. At the time there was only one other platoon of the company available, and the company commander, having organized the tanks to support him and reinforced by a platoon from C Company, started to attack and clear the wood. All enemy met were killed and, despite a delay in reorganizing afterwards, the force was on the move again within twenty minutes from the time of the first encounter. A farmhouse and orchard close to the route was next found to be held by bazooka and machine-gun teams. The company commander, leading one of the platoons, cleared the area and captured one of the bazooka teams.

Five hundred yards west of the Schlieffen line the tanks came under heavy and extremely accurate anti-tank fire, and could advance no further as it was still impossible for them to get off the road. The first five were knocked out and others, trying to pass, became bogged down. In the meantime the bridge over the stream had given way and the column was becoming very split up. It was therefore decided by the two commanding officers to reorganize and take up a battalion/regiment position in the area of the leading companies. By first light all four companies were in position, and once the bridge had been repaired the tracked vehicles, with anti-tank guns and mortars, followed on. The area was studded with a series of small woods and farms, many of which concealed SP guns. These gave the tanks a very worrying time, and it was not till several hours later, when they had ferreted out the offenders, that the group settled down to breakfast, consisting of the hot meal cooked the night before. Heavy NBW fire and shelling kept everybody in their trenches for the rest of the day, and several casualties were suffered. The battalion's casualties for these two days' fighting were 2 officers and 52 other ranks wounded, and 11 other ranks killed.

In the meantime, 3 Canadian Division was operating on the battalion's left and clearing the Hochwald forest feature. The enemy was still in occupation of the Schlieffen line, and on 2 March B Company, with one troop of 15th/19th Hussars in support, put in an attack to force a breach in the line. The forward platoon covered 200 yards of open country and was within 150 yards of its objective. Having allowed it to come completely in the open, the enemy opened up with heavy machine-gun and mortar fire. Further advance by the platoon was impossible under the withering fire, so the company commander decided to consolidate the position with the other two platoons. Three attempts were made to extricate the remnants of the pinned platoon, but each time intensified machine-gun, mortar and sniper fire was brought to bear on the company. The stretcher-bearers did gallant work crawling round with Red Cross flags and treating the most urgent cases. Evacuation of wounded was impossible.

In the evening, A Company passed through B Company and put in another assault on the same objective. It was a light night, made worse by artificial moonlight which silhouetted them as they moved. The leading platoon came under intense and accurate SA and mortar fire, and the leading section became casualties. There was no cover, which made movement extremely difficult. The NCO commanding the platoon displayed the finest gallantry. With complete disregard for his own safety, and with a coolness which reassured his men, he moved around organizing return fire and attending to the wounded. He reconnoitred the enemy positions and made a plan for their dispositions. During this time he was not more than 80 yards from the enemy and must have been clearly visible. He then left his platoon under the command of his platoon sergeant and took back the information to his company commander. Based on the information, a successful company left flanking attack was put in, and the company consolidated on its objective. As soon as they were established, C Company, with a troop of tanks, passed through. The enemy promptly reacted to the tanks more than to the infantry and started to engage them hotly with Spandaus from right, left and centre. However, the tanks' only concern was that bazooka teams might be lying in the ditches waiting for them to come along the road. Therefore, working in close cooperation with the troop, the leading platoon worked its way forward in single file along the ditches, ready to deal with any lurking bazooka teams. After the infantry had checked up to about 40 yards, the tanks advanced again, drawing all the enemy SA fire and allowing the platoon to advance unmolested. By this leap-frogging arrangement the platoon reached the first obstacle of the Schlieffen line, which was an anti-tank ditch. On reconnaissance of the bridge over it, the platoon commander considered it too flimsy to carry a tank, and the leading tank, trying to sheer off to the right, hit a mine. The others continued to give support and the platoon established itself in the excellent trenches provided by the enemy. By this time the enemy appreciated that their curtain of defensive artillery and machine-gun fire had failed to check the advance, and had evacuated the trenches. Patrols sent forward failed to contact the enemy, and the company therefore consolidated in the area, supported by a platoon of machine-guns from No. 2 Independent Machine-gun Company (4th RNF). The Schlieffen line had been breached, but only as a result of constant bombardment and persistent assault by 1st Herefords.

The enemy immediately commenced heavy shelling on the newly captured position and continued throughout the day. The battalion continued to hold these positions for the next two days, awaiting developments from 3 Canadian Division's sector. There was a noticeable decrease in shelling, and it appeared that the enemy were withdrawing their artillery.

On 5 March the battalion was regrouped, ready to continue operations towards Sonsbeck and Xanten, and 3 Mons passed through to carry out the first phase of the operation. In the meantime there had been considerable development on the right flank. 3 British Infantry Division operating on the immediate right, having driven the enemy out of Kervenheim, made rapid progress, as did the Guards Armoured Division from the direction of Geldern. These moves were made in conjunction with the American advance from the south, and the Allied armies were converging on Sonsbeck. 11 Armoured Division was halted while the other formations attended to the remaining enemy formations west of the Rhine.

The total casualties suffered in Operation Blockbuster were 28 killed and 124 wounded. On

9 March the division was withdrawn to Belgium to rest and refit. The battalion moved to Haecht, a small town north of Brussels. This was the longest and most enjoyable rest it had from battle during the campaign, and it was here that 29 Armoured Brigade rejoined with its new Comet tanks.

From the Rhine to the Leine: Operation Plunder

On 28 March, five days after the assault crossing of the Rhine, 11 Armoured Division left Belgium for a concentration area across the Rhine. 1st Herefords crossed the Rhine bridge at Wesel in the darkness at 2.00 a.m., and moved to the concentration area 4 miles to the north-east. On the 29th the battalion advanced to Earle, where it joined the Fife and Forfar Yeomanry, and continued through Legden and on to Osterwick. 7 Armoured Division on the left was unable to make such good progress, and the flank was exposed, but on the right, 6 Airborne Division, cooperating with an independent armoured brigade, was slightly ahead. On the 30th, 2nd Fife and Forfar Yeomanry and 1st Herefords occupied Metelon, and the next day the battalion was spread out on the road to Leer when it was ordered to deploy to meet a possible attack by 15th Panzer Grenadiers moving south-east towards Munster. B Company had had a slight brush with the enemy in the village of Stelen, but the anticipated attack did not materialize, and on 1 April 1945 the battalion continued through Burgsteinfurt, Emsdetten, Mesum and Riesenbeck, reaching the Dortmund–Ems Canal at Birgte on the Teutoburger Wald.

Dortmund–Ems Canal

During the night of 31 March/1 April 1945, 4 KSLI had secured a crossing of the canal and established a bridgehead facing the German positions on the high ground of the Teutoburger Wald. 159 Brigade was to cross the repaired bridge and continue the advance. However, the enemy fire held up 2nd Fife and Forfar Yeomanry and 1st Herefords for two-and-a-half hours after the bridge was completed at 2.30 p.m., and when they eventually attacked towards the wooded pass leading to Ibbenburen they made little progress in the face of fanatical opposition from men of the German Infantry NCOs' School at Hanover. The battalion suffered 12 killed, 38 wounded and 2 missing in the encounter.

On 3 April the battalion was relieved by 4th King's Own Scottish Borderers, and the next day continued the advance through Tecklenburg, Lotte and on to Osterkappeln, which was reached by 3.00 p.m., but enemy activity in the neighbourhood of Buttebohn made it necessary for the battalion to advance a further 20 miles before nightfall.

The Schlusselburg Bridgehead

On 5 April 1945 the battalion raced forward in an attempt to secure a bridge over the River Weser. D Company was detached to clear enemy resistance at Glissen, while the remainder advanced to the river. B Company, with its squadron of Fife and Forfar Yeomanry, advanced north-east and reached the river at Schlusselburg without opposition, while the remainder of the battalion continued along the main axis to Musleringen, due west of the point where B Company had rejoined after clearing the village of Diers.

There was no bridge at this point of the river, and B and C Companies crossed by assault

A Cromwell tank of the 2nd Fife and Forfar Yeomanry crosses the Dortmund-Ems Canal, Germany, 1945.

boats, rafts and ferry to form a bridgehead on the other side. A bridge across the river was under construction at Stolzenau, about 2 miles north of the battalion, but when nearing completion it came under very heavy air and ground attack and the crossing at this point was abandoned in favour of the bridge at Petershagen, built by 6 Airborne Division about 12 miles further up the river. The battalion bridgehead was therefore withdrawn and 1st Herefords concentrated on the evening of 6 April, ready to cross at Petershagen on the following day.

Loccum

The advance continued eastwards through Windheim and Dohren until the leading troops came under fire at the small town of Loccum, which was captured after a sharp battle in which at least seven German 88 mm guns were destroyed. B and C Companies were ordered to deploy left and right, and each was supported by a squadron of tanks. The heaviest fighting fell to B Company, which was engaged at close quarters for six hours, in conjunction with C Squadron of the Fife and Forfar Yeomanry.

11th Armoured divisional sappers ferry transport across the River Aller on a raft, Germany, 1945.

TO THE LEINE

The advance continued, and at 4.30 p.m. on 8 April the battalion moved through 1st Cheshires at Eilvese and continued northwards through the villages of Hagen, Dudensen and Laderholz towards the River Aller. The enemy resisted at Laderholz and B Company, with a squadron of tanks, was sent to clear the village, while C Company went on to Mandelsloh and, finding it clear, advanced north to Niederstocken, where it took 70 prisoners in a sharp engagement. The battalion remained in company areas that night and the next day battalion headquarters, with the rest of the group, moved to Rodwald, due west of Helstorf, to await completion of the bridge there, which would lead across the River Leine. The bridges at Neiderstocken and Helstorf had been blown.

The Final Days of the Campaign: April/May 1945 – Schwarmstedt

The plan was altered, and on 10 April the battalion group crossed the Leine over the 6th Airborne bridge at Neustadt, and returned to its own axis. It was ordered to clear a route northwards through the northern perimeter of the airborne bridgehead, and the advance to Esperke continued without opposition. However, just over a mile north of Grindau the enemy was encountered, and it was decided to launch a two-company attack to clear Schwarmstedt. B Company cleared the wooded hills on the right, and D Company the scrub on the left while C Company passed through to clear the village of Bothmer on the confluence of the rivers Leine and Aller. In the evening the battalion was relieved by 1 Commando Brigade, which was to force the crossing of the Aller at Essel, and withdrew to Grindau and Esperke, which had been cleared earlier in the day. The battalion remained in the area for the next two days.

On 12 April a deputation was received at 159 Infantry Brigade, then situated at Buch Holz, of German and Hungarian officers, including the commander of the German garrison troops, who crossed the Aller to negotiate for a neutral area. Beyond the river were situated a number of displaced persons, slave workers and concentration camps, including the notorious Belsen. An epidemic of typhus had broken out, and the German medical authorities feared that the displaced persons and internees would make a break for freedom and thus spread the disease. The terms laid down by the British commanders were not acceptable to the Commander of the German 1st Para Army controlling military operations in that area, and it was decided that the division would fight through the area, but special precautions were taken against infection.

Winsen (on the Aller)

By the morning of 13 April the bridge at Essel was secure. 1st Cheshires fought admirably to overcome enemy positions in the roadside woods leading to Winsen (on the Aller), but at midday on the 14th they were still 2 miles short of Winsen. Their approach was now assisted by 1st Herefords and 15th/19th Hussars attacking from the north-west. The battalion passed through the Cheshires at 12.30 p.m. and reached the Winsen–Ostenholz road, and in the evening advanced on the town, which was occupied by 8.00 p.m. About 30 prisoners of Battle Group Totzeck were captured, and a 75 mm gun limbered up ready to pull out was also captured with its half-track.

On the 15th the advance continued, both brigade groups of the division turning north. On the right, 2nd Fife and Forfar Yeomanry and 1st Herefords were in the lead, and fought a sharp engagement to clear Walthausen. Road blocks, bazookas and anti-tank guns continued to obstruct progress as far as Hessel, and in all twelve separate actions were fought by the companies. After passing through Hessel, the speed of the advance increased, and by the evening the leading tanks were in Muden.

The battalion reached Hermannsburg by 6.00 p.m. and was ordered to continue the advance to Muden. Here the bridge was blown behind the leading squadron, which was thus left in the gathering dusk on the far side of the river without infantry support. During the night, 1st Herefords formed a bridgehead to enable the Engineers to build a bridge, over which the advance continued to Poitzen the next day. At Muden, Lt-Col. R.C. Fripp DSO assumed command of 1st Herefords, and having previously served as second-in-command he had the advantage of knowing the men.

The battalion continued to advance, and on 16 April, after passing through Brambostel where the difficult cross-country track rejoined the main road, B Company, with its squadron of tanks of the Fife and Forfar Yeomanry, carried out a successful attack on Eimke.

On 17 April the battalion moved north to take over Ebstorf and then operated eastwards to Milzingen. The route was now diverted north to the Elbe, and in the afternoon of the 18th the new thrust commenced. The battalion moved in the direction of Winsen (on the Elbe) throughout the following day, passing through 1st Cheshires at Bardowick, just north of Luneberg. However, at Rottorf the bridge was blown behind the leading tanks, and a sharp engagement ensued in which A and D Companies formed a bridgehead. On the next day, the 20th, the advance to Winsen continued in the face of strong opposition, and it was not until the early afternoon that the battalion group entered the town. 1st Herefords remained in Winsen until 7 April, and during this period a composite group advanced to Hoopte on the river, where it was engaged in repelling enemy raids. On the 27th the battalion regrouped at Rottorf with 3rd RTR, and on 30 April crossed the Elbe by the Artlenberg bridge at midnight. After concentrating at Kollow at 5.00 a.m. on 1 May, it continued to advance in the general direction of Lubeck on the Baltic. Advancing on the left, the Herefords' group encountered many mines and roadblocks while penetrating to Schwarzenbeck, Havekost Mohnsen and Basthorst. The main centre of resistance, however, was Trittau, 5 miles further north. Here, 88 mm shells landed among A Company from the direction of the railway, and the enemy had to be routed by a flanking sweep before the battalion could advance to Gronwohld.

Citation for Military Medal for Cpl H.T. Royster, Herefordshire Regiment

At Rottorf (map reference 728300 – 1/100,000 Sheet L4) on 20 April 1945, Cpl Royster was riding on a tank which was bazooked. His Pl Comd and two other men on the tank became casualties. Although severely shaken, Cpl Royster took control over the remainder of the men who he organised for the necessary wood clearing immediately. Owing to the nature of the country the tanks were unable to deploy. In this operation his platoon came under sniping fire, and the platoon sergeant was wounded. Cpl Royster took command of the remainder of the platoon which now numbered 15, and led them on to the located enemy posts.

He personally destroyed one Spandau post and killed the crew of four. On reaching the objective his platoon came under heavy fire from another enemy position, but he re-organised his platoon, and beat off one enemy counter-attack before being reinforced by another platoon.

By his determined leadership and disregard for personal safety Cpl Royster ensured the success of an operation, which might otherwise have proved expensive in tanks and men.

Award approved by B.L. Montgomery, Field Marshal
Commander-in-Chief 21 Army Group

The Unconditional Surrender

On the following day, 2 May 1945, the 4 KSLI group passed through 1st Herefords and proceeded to Barkhorst, and in the afternoon received the surrender of Bad Oldesloe. 1st Herefords, having followed up, cleared the village of Rethwischdorf, taking 20 guns and 500 prisoners, and headed for Reinfeld. It was soon realized that the German resistance had collapsed and that the enemy was surrendering by the thousand. On 3 May the battalion reached Bad Segeberg and remained there for the next week, during which time the town sports ground was established as a prisoner of war collecting point through which many thousands passed.

Finally, at 8.00 a.m. on 5 May 1945, German forces in north-west Europe surrendered unconditionally, the instrument of surrender being signed by Gen.-Adm. Von Friedeberg at the headquarters of FM Montgomery at Luneburg Heath at 6.20 p.m. on 4 May.

Hordes of surrendering enemy had to be rounded up, marshalled and sent to concentration areas; guards and escorts had to be provided; and war equipment had to be collected and destroyed. In addition there were countless civilian problems to be attended to until the military government organization commenced functioning.

Herefordshire Regiment insignia, 1939–47.

On 13 May the battalion made its last operational move to occupy Flensburg in the north of Schleswig-Holstein. Here it took over a splendid *Wehrmacht* barracks and assumed the duties incidental to an army of occupation. Quickly the battalion shed its campaign dress and a high standard of turn-out was required.

Operation Blackout, 23 May 1945

After the German collapse on 4 May 1945, Grand Adm. Doenitz formed a 'puppet' government with which he intended to carry out the government of Germany. At first this was considered a convenient arrangement by the British authorities, as the country was in such a state of chaos that only the Germans were capable of regaining a certain amount of order. It was soon realized, however, that the Doenitz administration was not particularly efficient, and that dangerous elements existed in its ranks.

So Operation Blackout was conceived, the object of which was to liquidate the 'puppet' government, and also the OKW administration, with a single stroke. 1st Battalion the Herefordshire Regiment was to carry out this operation in conjunction with 1st Battalion the Cheshire Regiment and 15th/19th Hussars, all units of 11 Armoured Division. Each unit was provided with a long list of 'wanted' persons, divided into four categories according to their

Operation Blackout, 23 May 1945. Col.-Gen. Jodl, Dr Albert Speer (Reichs Armaments Minister), and Grand Admiral Doenitz under arrest at Flensburg.

Pennants taken from the car of Grand Admiral Doenitz.

importance. The two infantry battalions were to search for and arrest these people, while 15th/19th Hussars were to assist in sealing off the area to prevent any people escaping.

The Herefords moved off at 9.30 a.m. from their barracks and were ready in position just outside the area five minutes before zero hour (10.00 a.m.). On the codeword given by Brig. J.B. Churcher, who was commanding 159 Infantry Brigade, all units made a simultaneous pounce.

Grand Adm. Doenitz, Gen.-Adm. Von Friedeburg and Col.-Gen. Jodl were among the first to be captured, and they objected strongly to being taken away in an ordinary three-ton lorry. They were transported to the *Patria*, a ship used for the headquarters of the Allied Commission, for a conference with the Allied leaders, after which they requested permission to collect their personal belongings. Adm. Von Friedeberg took the opportunity thus provided to end his short career as commander-in-chief of the German Navy by committing suicide in the lavatory.

Very soon after 10.00 a.m., large numbers of 'prisoners' began to pour into the compound which had been hastily prepared for them, and there they were segregated into their various categories. This was not an easy task, but the F.S. personnel were of great assistance as they could almost 'smell' a man's category before asking for his name or his papers.

During the searching of the marine barracks, all those in the building were paraded in the corridors with their faces to the walls while the rooms were searched. Since many had been caught 'napping', the state of their attire did not in all cases comply with normal convention, and two or three Herefords were lucky enough to find a bevy of German Wrens having a shower. The women did not resent this intrusion, although, according to the men's story, the Herefords beat a hasty retreat. As was usual in those days when searching a German headquarters, large stocks of ham and wines were discovered, and it was interesting to note the ruses adopted by the high German officials to conceal small belongings about their persons. Reichminister Schwerin von Krosigk, for example, produced his watch from a shoe, and a very small, tight-fitting wallet containing important papers from underneath his vest. Pennants used by Grand Adm. Doenitz are now proudly displayed in the Officers' Mess of 1st Battalion the Herefordshire Light Infantry.

The operation was a complete success, as the Germans had been taken completely by surprise, and during the day a total of 756 arrests were made, among them many high Nazi officials.

The Army of Occupation

On 7 February 1945 Brig. J.B. Churcher DSO was appointed honorary colonel of 1st Battalion the Herefordshire Regiment. The termination of hostilities saw the start of a new phase in the activities of the battalion, namely internal security duties. This work, consisting largely of guard duties, patrols and searches, was distinctly boring, especially to men who shortly expected to return to civilian life. One of the greatest difficulties, therefore, was to keep them interested and maintain morale. This was achieved by organizing special training classes and sporting competitions.

Freedom of the City of Hereford

On 29 September 1945 the Herefordshire Regiment received the Freedom of the city of Hereford, and a detachment under the command of Maj. W.A.P. Crofts MC, together with the 159 Infantry Brigade band, was sent home for the ceremony. The mayor, Mr T. Powell, in his address said: 'The citizens of Hereford are proud of their Regiment. They give thanks to those

As a part of the Army of Occupation in Germany at the end of hostilities, the 1st Herefords were garrisoned in the badly bombed German city of Krefeld in the Ruhr, from February to July 1946. Above, Officers of the 1st Bn. Below, Sergeants' Mess.

The title deed granting the Freedom of the City of Hereford to the Herefordshire Regiment on 29 September 1945.

who have come safely through the fires of battle. They remember with deepest sympathy those who are left to mourn.' The recorder, Mr R.F. Lyne, then read the deed:

Whereas the Mayor, Aldermen and Citizens of the City of Hereford, being sensible of the great record and glorious traditions created by the *Herefordshire Regiment* over many years of loyal and devoted service to the Sovereigns of this Realm, and being desirous of recognising, cementing and fostering the long and intimate association which has been enjoyed between the City and the Regiment in which so many of the Citizens of Hereford have been proud to serve,

Do Hereby Confer upon the *Herefordshire Regiment* in perpetuity, the right, title, privilege, honour and distinction of marching through the streets of the City of Hereford on all ceremonial occasions, with drums beating, bands playing, Colours flying and bayonets fixed.

In Witness whereof the Corporate Seal of the Mayor, Aldermen and Citizens of the City of Hereford has been affixed in pursuance of a Resolution of the Council of the 29th May 1945.

The chief steward, Sir John Arkwright, then presented the deed of gift to Brig. J.B. Churcher DSO, honorary colonel of the regiment. The ceremony was broadcast to the battalion in Flensburg by Chester Willmott of the BBC, who became famous as the author of *The Struggle for Europe*. On the same day the mayor and corporation granted the regiment the use, on ceremonial occasions, of the silver of the old Hereford Militia, which had been entrusted to the corporation on its disbandment in 1908.

Freedom of the City of Hereford Parade, 29 September 1945. (Both photographs courtesy Hereford
Times)

The Guard of Honour

On 3 November 1945 1st Battalion the Herefordshire Regiment was honoured by being chosen to provide the guard of honour on the occasion of the visit of FM Montgomery to the headquarters of 159 Brigade at Flensburg. Shortly afterwards, on 16 November, the battalion took over responsibility for Keis Sud Tonder from the Inns of Court. A and C Companies took over Leck, while the remainder of the battalion was stationed at Niebull. On 6 January 1946 the battalion gave a great send-off to Lt-Col. R.C. Fripp DSO, who left the battalion on release, and he was succeeded by Lt-Col. H.H. Barneby.

Return to 53 (Welsh) Division

In January 1946 11 Armoured Division was disbanded and 159 Brigade was returned to 53 (Welsh) Division, then stationed in the Ruhr. In consequence of this reorganization, 1st Herefords moved from Schleswig-Holstein to Krefeld on 6 February 1946.

After the termination of hostilities in the Far East on 2 September 1945, demobilization of the wartime forces proceeded smoothly by release groups and the men were transferred to the Reserves automatically but were not discharged. This gradual reduction in manpower caused a corresponding reduction in the establishment, and units whose disbandment was to be only temporary pending resuscitation as part of the peacetime army were placed into suspended animation.

The Victory Parade

In May the Hereford T & AFA asked the battalion to provide a contingent for the victory parade in London on 8 June 1946. It was intended that those selected should be Territorials, and preferably men who had taken an active part in the war. Owing to the rate of demobilization there were very few such men still serving with the battalion in the British Army of the Rhine, and Lt-Col. Barneby decided to enlist the services of some who had already been demobilized. Lt-Col. R.C. Fripp DSO was asked to command the contingent, while Maj. W.A.P. Crofts MC and Maj. A.J.W. Phillips MC were selected to carry the colours, which were taken out of Hereford Cathedral where they had been lodged for the duration of the war. The other members of the contingent were RSM H.H. Rollings, CSM W. (Paddy) Mason, CSM Benfield, Sgts Rogers, Pye, and A.A. Perkins, Cpls L. Jones, Barnham and W.E. Williams MM, L/Cpl W.J. Holland and Ptes T.E.A. Morgan and L. Perkins.

Suspended Animation

On 17 June 1946 Maj.-Gen. J.B. Churcher DSO visited the battalion in Krefeld for the last ceremonial parade, as the battalion had been ordered into suspended animation by 15 July. Those men remaining were posted to other units, notably 4 KSLI and 1st Cheshires, and 159 Brigade ceased to exist.

CHAPTER 18

2nd Battalion the Herefordshire Regiment, 1939–44

It was recorded in Chapter 12 that in March 1939 it was decided to double the strength of the Territorial Army and to form the second line. This was achieved by each first line unit intensifying its recruiting programme and providing a nucleus for its duplicate unit. In this manner the original 53 (Welsh) Division raised the duplicate 38 (Welsh) Division.

The Herefordshire Regiment had a peacetime establishment of one battalion, and on 31 March 1939 orders were received to raise a duplicate battalion and to submit recommendations for the division of the county into two battalion areas. In April 1939 1st Battalion the Herefordshire Regiment was divided to form two battalions, 1st and 2nd, and Capt. N.G. Blake MBE of B Company (Ross-on-Wye) was promoted to Lt-Col. to command the latter.

The manner in which this division was achieved by allocation of companies has been described already, but it is of interest to note that both battalions were, in fact, lineal descendents of the original 1st Battalion. This is in contrast with the status of 2nd/1st and 3rd/1st Battalions raised during the First World War, which, it will be remembered from Chapter 11, were supernumerary and did not affect the lineage of the 1st/1st Battalion, as the original was then known.

1st and 2nd Battalions continued to function together until separated for annual camp, which was held in 1939 at Locking, Weston-Super-Mare. 2nd Battalion followed 1st Battalion to camp in August 1939. Towards the end of the camping period it became obvious that hostilities were about to begin, and a very detailed programme was drawn up regarding the disposition of personnel on orders for embodiment. In fact, the battalion was still in camp when the order to embody was received at divisional headquarters on 1 September 1939.

2nd Battalion the Herefordshire Regiment was mobilized as part of 114 Infantry Brigade of 38 (Welsh) Division on 3 September 1939. The brigade comprised:

5th Battalion KSLI (duplicate of 4th Battalion)
1st Brecknockshire Battalion South Wales Borderers (duplicate of 3rd (Brecknockshire & Monmouthshire) Battalion the Monmouthshire Regiment
2nd Battalion the Herefordshire Regiment (duplicate of 1st Battalion)

The battalion organization at the outbreak of war was as follows:

Company		Old company	
Headquarters	Hereford	Headquarters	Hereford (part)
W	Hereford	A	Hereford (part)
X	Ross	B	Ross
Y	Ledbury (one Platoon Colwall)	C	Ledbury
Z	Bromyard	D	Leominster (Bromyard Platoon)

The battalion remained at Locking, Weston-Super-Mare, until 10 September 1939, when each company returned to its normal location in Herefordshire prior to the battalion taking up its home defence duties on 13 September 1939. Col. H.E.P. Pateshall CB DSO TD DL was appointed honorary colonel of 2nd Battalion on 2 September 1939.

The battalion was at first located at Hereford, and later at Glen Usk Park, Crickhowell. In May 1940 it received orders to move to Rugeley camp on Cannock Chase, Staffordshire, and afterwards to Oulton Park, Cheshire. While there, the evacuation from Dunkirk took place between 27 May and 3 June, and the battalion was ordered to prepare to receive evacuated troops. About a thousand men were received, documented and sent on leave.

In June 1940 the battalion was warned for service in the tropics, embarkation leave was completed and the strength was made up to approximately a thousand in all ranks, but this move was cancelled, and the battalion was retained in the United Kingdom with the remainder of 38 (Welsh) Division on home defence. Soon afterwards the battalion was ordered to Aintree, Liverpool, to join the city defences.

In November 1940 the battalion moved to Camberley to begin a new type of training. The divisional commander, Maj.-Gen. Irwin, called a conference of all officers and senior NCOs and made it known that the division was to be prepared for active service and that he wished it to emulate the original 38 (Welsh) Division of the First World War. At last it seemed as though those wearing the yellow cross of St David of Wales on the black shield were about to serve overseas, and in January 1941 Lt-Col. W.A. Grey (KSLI) succeeded to the command of the battalion.

Towards the end of February 1941 the battalion had its first experience of a regular barracks, when it moved to Oudenarde Barracks, Aldershot. Training continued in conjunction with the Canadian Army, but gradually the hope of active service began to fade, and orders were received to proceed on coastal defence. The battalion moved to Bognor Regis and elsewhere in Sussex. Brigade and divisional training were continued, together with the normal coastal defence duties, until orders were received that the division was to concentrate in Dorset in November 1941 to prepare for further advanced training, with a view to overseas service.

In May 1942 the battalion was ordered to draft, and in addition special platoons were selected from each battalion in the division and sent on combined operations training. The strength of the battalion thus gradually diminished, and with it the prospect of overseas service, so in due course coastal defence duties were resumed.

In May 1943 the battalion was given a much more important role than it had hitherto fulfilled when a sector of 'Hell's Corner' in the Hythe area of Kent was taken over. After air-raids, shelling and constant patrolling, with the cliffs on Boulogne in view, the battalion moved at the end of October 1943 to Alnwick, Northumberland, for further training. After taking part in Exercise Eskimo, hopes of active service were again raised, only to be dashed when on 17 January 1944 the division was again committed to coastal defence.

The battalion moved with 114 Brigade to Sandown on the Isle of Wight, and among its duties was the defence of what was then known only as a vulnerable point, but which has since been identified as Pluto, the pipeline which carried petrol under the sea to Normandy.

In March 1944 Lt-Col. C.D. Barlow (KSLI) succeeded to the command of the battalion.

Shortly after D-Day, 38 (Welsh) Infantry Division ceased to exist as a field force unit. All available officers and men of the battalion were drafted to the British Liberation Army, and the remainder – some 17 other ranks – were transferred to 5th Battalion KSLI on 14 July 1944. 2nd Battalion the Herefordshire Regiment lapsed into abeyance on 15 July 1944.

On 15 August 1944, 38 (Welsh) Division 'ceased to command its units' and began to disperse. On 1 September 80 Division, which had been formed on 1 January 1943, was redesignated 38 (Reserve) Division.

The cadre of 5th Battalion KSLI moved on 26 July 1944 to Lancaster, where Lt-Col. W.R. Lawton, (North Staffordshire Regiment) succeeded Lt-Col. J.H. Blackburn to its command. 5th Battalion KSLI now became a composite battalion, including KSLI, Herefordshire Regiment and North Staffordshire Regiment personnel. This followed the organization of 20th Infantry Training Centre at the depot, Copthorne Barracks, Shrewsbury, which replaced the Infantry Training Centre of the KSLI.

After two months in Lancaster, 5th Battalion KSLI moved nearer to its home counties when, in September 1944, it moved to the hutted camp known as Anzio Camp, Crickhowell, near Abergavenny. Here, reserve division training continued until VJ Day (2 September 1945), up to which date 100 officers and 4,000 other ranks had been drafted to combat units. 5th Battalion KSLI was placed into suspended animation on 28 February 1946.

Officially, on 1 January 1947, 4th and 5th Battalions KSLI and 1st and 2nd Battalions the Herefordshire Regiment were amalgamated to form 4th Battalion KSLI and 1st Battalion the Herefordshire Regiment respectively, thereby reverting to the organization which existed prior to April 1939. On 28 May 1947 the title of the Herefordshire Regiment was changed to the Herefordshire Light Infantry, as recorded in Chapter 19.

It will be appreciated that 2nd Battalion the Herefordshire Regiment was frustrated in its desire to see active service overseas in the Second World War, just as were 2nd/1st and 3rd/1st Battalions of the regiment in the First World War. However, in view of the danger of invasion and the intensity of air-raids which were experienced in the Second World War, service in the defence of the United Kingdom was recognized by the award of the undernoted medals to members of 2nd Battalion the Herefordshire Regiment:

Defence Medal (1939–1945) (qualification period 3 years)
War Medal (1939–1945) (qualification period 28 days)

PART FOUR: THE HEREFORDSHIRE LIGHT INFANTRY

1st Battalion the Herefordshire Light Infantry, 1947–67

The Cold War

In view of British military commitments abroad and the unsettled conditions prevailing throughout the world, compulsory military service was retained at the end of the Second World War as the basis of the Armed Forces of the Crown. The National Service Acts of 1948–1955 (1948 11–2 Geo VI Ch 64 *et sequi*) imposed a liability on all male British subjects resident in Great Britain who had attained age 18 but not 26 to serve twenty-four months' whole time in the Armed Forces, and thereafter forty-two months, part time, in the Auxiliary Force. While serving in the Regular Force under those Acts, Herefordshire men were engaged in military operations in Germany, the Middle East, the Far East, Korea and Kenya. In 1951 Z Reservists were recalled for fifteen days' training and mobilization exercise, but fortunately the international situation did not require this to be repeated.

Similarly, under the authority of the Home Guard Act of 1951 (15 Geo VI Ch 8), the Home Guard was re-formed by 1952, and remained active until 1956, when it was decided that the international situation no longer justified its retention. It was placed into suspended animation and finally disbanded in 1957.

With the return to more peaceful conditions, provision was made for the discharge from the Reserves of war veterans and national servicemen under the terms of the Navy, Army and Air Force Reserves Act of 1954 (2–3 Eliz II Ch 10), and it was decided in 1957 that National Service should be abolished by 1963 (Command White Papers 124 and 230 of 1957).

The Reconstitution of the Territorial Army

It has been recorded that in April 1939, 1st Battation the Herefordshire Regiment was divided to form two battalions, and that at the end of their war service both battalions were placed into suspended animation pending the reconstruction of the Territorial Army. The Territorial Army was re-formed on 1 January 1947, and officially at that date 1st and 2nd Battalions of the regiment were amalgamated to form 1st Battalion the Herefordshire Regiment (TA), but recruiting did not commence until 1 April 1947.

The Herefordshire Light Infantry

In the post-war reorganization of the Regular Army in 1946, the infantry regiments were grouped and the KSLI formed part of the Light Infantry Group – Corps J – which comprised:

Somerset Light Infantry (Prince Albert's)
Duke of Cornwall's Light Infantry
Oxfordshire and Buckinghamshire Light Infantry
King's Own Yorkshire Light Infantry
King's Shropshire Light Infantry
Durham Light Infantry

(The term Light Infantry Group was altered to Light Infantry Brigade on 21 June 1951.)

In view of the peculiar position of the Herefordshire Regiment within the Corps of the KSLI, it was necessary to give serious consideration to the possible future of the regiment when the Territorial Army was re-formed. As a result of letters between Gen. Sir Charles Grant (Colonel of the KSLI), Maj.-Gen. J.B. Churcher (honorary colonel the Herefordshire Regiment) and Col. H.E.P. Pateshall (chairman of the Herefordshire Territorial Association), it was agreed at a County Territorial Association meeting held at Hereford in August 1946 that application should be made for the regiment to be re-formed as infantry. It was also felt that as the regiment and the rifle volunteers had been so closely affiliated to the KSLI for sixty-five years, it would strengthen their claim to remain infantry if they could be included in the Light Infantry Group. In consequence, in order to preserve the regiment's oustanding history in two world wars, it was decided to request that,

in the interests of the Army, the Corps of the KSLI and the County of Herefordshire, that the honour of becoming Light Infantry be conferred on the Regiment, and further that the name and title should be The Herefordshire Light Infantry.

1st Battalion the Herefordshire Regiment (TA) was re-formed on 29 April 1947 under the command of Lt-Col. H.H. Barneby with Maj. G.M. Singleton MC as second-in-command. Capt. M.P. Carr (KSLI) was adjutant and the quartermaster was Capt. G. Broad (KSLI). Recruiting for other ranks opened on 16 June 1947, and the battalion was organized as follows:

Company	Location	Commanding officer
Headquarters	Old Barracks, Hereford	Capt. R.W. Little
Support	Drill Hall, Hereford	Maj. P.E. Barnsley DSO
B	Drill Hall, Ross	Maj. R.V. Webb
C	Drill Hall, Ledbury	Maj. D.S. Daly
D	Drill Hall, Leominster	Maj. J.A. Watkins MC

(A Company was not raised at Kington until 1948, in view of the dilapidated state of the drill hall.)

The battalion formed part of 159 (Welsh Border) Infantry Brigade of 53 (Welsh) Infantry Division (TA), which comprised:

7th Battalion the Worcestershire Regiment
4th Battalion the King's Shropshire Light Infantry
1st Battalion the Herefordshire Regiment

(7th Battalion the Worcestershire Regiment was replaced by 2nd Battalion the Monmouthshire Regiment in 1957.)

Change of Title

Although the regiment appeared in Infantry Corps J (the Light Infantry Group), it originally retained its old title of the Herefordshire Regiment. Two months later, however, the following Royal Warrant appeared in Army Order 67 of 1947, granting the request to become light infantry:

The Herefordshire Regiment
Change of Title and Corps – Warrant Amendment
George RI
Whereas we deem it expedient to change the designation of The Herefordshire Regiment.
Our will and pleasure is that this regiment shall henceforth be entitled The Herefordshire Light Infantry
Our further will and pleasure is that the Schedule
attached to the Warrant of His late Majesty King
George V dated 27th February 1926, declaring what
bodies of Our Military Forces shall be corps for
the purpose of the Army Act, the Reserve Forces Act
1882, and the Territorial and Reserve Forces Act
1907, shall be amended as follows:

Under Infantry Corps 'J' for The Herefordshire
Regiment (Territorial Army).

Substitute The Herefordshire Light Infantry
(Territorial Army).

Given at our Court at St. James's this 28th day
of May 1947 in the 11th year of our Reign.

By His Majesty's Command.
F.J. Bellenger

The Regimental Cap Badge

The regimental cap badge was redesigned to incorporate the bugle horn, but it retained the lion and included the motto 'Manu Forti' for the first time. It is described as

a bugle horn stringed, mouthpiece to the right, thereon a lion passant guardant, holding in the dexter paw a sword, point uppermost, standing on a tablet inscribed with the motto 'Manu Forti'. In silver plate for officers and in white metal for Other Ranks.

The design was approved in 1950 and the badges were taken into use as supplies became available.

Battle Honours

The battle honours awarded to the regiment for service in the Second World War were notified in Army Order 58 of 1957, and in consequence the following ten honours were emblazoned on the horizontal arm of the cross of St George of the Queen's colour of 1st Battalion the Herefordshire Light Infantry.

Odon
Bourguebus Ridge
Souleuvre
Falaise
Antwerp
Hechtel
Venraij
Hochwald
Aller
North West Europe 1944–45

National Service

Up to 1950, 1st Battalion the Herefordshire Light Infantry consisted entirely of volunteers, but in that year the first men recruited through National Service joined in accordance with the obligations imposed by the National Service Acts of 1948–1955. In 1951 Z Class Reservists were called to the colours for fifteen days' training and mobilization exercise, and thus the battalion was brought up to strength during summer camp. However, following the suspension of the National Service commitment in 1957, the battalion was again composed entirely of volunteers, and so the traditional role of the Herefordshire Rifle Volunteers was continued.

Organization

The organization of 1st Battalion the Herefordshire Light Infantry remained unchanged until 1952, when a platoon of B Company (Ross) was raised at Cinderford in the Forest of Dean, just over the county boundary in Gloucestershire. This platoon increased in strength and in October 1953 the headquarters of A Company were transferred from Kington to Cinderford. The Kington volunteers reverted to the pre-war establishment and in November 1953 formed a platoon of D Company (Leominster).

The Cinderford Company adopted the title 'the Foresters', and is successor to the old Ruardean Company of 1908. Traditionally the area had formed part of 28th Regimental District with headquarters in Gloucester. The Forest of Dean Rifle Volunteers were 12th Gloucestershire VRC and formed part of 1st Administrative Battalion of Gloucestershire Rifle Volunteers, which became 2nd Volunteer Battalion the Gloucestershire Regiment following the reorganization of 1881, and 5th Battalion the Gloucestershire Regiment (TF) in 1908. The Gloucester T & AFA administer A Company, and that association built the Cinderford drill hall, which was opened on 22 April 1957.

Consequent on the 1961 reorganization of the Territorial Army, support company ceased to exist as such, being replaced by a support group. Support platoons were retained in Hereford and cadre support platoons were raised at Cinderford and Ross, with A and B Companies respectively. Finally, in May 1962 a platoon of C Company (Ledbury) was raised at Bromyard, and thus the battalion state in October 1962 was as undernoted:

Honorary Colonel Brig. Copland-Griffiths, F.A.V. DSO MC DL JP

Battalion headquarters

Rank	Name	Engagement	Appointment
Lt-Col.	Hill, T.J.B. MBE, KSLI	Regular	Commanding officer
Maj.	Priddle, G.S. TD	TA	Second-in-command
Capt.	Haszard, J.R. KSLI	Regular	Adjutant
Maj.	Sutton, E.H. KSLI	Regular	Quartermaster & PMC
Maj.	Watkinson, R.G. RAMC	TA	Medical officer
Maj.	Dukes, A.F. RAMC	TA	Medical officer
Capt.	Nicklin, F.N. RAPC	TA	Unit paymaster
CF4 CL	Coombs, R.J.	TA	Padre
2/Lt.	Quartermain, R.M.	TA	Intelligence officer
WO1	Lloyd, D.L.	Regular	Regimental sergeant-major
WO2	Sharman, J.H.	TA	Orderly room quartermaster-sergeant
WO2	Healey, W.V.	TA	Regimental quartermaster-sergeant

Headquarters Company, Hereford

Rank	Name	Engagement	Appointment
Maj.	Lewis, R.R. TD	TA	Commanding officer & PRI
Capt.	Jolly, M.	TA	Second-in-command
Lt.	Bulmer, D.E.	TA	Regimental signals officer
2/Lt.	Peach, W.R.	TA	Assistant regimental signals officer
Lt.	Barneby, R.H.H.	TA	Motor transport officer
WO2	Warr, F.C.	TA	Company sergeant-major
Sgt	Noble, N.E.	Regular	Permanent staff instructor
Col.-Sgt	Knight, C.G.	TA	Company quartermaster-sergeant

Support Group, Hereford

Capt.	Buckley, C.N.	TA	Commanding officer
WO2	Knight, A.W.	TA	Assault pioneer platoon commander
Sgt	Bowtell, J.D.	Regular	Permanent staff instructor
Col.-Sgt	Chadd, D.C.	TA	Company quartermaster-sergeant
Sgt	Gallagher, B.	TA	Machine-gun/recce platoon

A Company (The Foresters), TA Centre, Valley Rd, Cinderford

Capt.	Hawkins, M.	TA	Commanding officer
Capt.	Thompson, A.F.	TA	Second-in-command
Capt.	Ursell, D.J.V.	TA	Sp platoon commander
2/Lt.	Field, R.J.	TA	Platoon commander
WO2	Sims, R.M.J.	TA	Company sergeant-major
Sgt	Huff, D.C.	Regular	Permanent staff instructor
Col.-Sgt	Holder, D.J.	TA	Company quartermaster-sergeant

B Company, TA Centre, Alton Rd, Ross-on-Wye

Maj.	Bristow, H.M.	TA	Commanding officer
Capt.	Alsop, J.E.	TA	Second-in-command
Lt.	Lee, P.L.	TA	Platoon commander
Lt.	Cleland, G.J.	TA	Battalion mortar officer/ Sp platoon commander
Lt.	Williams, T.L.	TA	Platoon commander
Col.-Sgt	Matthews, T.A.	TA	A/company sergeant-major
WO2	Venn, S.R.	Regular	Permanent staff instructor
Col.-Sgt	Wragg, H.H.	TA	Company quartermaster-sergeant

C Company, Drill Hall, Ledbury
(one platoon at Drill Hall, Bromyard)

Maj.	Feltham, G.D.F. TD	TA	Commanding officer
Capt.	Jeffrey, J.W. de M.	TA	Second-in-command
Capt.	Cottle, P.	TA	Sp platoon commander/ battalion anti-tank officer
Lt.	Hopton, J.S.	TA	Platoon commander
Lt.	Yates, B.R.P.	TA	Platoon commander
Lt.	Cope, R.G.	TA	Platoon commander
Col.-Sgt	Powell, W.J.A.	TA	A/company sergeant-major
WO2	Gandon, H.	Regular	Permanent staff instructor
Sgt	James, S.D.	TA	A/company quartermaster-sergeant

D Company, Drill Hall, Leominster
(one platoon at Drill Hall, Kington)

Maj.	Rollings, W.R.P.	TA	Commanding officer
Capt.	Wardman, A.R.	TA	Second-in-command
Lt.	Coates, P.M.	TA	Platoon commander
Lt.	Miller, D.A.	TA	Sp platoon commander
Lt.	Meredith, J.C.C.	TA	Platoon commander
Sgt	Kenward, P.A.	Regular	Permanent staff instructor
Col.-Sgt	Jones, T.	TA	Company quartermaster-sergeant
WO2	Greenhouse, A.J.	TA	Company sergeant-major

Miscellaneous Appointments

Unit security officer	Capt. Haszard, J.R. (KSLI)
Unit fire officer	Capt. Haszard, J.R. (KSLI)

The immediate post-war concept that the Territorial Army should be a force of all arms manned in key positions by long-term volunteers, and brought up to full establishment by trained National Servicemen, so that in an emergency it could take its place on the Continent with the other NATO forces, was not to endure.

In 1955 and 1956, far-reaching reforms were conceived, whereby the Territorial Army reverted to its traditional role of home defence, but with emphasis on civil defence in the nuclear age. Only two divisions, 43 (Wessex) and 53 (Welsh), were to remain at full scale in order to fulfil the British Army's commitment to NATO.

1st Battalion the Herefordshire Light Infantry, as part of 159 (Welsh Border) Infantry Brigade, remained in 53 (Welsh) Division until 1 February 1961, when the brigade was transferred to the newly re-formed 48 Division, with headquarters at Shrewsbury. The brigade, with headquarters at Worcester, comprised:

7th Battalion the Worcestershire Regiment
4th Battalion the King's Shropshire Light Infantry
1st Battalion the Herefordshire Light Infantry

The battalion took down the Welsh W of 53 Division and replaced it with the formation sign of 48 Division, the design of which incorporates the gold crown of Offa, King of Mercia (AD 757) superimposed on the red cross of St Chad, the whole on a green square with a gold border. St Chad was Bishop of Mercia during the first century AD.

In 1962 the Territorial Army Emergency Reserve was formed with the object of creating a reserve of 'ever readies', liable to be called on to reinforce the Regular Army in any emergency. Although they will be called on only in an emergency, their obligation to serve overseas with the Regular Army, without the Territorial Army being embodied, is an entirely new concept of Territorial soldiering.

While these changes were taking place in the Territorial Army, the Regular Army was further reorganized and consequent on the policy of reducing the infantry of the Regular Army, 1st and 2nd Battalions KSLI were amalgamated on 12 June 1948 to form the present 1st Battalion, in which many Herefordshire men completed their National Service before transferring to 1st Battalion the Herefordshire Light Infantry (TA).

Similarly, 1st and 2nd Battalions the Worcestershire Regiment were amalgamated and on 17 April 1948, certain items of silver, formerly belonging to 36 Herefordshire Regiment of Foot, were presented to the Herefordshire Light Infantry, in trust, as a constant reminder of the ancient ties between the regiments of Worcestershire and Herefordshire.

In 1953 the Militia element of the corps of the KSLI finally ceased to exist when, by Army Order 47 of April 1953, 3rd Battalion KSLI (late the Shropshire Militia) was formally disbanded. The battalion had been in suspended animation since 8 August 1919.

It has been recorded that 4th (Herefordshire Militia) Battalion KSLI was disbanded on 13 April 1908, and until 1919 the Herefordshire members of the Special Reserve served in 3rd Battalion.

In July 1957 a major reorganization of the Regular Army was initiated, which provided for the infantry to be regrouped into fourteen brigades and the Parachute Regiment by 1962 (Command White Paper 230).

The KSLI forms part of the Light Infantry Brigade, the headquarters of which are situated at Copthorne Barracks, Shrewsbury. The brigade comprises the following regiments and battalions:

Somerset & Cornwall Light Infantry
Somerset Light Infantry (Prince Albert's) (TA)
Duke of Cornwall's Light Infantry (TA)
King's Own Yorkshire Light Infantry
King's Shropshire Light Infantry
Herefordshire Light Infantry (TA)
Durham Light Infantry

The Oxfordshire and Buckinghamshire Light Infantry severed connection with the Light Infantry Group and joined the Green Jackets Brigade as 1st Green Jackets 43rd and 52nd, the former title being retained by their Territorial battalion.

The Highland Light Infantry had not formed part of the original Light Infantry Group, and in this reorganization was amalgamated with the Royal Scots' Fusiliers to form the Royal Highland Fusiliers (Princess Margaret's Own Glasgow and Ayrshire Regiment) in the Lowland Brigade.

Sixteen eventful years

The regimental journal contains a full account of the activities of 1st Battalion the Herefordshire Light Infantry during the years 1946 to 1962, and it is only necessary here to record those events of historical interest.

Freedom of the City Reunion, 28 September 1946

The first all ranks reunion was held at the Shirehall, Hereford, to commemorate the first anniversary of the conferring of the freedom of the city of Hereford on the regiment. It was decided that this should become an annual event, and in consequence the 'Regimental Days' are now as follows:

Suvla Bay: second Friday in September to celebrate the landing and battle at Suvla Bay, 9 August 1915;
Freedom of the City: annual reunion held to celebrate the granting of the freedom of the city of Hereford to the regiment on 29 September 1945, normally held on the third Saturday in September.

The Lion Club

This social club was opened at the Old Barracks, Hereford, on Saturday 6 March 1948 by the Lord Lieutenant of Herefordshire, Sir Richard Cotterell Bt.

Col. H.E.P. Pateshall CB DSO TD DL

The death occurred of Col. Pateshall at Allensmore Court, Hereford, on 18 October 1948. He was gazetted to the East Yorkshire Regiment from Sandhurst in 1899. After 15 years service he retired, and a few months later was gazetted major to 1st Battalion the Herefordshire Regiment. On mobilization in 1914 he was appointed staff captain to 160 Brigade, in which capacity he took part in the Suvla Bay landing. He was later DAA and quartermaster-general of 53 Division and served in Egypt and Palestine, being twice mentioned in despatches and awarded the DSO in 1918. Col. Pateshall commanded 1st Battalion the Herefordshire Regiment from 1920 to 1926, and he served as chairman of the Herefordshire Territorial Army Association from 1929 to 1947. In recognition of his service in that capacity he was made a Companion of the Order of the Bath in the New Year's Honours list of 1942 and in the same year was awarded the Territorial Decoration. In 1940 he was appointed honorary colonel of 2nd Battalion and he more than earned the affectionate title of 'The Father of the Regiment'. The regiment provided a detachment as escort, bearers and firing party at his funeral on 21 October 1948.

The Territorial Army Review

On 31 October 1948 HM King George VI reviewed the Territorial Army in Hyde Park. The battalion provided a colour party and representative detachment. The colour party consisted of

Lt. L.A. Sturley, Lt. H.J. Downes, Col.-Sgt C. Griffiths, Pte D.C. Chadd and Pte G.V. Cole. The detachment was commanded by Maj. W.D.A. Clare.

The regimental war memorial chapel – St Aidan's Chapel, St Chad's Church, Shrewsbury

On 10 February 1951 Lt-Col. R.C.B. Armitstead succeeded to the command of the battalion and one of the first ceremonies to take place during his term of command was the dedication of the memorial chapel on Sunday 10 June 1951. The Lord Bishop of Lichfield performed the dedication and he was assisted by the Dean of Hereford, the Archdeacons of Salop and Ludlow, and other distinguished clergy. Among the guests were the Lord Lieutenant of Herefordshire, Sir Richard Cotterell and many members of the Hereford O.C.A. The battalion provided a colour party and detachment of seventy-five all ranks.

The regimental memorial chapel is dedicated

To the Glory of God and in memory of The Officers and Men of the Corps of The King's Shropshire Light Infantry, in which is incorporated the King's Shropshire Light Infantry and The Herefordshire Regiment (TA), who laid down their lives in the Service of their Country.

St Aidan's Chapel was dedicated in 1914 to the memory of Richard Eden St Aubyn Arkwright, Vicar of the Parish of St Chad, Shrewsbury, 1906–1913, and rededicated also as a memorial chapel to the KSLI and the Herefordshire Regiment on 10 June 1951.

The Herefordshire memorial is situated beneath the east window and comprises three carved

The colour parties of the 4th Bn, KSLI, and 1st Bn Hereford LI, at St Chad's Church, Shrewsbury, 10 June 1951, on the occasion of the re-dedication of the memorial chapel to the two regiments.

oak panels. In the centre is inscribed '*Manu Forti*. The Herefordshire Regiment, formerly The Herefordshire Rifle Volunteer Corps, now The Herefordshire Light Infantry (Territorial Army).' On either side are inscribed the battle honours; on the left, beneath the badge of the Herefordshire Regiment, the battle honours awarded from 1900–1918; and on the right, beneath the badge of the Herefordshire Light Infantry, those awarded from 1939 to 1945:

1900–1918	1939–1945
South Africa 1900–02	Odon
Soissonnais-Ourcq	Bourguebus Ridge
Ypres 1918	Souleuvre
Courtrai	Falaise
France and Flanders 1918	Antwerp
Landing at Suvla	Hechtel
Rumani	Venraij
Gaza	Hochwald
El Mughar	Aller
Jerusalem	North West Europe 1944–45
Tell Asur	

Col. Gilbert Drage

The death occurred of Col. Gilbert Drage on 6 May 1952 at Norton, Radnorshire. After serving twenty-three years in the Royal Marines, Col. Drage took command of 1st Battalion the Herefordshire Regiment in 1914. He served with the battalion in Gallipoli, Egypt and Palestine, being wounded at Suvla Bay. He received the DSO and retired in 1918. The Herefordshire Light Infantry was represented at his funeral by Lt-Col. R.C.H. Armitstead and the Herefordshire Regiment O.C.A. by Maj. L.B. Green.

Coronation of HM Queen Elizabeth II

The regiment took part in the Coronation of HM Queen Elizabeth II on 2 June 1953 by providing personnel for the procession from Westminster Abbey, and also a street-lining party. Those taking part in the Procession were Maj. R.V. Webb TD, WO I.F. Freeman, Sgt E.J. Griffiths, L/Cpl F. Druce and L/Cpl S.L. Gordon, and the street-lining party comprised Lt. E.S.H. Bulman, Col.-Sgt F.C. Warr and Sgt H.S. Parry (colours and escort), and CSM A.J. Greenhouse, Sgt G.V. Cole, Sgt A.W. Wood, Sgt M.T.F. Hickey, Cpl J. Chambers, L/Cpl B. Daffurn, L/Cpl F.C. Roberts, L/Cpl T.A. Matthews, Pte J. Marks, Pte J.V. Lucas, Pte R.C. Lawrence, Pte R. Billingham, Pte R. Payne, Pte D. Minton, Pte K.V. Winney and Pte D. Cotterell.

Contingents from the regiment also took part in special coronation services in Hereford and Leominster. Members awarded the Queen's Coronation Medal were Lt-Col. R.C.H. Armitstead, Maj. G. Broad MBE, Maj. R.V. Webb TD, RQMS W.V. Healey, CSM A.J. Greenhouse, Col.-Sgt F.C. Warr, Sgt W.L. Oakey and Sgt C.G. Weaver.

New TA centres

Lt-Col. G.M. Thornycroft succeeded to the command of the battalion in February 1954, and during his command two new TA centres were opened. In 1956 the TA centre at Harold Street, Hereford, was completed, and this very fine building was formally opened at a ceremony held on 22 September 1956 by the Lord Lieutenant of Herefordshire, Lt-Col. Sir Richard Cotterell Bt. The opening ceremony was attended by Lt-Gen. Sr Lashmer Whistler KCB KBE DSO (GOC-in-C Western Command), the Lord Bishop of Hereford and members of the Territorial Association. On 22 April 1957 the TA centre at Cinderford was opened.

No. 1 dress

The Coronation Detachment had worn no. 1 dress of light infantry green in June 1953, but it was not until 1956 that the band received no. 1 dress, in which it paraded for the first time on Armistice Day 1956.

Maj.-Gen. J.B. Churcher CB DSO

In February 1957 Maj.-Gen. Churcher relinquished the honorary colonelcy of 1st Battalion the Herefordshire Light Infantry, and he was succeeded by Brig. F.A.V. Copland-Griffiths DSO MC DL JP. Maj.-Gen. Churcher had commanded the battalion from 1942 until 1944, and he had been honorary colonel since 1945. He was presented with a suitably inscribed cigarette box by Lt-Col. G.M. Thornycroft on behalf of all ranks of the battalion, in recognition of his great services to the regiment.

The guard of honour for HM the Queen, Hereford, 24 April 1957

On the occasion of the visit to Herefordshire of HM the Queen and HRH the Duke of Edinburgh, 1st Battalion provided a guard of honour at Hereford, and street-lining parties at Ledbury and Ross. The guard of honour was commanded by Maj. G.S. Priddle TD.

The Golden Jubilee of the Territorial Army, 1908–1958

On 18 December 1957 Lt-Col. J.D. Sale succeeded to the command of the battalion and he was soon involved in the preparations for the celebration of the TA Golden Jubilee in 1958. The highlight of the celebrations was Her Majesty's Royal Review in Hyde Park, London, on 22 June. The regiment provided a contingent of thirty for this review, under the command of Maj. G.H. Mason. The colours were carried by Lt. J.W. de M. Jeffrey and Lt. M. Jolly, and the escort to the colours consisted of CSM F.C. Warr, CSM A.J. Greenhouse and Col.-Sgt D.C. Chadd. The Golden Jubilee was further marked by a parade to Hereford Cathedral on Sunday 13 July, followed by a march past, when the Lord Lieutenant of Herefordshire, the Viscount Cilcennin PC took the salute in High Town. There was an almost complete turn-out of the regiment on this day, and the marching column also included many of the Old Comrades and Cadet Detachments.

The regimental museum

Lt-Col. G.M. Thornycroft initiated a collection of uniforms and other relics of the regiment, which formed the basis of a small regimental museum that was developed by Lt-Col. J.D. Sale. In 1960 Lt-Col. T.J.B. Hill MBE succeeded to the command of the battalion, and under his guidance the museum has become a source of pride to all members of the regiment, past and present. In order that the valuable exhibits are preserved for posterity, they have been made the subject of a trust deed under the aegis of the Army Museum Ogilby Trust.

The visit of HM The Queen to Hereford on 24 April 1957.
Above: The Royal salute. Below: The Queen inspects the Guard of Honour provided by the 1st Bn the
Hereford Regiment, commanded by Maj. G.S. Priddle TD.

Centenary Celebrations.
The centenary parade in High Town, 27 November 1960, marking 100 years of continuous service from
the revival of the Herefordshire Rifle Volunteers in 1860. The salute was taken by the Lord Lieutenant
Col. J.F. Maclean and the parade led by the commanding officer, Lt-Col. T.J.B. Hill MBE.

Lt-Col. T.J.B. Hill MBE displays the regimental colours.

Millom Camp, 1960. Front row, from fourth left: Capt. Monk (Adjutant), RSM Baines, Lt-Col. Hill MBE (CO), RQMS Healey, Maj. Sutton (QM), CSM Greenhouse, CSM Knight, ORQMS Sharman.

1st Bn Hereford LI, Western Command Cross-Country Championship, 1961. The team leader, J. Tarrant, receives the cup from the CO, Lt-Col. T.J.B. Hill.

Centenary of the regiment

In 1960 the regiment celebrated 100 years of continuous service from the revival of the Herefordshire Rifle Volunteers in 1860. The centenary was celebrated on Sunday 27 November 1960 by a thanksgiving service in Hereford Cathedral, followed by a parade through the city, with a march past in High Town. The salute was taken by the Lord Lieutenant Col. J.F. Maclean. The colour party consisted of Lt. A.F. Thompson, Lt. R.G. Cope, CSM A.J. Greenhouse, Col.-Sgt D.C. Chadd and Col.-Sgt C.G. Knight, and the two divisions were commanded by Maj. G.D.F. Feltham and Maj. R.R. Lewis TD respectively. The parade was led by the commanding officer, Lt-Col. T.J.B. Hill MBE.

Conclusion

During the period 1947–1967, the regiment has grown in strength and acquired a fine reputation, in both training achievements and sporting activities. The Herefordshire Light Infantry has a proud place in the annals of the Territorial Army, and it was a sad day in 1967 when Herefordshire lost its own Territorial battalion on the disbandment of 1st Battalion the Herefordshire Light Infantry. In consequence of the Territorial Army reductions and reorganization, Shropshire and Herefordshire were joined together as part of the Light Infantry Volunteers. In 1972 they became 5th Battalion the Light Infantry (Volunteers) with two companies in Herefordshire, one in Hereford and the other at Ross-on-Wye.

CHAPTER 20

Dress and Insignia, 1860–1967

Introduction

The infantry of the Volunteer Force dressed in the 'Rifle' tradition until the battalions became part of the Territorial regiments after 1881, when they adopted the uniform of their county regiments.

In Herefordshire the reluctance to become 3rd Volunteer Battalion K(SLI) was reflected in the fact that 1st HVRC retained the rifle title and black facings until 1908, when it became 1st Battalion the Herefordshire Regiment.

In 1908 the Territorial Force adopted khaki service dress in addition to full dress, but a limited use of khaki service dress had followed the South African War, when the Volunteers affected the slouch hat and campaign dress of the Service Companies.

The 'Sam Browne' belt was worn by officers in service dress when on duty until 1916, but in that year it was ordered to be worn on all occasions.

Full Dress was not revived after the First World War except by the bands, and service dress was in sole use until 1937 when, following the coronation of HM King George VI, a blue patrol uniform was made optional.

In 1940 the service dress for other ranks was replaced by the battle dress and at the same time the SD cap was replaced by the field service cap. This head-dress continued until 1944, when it was replaced by the general service cap. The beret evolved naturally, and in 1947 khaki berets were issued, which were replaced by light infantry berets in 1948.

The coronation of HM Queen Elizabeth II in 1953 was the occasion of the limited introduction of no. 1 dress of light infantry green, and by 1956 it had been made available to the band and senior WCOs.

The Arms of the City of Hereford

The Herefordshire Light Infantry and its predecessors have taken their insignia from the arms of the city of Hereford: a shield, charged with the three lions of England (from the royal arms of Richard I), surrounded by a border bearing ten St Andrew's crosses, supported by two silver lions rampant guardant, each with a collar charged with three gold buckles and having as a crest a lion passant guardant holding in the dexter paw a sword, the motto being '*Invictae fidelitatis praemium*'.

The city received its first charter from Richard I (1189–1199), since when lions have appeared in its arms. In 1645, as a Royalist stronghold, it was besieged by the Scots under Leslie Earl of Leven, and in token of its loyalty the city received a grant of arms, which not only recognized the arms which it had been using, but added emblems commemorating the siege. The lions surrounded by saltires represent the Royalist forces hemmed in by the insurgent Scots, and the buckles on the collars of the supporting lions are from the arms of the Earl of Leven. The sword held by the lion crest similarly commemorates the service to the Crown, as does the motto: 'The reward of faithfulness unconquered'.

The following is an extract from the Grant of Arms:

Colours and Uniforms 1860–1960
Left: Full dress 1908–14; Centre: No. 1 Dress 1956–62; Right: HVRC 1860–75.

for there hath not any City since this un-natural rebellion expressed greater fidelity and courage than the City of Hereford, in continuing their allegiance and resisting the many attempts of the rebels. But the greatness of their loyalty, courage and undaunted resolution did then most eminently appear when, being straitly besieged for a space of five weeks by a powerful army of rebellious Scots, and having no hopes of relief, they, joining with the garrison and doing the duty of soldiers, then defended themselves with so great destruction of the besiegers that they became the wonder of their neighbouring garrisons and therefore do justly deserve such characters of honour.

The Facings and Insignia of 36th Foot and the Herefordshire Militia

In 1908 the Herefordshire Regiment wished to remember 36th (Herefordshire) Regiment of Foot, which became 2nd Battalion the Worcestershire Regiment in 1881, and did so by adopting the grass-green facings of 36th Foot, together with the gold lace and brass appointments, in place of the black facings and silver lace of the HRVs.

The Herefordshire Militia was similarly remembered by the officers of the Herefordshire Regiment adopting the badge of an apple on their buttons. The Herefordshire Militia became 4th (Militia) Battalion KSLI in 1881, and was disbanded in 1908.

The insignia and facings of the Herefordshire Regiments are easily confused because the Volunteers and Militia both used the arms of the city of Hereford, and while the facings of 36th Foot were described as grass green after 1830, they were previously, on occasions, described also as willow green and gosling green, which was also the colour of the facings of the Herefordshire Militia in the nineteenth century, but their facings in 1778 were described as being of apple green.

The Light Infantry and Rifle Tradition

On becoming the Herefordshire Light Infantry in 1947, the regiment adopted the dress and traditions of the light infantry and included the bugle horn in the cap badge. This was not such an innovation as is sometimes suggested, because the bugle badge had been worn by the HRVs from 1860 to 1908.

The Light Infantry Bugle Horn

The badge was authorized for the British Army under Horse Guards General Order No. 282 of 28 December 1814:

> His Royal Highness the Prince Regent having been pleased to command 'that the caps of the Rifle and Light Infantry Corps, and the Rifle and Light Infantry Companies of Regiments, shall have a bugle horn with the number of the Regiment below it, instead of the brass plate worn by the rest of the Infantry'. The Commander-in-Chief has directed that the same shall be established throughout the several Companies and Corps of Riflemen and Light Infantry in His Majesty's service.

Pictures and prints of officers and men of the light division show the bugle horn being worn prior to the date of the general order quoted above. The bugle horn is traditionally the sign of the Forester or hunter, and has been used for centuries by the foresters of Germany in conjunction with the jaeger green clothing as a symbol of trade. It was first used in military uniform by the Prussian Field Jaeger Corps in 1744.

The light companies of foot regiments added to the British Establishment in 1770 (W.O. 26/28 pp. 360–1), adopting the bugle horn from the Jaeger Regiments, and it naturally followed that the rifle and light infantry regiments, subsequently formed, continued that tradition. The bugle badge was similarly adopted by 4 KSLI and 1st Hereford Light Infantry from their inception as Rifle Volunteers.

The formation of the Light Infantry Group of regiments in 1946 brought with it the adoption of a light infantry bugle cap badge (Oxfordshire and Buckinghamshire Light Infantry large pattern) for National Service recruits at Light Infantry Training Centres, together with the shoulder title 'Light Infantry' (*Vide* C.4512 Vol. LXI List of Changes in War materials dated 31 May 1951 and confirmed by the Light Infantry Colonels Committee Meeting).

The 1957 reorganization of the Regular Army was accompanied by the abolition of the regimental cap badges for regular personnel and the substitution of brigade badges. The Light

Top: 1st Herefordshire Rifle Volunteer Corps Officers'/ NCOs' pouch belt, c. 1883; above: silver buckle as worn on walking out dress belt of the Herefordshire Rifle Volunteers; right: helmet plate, HRVC, 1878–1901.

Infantry Brigade continued the practice instituted by the Light Infantry Group, but as the Oxfordshire and Buckinghamshire Light Infantry were brigaded with the KRRC and the Rifle Brigade as 1st Green Jackets 43rd and 52nd, their pattern bugle was not continued, and instead the original design of 1814 was reintroduced and the badges were issued on October 1959. The Territorial battalions continued to wear their regimental cap badges.

The light infantry green is a reminder of the original role in the forests of North America and the first battle dress.

The Bugle badge is a reminder that the light troops skirmished and scouted ahead of the main body of the army where the cumbersome drum was replaced by the bugle for conveying orders in the field.

The green whistle cords are worn by officers, warrant officers and sergeants as a reminder of the nature of the original tactical employment which required commissioned and non-commissioned officers to take control while skirmishing, and to give orders by the whistle. Pouch belts and whistles were worn by officers of the light infantry and rifles.

The drill is another reminder of the days when the light infantry was equipped light and required to march faster and further than the remainder of the army to outflank the enemy and to advance at the bugle call.

Light infantry march past at 140 paces to the minute, carry their arms 'at the trail', ready at all times for immediate use, and carry out all movements from and to the 'stand at ease' position, thus signifying that they are alert at all times.

Roll of Honour

The following are lists of the officers, WOs, NCOs and men who gave their lives in the South African War, the First World War and the Second World War.

> We will remember them when the sun rises up, and at even,
> Long as the winds of the West shall sing through the hills
>   of the free;
> Long as the stream shall flow, and Wye go down to the Severn,
> Long as the tide shall roll and Severn sweep to the sea.

Extract from 'Of The Men of an Inland County', John S. Arkwright.

The South African War, 1900–1902

1st Herefordshire Rifle Volunteer Corps serving at the time of death with 1st Volunteer Service Company KSLI:

Pte Adams, H.H.
L/Cpl Oakley, F.R.

1st Herefordshire Rifle Volunteer Corps serving at the time of death with 2nd Volunteer Service Company KSLI:

Cpl James, A.
Pte Smith, J.P.

The Welsh Border Brigade Bearer Company RAMC (V):

Cpl Figg, H.
Sgt Hickman, G.
Pte Smith, A.E.
L/Cpl Vaughan, C.M.E.

4th (Herefordshire Militia) Battalion KSLI serving at the time of death with 2nd KSLI:

Pte Gingell, A.
Pte Goodwin, A.
L/Cpl Morgan, W.J.
Pte Mountain, D.
Pte Russell, J.
Pte Tinson, G.

Pte Vickerage, W.
Pte West, C.

The roll of honour for the South African War is displayed on a tablet in Hereford Cathedral and on the South African war memorial, St Chad's Terrace, Shrewsbury.

The First World War, 1914–1919

The Herefordshire Regiment

Officers:

Maj.	Carless, W.T.	Maj.	Whitehouse, A.G.R. MC
Capt.	Berney, G.N.	Capt.	Carver, W.L.
Capt.	Croft, Sir Herbert Archer Bt	Capt.	Jordan, L.O. MC
Capt.	Holman, A.V.	Capt.	Lloyd, W.H.
Capt.	Levason, D.G.G.	Capt.	Sale, R.C.
Capt.	Russell, E.S. MC	Capt.	Yeomans, H.W.
Capt.	Wilson, A.	Lt.	Duff-Gordan, C.L.
Lt.	Crossley, A.H.	Lt.	Mitchell, P.M.
Lt.	Howells, R.	Lt.	Pritchett, E.G.
Lt.	Pettigrew, G.T.R.	2/Lt.	Court, R.W.S.
Lt.	Whittaker, W.R.	2/Lt.	Marshall, A.
2/Lt.	Jones, F.T.A.	2/Lt.	Vaughan, C.
2/Lt.	Reeve, H.J.	2/Lt.	Wells, N.A.
2/Lt.	Watts, J.H.		

Other ranks:

Serving at the time of the death with 1st/1st Battalion the Herefordshire Regiment:

Pte	Adams, F.	Pte	Adams, G.	Pte	Amos, J.
L/Cpl	Andrews, F.	Pte	Arnold, A.	Pte	Arnold, E.W.
Pte	Arnold, W.J.	Pte	Ashurst, A.A.L.	Pte	Attwood, W.
Pte	Averill, T.	Pte	Baker, E.G.	Pte	Bannister, J.
Pte	Barber, A.O.	Pte	Barber, H.	L/Cpl	Barnett, R.W.
Pte	Beaumont, W.	Pte	Bell, J.	Pte	Bendall, L.G.
Pte	Berrow, J.A.	Pte	Bevan, W.N.	L/Cpl	Bezant, E.W.
Pte	Bird, C.	Pte	Birks, G.A.	Pte	Blake, E.
Pte	Bond, C.T.	Pte	Boscoe, W.	Pte	Bosley, H.T.
Pte	Boucher, W.I.	A/L/Cpl	Bounds, G.T.	Pte	Bowkett, A.
Pte	Bowkett, J.W.	Pte	Bradley, W. (Newtown, Ledbury)	Pte	Bradley, W. (Holmer)
Pte	Bridges, J.	Pte	Briggs, C.F.	Pte	Brimfield, H.
Pte	Brookes, R.W.	Pte	Brown, W.	Pte	Bryant, W.
Pte	Bull, T.	Pte	Caines, A.	Pte	Caines, H.

Pte	Campbell, A.W.	Sgt	Chadd, W.C.	Pte	Chamberlaine, T.
Pte	Cheffers, C.	Sgt	Chirnside, C.	Pte	Clarke, H.
Pte	Clarke, T.	Pte	Clarkson, D.H.	Pte	Clayton, A.
Pte	Clayton, W.	Pte	Cleaton, T.C.	Pte	Cobbledick, A.H.
Pte	Collins, T.G.	Sgt	Colwell, C.J.	Pte	Cook, T.G.
Pte	Cooke, W.	Pte	Cooke, W.H.	Pte	Counsell, T.L.
Pte	Crump, P.	Pte	Dallow, H.	Pte	Dance, W.E.
Pte	Davies, A.H.	Pte	Davies, A.T.	Pte	Davies, F.
Pte	Davies, H.T.	Pte	Davies, J.	A/L/Cpl	Davies, O.
L/Cpl	Davies, L.A.	Pte	Deakin, J.	Pte	Dobson, J.
Pte	Donovan, A.E.	Pte	Doyle, J.	Pte	Duffty, T.C.
Pte	Dutton, F.A.	Pte	Dyke, A.	Pte	East, H.H.
Pte	Easthope, D.E.	A/L/Cpl	Edmonds, R.	Pte	Edmundson, H.
Pte	Edwards, F.E.	Pte	Edwards, G.H.	Pte	Edwards, R.
Pte	Edwards, W.	Pte	Ellis, D.	Pte	Evans, D.
A/L/Cpl	Evans, J.	Pte	Evans, J.	Pte	Evans, L.C.
L/Cpl	Evans, W.A.	Pte	Eversham, H.A.	L/Cpl	Falconer, E.
Pte	Faulkner, W.	CSM	Faulkner, W.H.	Pte	Fell, R.
Pte	Fleetwood, W.	A/CQMS	Fletcher, E.A.G.	L/Cpl	Fowler, G.
Pte	Fowler, H.	Pte	Fowler, W.H.	Pte	Fox, H.
Pte	Fry, W.J.	Pte	Fuller, F.W.	Pte	Gardiner, A.
Pte	Girling, S.G.	Pte	Gittins, A.	Pte	Grainger, J.
Pte	Green, C.	Cpl	Green, J.	Cpl	Green, J.H.
Pte	Griffiths, J.	Pte	Griffiths, W.	Pte	Gummer, T.
Pte	Gunn, R.E.	A/L/Cpl	Gurney, H.V.	Pte	Hall, W.
Pte	Hands, W.	Pte	Hanks, E.T.	Pte	Hards, G.A.
Pte	Hargest, R.	Pte	Harley, A.	Pte	Harris, G.M.
Pte	Harris, J.	CQMS	Harris, J.F.	Pte	Harris, S.
Pte	Harris, W.H.	Pte	Hatton, F.W.L.	A/Sgt	Herbert, A.
Pte	Hicks, G.	Pte	Higley, P.	Pte	Hiles, E.
Pte	Hill, A.	Pte	Hill, F.	Pte	Hill, T.
L/Cpl	Hodges, A.	Pte	Hodges, R.A.	Pte	Hodges, W.A.
Pte	Hodnett, E.J.	Pte	Holloway, F.R.	L/Cpl	Holmes, A.
Pte	Hope, J.	Pte	Horton, J.	A/L/Cpl	Howells, G.B.
Pte	Howse, W.H.G.	A/Sgt	Huckson, J.	Pte	Hughes, G.
Pte	Hughes, H.	Pte	Hughes, W.R.	Pte	Hunt, H.
Pte	Husbands, A.	Pte	Innes, J.	Pte	Izzard, H.
Pte	James, H.T.	Pte	Jay, H.S.	Pte	Jenkins, A.
Pte	Jenkins, F.	Pte	Jones, A.	Pte	Jones, C.
Pte	Jones, E.	A/L/Cpl	Jones, F.C.	Pte	Jones, F.J.
Pte	Jones, Harold	Pte	Jones, Harry	Pte	Jones, Henry
Pte	Jones, P.T.	Pte	Jones, Wallace	Pte	Jones, William
Pte	Jones, W.C.T.	Pte	Jones, W.J.	Pte	Jordan, H.G.E.
Pte	Keay, E.J.	Pte	Kitson, D.	A/L/Cpl	Knight, W.
Pte	Knott, F.	Pte	Ladmore, H.	Pte	Lane, J.
Pte	Langford, G.	Pte	Lawrence, G.	Pte	Lawrence, J.W.
Pte	Leach, S.T.	L/Cpl	Leddington, B.G.	Pte	Lewis, J. (Clewstone)
Pte	Lewis, J. (Pembridge)	A/Sgt	Lewis, W.E.	Pte	Lilwall, G.

Pte	Lloyd, E.	Pte	Lloyd, W.J.	A/Sgt	Longford, W.
Pte	Low, F.	Pte	Mainwaring, R.T.	Pte	Mansell, S.H.
Pte	Mantell, H.	Pte	Mapp, W.J.	Pte	Marchant, W.G.
Pte	Marklove, H.H.	Pte	Marshall, N.H.	L/Cpl	Marston, R.E.
Pte	Mason, C.	Pte	Mason, G.A.	Pte	Mason, H.J.
Pte	Mason, S.	Pte	Matthews, A.	Pte	Matthews, E.
Pte	Matthews, E.J.	Cpl	Meek, E.J.	Pte	Meek, N.
Pte	Meredith, E.	Pte	Miles, C.	Pte	Miles, L.T.
Pte	Millar, J.	L/Cpl	Mills, T.	Pte	Mince, S.
Pte	Minchin, E.	Pte	Moore, W.	Pte	Morgan, F.J.
Pte	Morgan, G.	Pte	Morgan, O.J.	Pte	Morgan, W.
A/CSM	Morris, E.G.	Pte	Morris, J.	Pte	Morris, W.
Pte	Moss, E.	Pte	Mutlow, C.W.	Pte	Naylor, J.
Pte	Newman, A.	Pte	Newns, W.	Pte	Nicholls, E.D.
Pte	Nicholls, R.	Pte	Nicholls, W.T.	L/Cpl	Noble, E.G.
Pte	Norgrove, R.M.	Pte	Oliver, F.	Cpl	Oliver, W.
Pte	Oliver, W.H.	L/Cpl	Osborne, T.J.	Pte	Owen, G.T.
Pte	Owens, W.T.	Pte	Page, R.H.	Pte	Parker, J.
Pte	Parry, A.E.	Pte	Parsons, J.A.J.	Pte	Partridge, W.
Pte	Peters, W.	Pte	Pike, D.H.	Pte	Pinches, W.
Pte	Pitt, J.C.	Pte	Pitt, T.	Pte	Pocknell, W.J.
Pte	Ponfield, W.J.	Cpl	Poole, H.W.	Cpl	Pope, G.
Pte	Porter, B.J.	Pte	Porter, L.	Pte	Poyner, W.H.
Pte	Preece, C.B.	Pte	Preece, J.	Pte	Price, E.
Pte	Price, E.H.	Pte	Price, J.W.	Pte	Prowlin, H.
Pte	Pugh, T.	Pte	Ratcliffe, T.	Pte	Rawlings, J.E.
A/Sgt	Raymond, A.L.	Dmr	Raymond, H.	Pte	Reynolds, J.C.
Pte	Richards, A.	Cpl	Richardson, A.J.	Pte	Roberts, E.H.
Pte	Rock, C.	Cpl	Rogers, C.L.	Pte	Rogers, D.R.
Pte	Ryder, C.	Pte	Saunders, A.	Pte	Savigar, G.
Pte	Savory, H.	Pte	Savory, W.F.C.	Pte	Shears, J.S.
Dmr	Sherwood, B.M.	Pte	Skyrme, L.	Cpl	Smith, G.R.
Pte	Smith, P.	Pte	Smith, S.H.	Sgt	Smith, W.
Pte	Soane, J.	Pte	Solomon, E.T.	Pte	Spencer, H.G.
Pte	Stallard, F.	Pte	Stephens, T.R.	L/Cpl	Stokes, L.C.
Pte	Stone, W.G.	Pte	Swaincot, A.	Pte	Swift, T.W.
L/Sgt	Symonds, J.B. DCM MM	Pte	Tanswell, H.	Sgt	Taylor, G.R.
L/Cpl	Taylor, H.	Pte	Taylor, J.	Pte	Taylor, J.T.
Pte	Taylor, P.G.	A/Sgt	Teague, A.H.	L/Sgt	Thackway, J.
Pte	Thomas, H.W.	Pte	Thornton, S.J.	Pte	Tippins, F.
Pte	Todd, H.L.	Pte	Tongue, W.A.	Pte	Tristram, A.
L/Cpl	Trumper, B.C.	Pte	Tuckwell, H.	Pte	Turner, W.J.
L/Cpl	Tyler, W.	Pte	Vaughan, G.	L/Cpl	Waites, L.A.
Pte	Walker, J.J.	Pte	Walters, C.E.	Pte	Walters, C.H.
Sgt	Wargent, C.W.	Pte	Warren, C.D.	Pte	Watkins, F.G.
Pte	Watkins, H.L.	Pte	Watkins, J.	Pte	Webb, W.E.
Pte	Whitcombe, G.	Pte	Whiting, R.	Pte	Whitney, J.

Pte	Whittaker, H.T.	Pte	Whittaker, H.W.	Pte	Wild, J.J.
Pte	Wilkins, P.C.	Pte	Wilkinson, C.	Pte	Williams, A.J.
Pte	Williams, A.R.	Pte	Williams, F.	Pte	Williams, G.T.
Pte	Williams, J.	Pte	Williams, J.E.D.	Pte	Williams, R.
Sgt	Williams, T.	Pte	Williams, W.C.	Pte	Wilson, W.
Pte	Winters, J.	Pte	Witherstone, A.H.	Pte	Withington, F.
Pte	Withington, T.H.	Pte	Wood, S.R.	Pte	Wright, C.
Pte	Wright, J.	Pte	Wright, S.A.	CSM	Yemm, R.G.

Serving at the time of the death with 3rd/1st Battalion the Herefordshire Regiment:

Pte	Baker, R.C.	Pte	Jones, T.	Pte	Mayo, A.
Pte	Mills, A.W.	L/Cpl	Mutlow, T.J.	Pte	Rowbrey, G.T.
Pte	Skyrme, M.	Pte	Tuberfield, W.	Pte	Wills, G.

Serving at the time of death with 1st Reserve Battalion the Herefordshire Regiment:

Pte	Adams, C.	Pte	Drew, J.W.	Pte	Gibbs, P.C.
Pte	Hassall, G.	Pte	Hope, L.	Pte	Jones, D.M.
Pte	Lewis, E.	Pte	Morgan, L.S.	Pte	Morris, D.
Pte	Owens, I.	Pte	Preece, F.M.	Pte	Pritchard, J.
Pte	Probert, A.I.	Pte	Smith, S.	Pte	Taylor, J.
Pte	Verry, W.J.				

Serving at the time of death with the KSLI:

Pte	Abberley, J.	Pte	Barrell, V.	A/Cpl	Bailey, G.E.
Pte	Banchini, W.H.	L/Cpl	Beazley, A.	Sgt	Bratt, A.J.
Pte	Chapman, G.	Pte	Gibbons, A.C.	Sgt	Grady, J.T.
Pte	Good, S.G.	A/Sgt Instr.	Jackson, E.C.	Pte	James, J.H.
Pte	Jay, W.J.	Pte	Jones, E.J.	Pte	Jones, G.
Pte	Jones, W.E.	Pte	King, H.A.	Pte	Mace, W.W.
Pte	Manns, A.S.	Sgt	Mapp, C.R.	Pte	Meredith, J.S.
Cpl	Millichamp, W.G.	Pte	Morgan, W.	Pte	Oakley, J.
Pte	Powell, A.J.	Pte	Preece, R.	Pte	Price, A.
Pte	Price, G.H.	Sgt	Taylor, R.F.	Pte	Townsend, A.
Pte	Turbill, T.	Pte	Turner, R.	Pte	Weaver, F.C.
Pte	Wilcox, F.H.	Pte	Williams, G.		

Serving at the time of death with 5th Battalion South Wales Borderers:

Pte Cooke, A.E.

Serving at the time of death with 12th/13th Battalion Northumberland Fusiliers:

Pte Crosthwaite, A.F.

KSLI serving at the time of death with 1st/1st Battalion the Herefordshire Regiment:

L/Cpl	Barnsley, H.		Pte	Mitchell, T.
Pte	Bright, W.G.		Pte	Moore, G.
Pte	Bubb, G.A.		Pte	Munden, A.G.
Pte	Cardwell, A.		Pte	Murray, H.
Pte	Carrier, T.E.		Pte	Musk, E.E.
Pte	Fischer, E.J.		Pte	Parkinson, J.
Pte	Fox, W.		Pte	Philpott, C.
Pte	Gorrell, J.H.		Pte	Quilliam, T.C.
Pte	Harvey, F.S.		Pte	Reed, G.
Pte	Hotchkiss, F.		Pte	Rees, S.G.
Pte	Hudson, A.C.		Pte	Revell, J.
Pte	Jackman, A.		Pte	Smallridge, H.
Pte	Jackson, T.		Pte	Soper, F.H.
Pte	Jones, J.		Pte	Southern, S.H.
Pte	Jones, T.		L/Cpl	Stevens, W.C.
Pte	Lanyon, S.		Pte	Strugnell, G.E.
Pte	Long, M.W.		Pte	Sykes, H.
Pte	Lunt, G.T.		Pte	Taylor, C.
Pte	McCaig, W.		Pte	Taylor, J.
Pte	Mason, C.		Pte	Weaving, F.E.
Pte	Mawer, E.L.		Pte	Willis, H.

The roll of honour for the First World War is illuminated and displayed in a case in Hereford Cathedral. A copy was published by the Herefordshire Regiment Old Comrades' Association in 1932.

The roll of honour of the KSLI serving at the time of death with 1st/1st Battalion the Herefordshire Regiment is recorded in *The History of the KSLI in the Great War, 1914–18*, edited by W. de B. Wood.

The Second World War, 1939–1945

The Herefordshire Regiment

Serving at the time of death with 1st Battalion the Herefordshire Regiment in the North West European Campaign (in date order):

Officers killed in action:

Company	Number	Rank	Name	Date	Location
A	243033	Capt.	Boddy, S.H.	30 Jul 44	La Vacquerie
B	87117	Capt.	Bulmer, O.T.	9 Sep 44	Helchteren
D	285429	Lt.	Creamer, F.B.	9 Sep 44	Helchteren
C	Cdn/270	Lt.	Kotchapaw, W.J.	10 Sep 44	Hechtel
A	Cdn/160	Lt.	Hopkinson, G.G.	1 Apr 45	Birgte
A	?	Lt.	Spittall, A.J.	1 Apr 45	Birgte
B	330179	2/Lt.	Hancox, T.E.	10 Apr 45	Grindau

Officers who died of wounds received in action:

Company	Number	Rank	Name	Date	Location
S	63916	Capt.	Barneby, R.P.	1 Jul 44	Tourmaville

Other ranks killed in action:

Company	Number	Rank	Name	Date	Location
A	4041922	Pte	Ward, F.	28 Jun 44	Tourmaville
C	4105557	Pte	Davies, V.J.	29 Jun 44	Tourmaville
D	4104881	Pte	Cooke, G.H.	30 Jun 44	Tourmaville
D	14645780	Pte	Higgins, E.R.	30 Jun 44	Tourmaville
A	4032353	L/Cpl	Rycroft, W.A.	30 Jun 44	Tourmaville
S	4036562	Cpl	Curtis, J.A.	1 Jul 44	Tourmaville
A	4039548	Pte	Jones, A.E.	1 Jul 44	Tourmaville
B	5127583	Pte	Jones, J.H.	1 Jul 44	Tourmaville
S	4041611	Pte	Bell, C.V.	1 Jul 44	Tourmaville
S	4042325	Pte	Evans, S.C.	1 Jul 44	Tourmaville
HQ	4105413	Pte	Lloyd, G.H.	1 Jul 44	Tourmaville
C	5436676	Pte	Chivers, G.J.	18 Jul 44	Ranville
S	4037012	L/Cpl	Millington, T.E.	18 Jul 44	Ranville
HQ	4105695	L/Cpl	Carey, R.W.	18 Jul 44	Ranville
C	5441913	Pte	Andrews, E.	18 Jul 44	Ranville
C	4042750	Pte	Morrisey, J.H.	18 Jul 44	Ranville
A	4036343	L/Cpl	Baker, D.	18 Jul 44	Ranville
S	4105451	Pte	Jones, W.J.	18 Jul 44	Ranville
B	4105788	Pte	Finney, D.L.	19 Jul 44	Demouville
HQ	4036283	Pte	Skinner, B.	19 Jul 44	Demouville
HQ	4105875	Pte	Ritterband, B.	19 Jul 44	Demouville
A	4041839	Pte	Carberry, W.H.	21 Jul 44	Caen
A	4034609	Pte	Hill, J.E.	30 Jul 44	La Vacquerie
HQ	4105772	Pte	Dodd, W.	30 Jul 44	La Vacquerie
A	4036863	Pte	Ansell, R.	30 Jul 44	La Vacquerie
A	14585610	Pte	Ford, J.J.	30 Jul 44	La Vacquerie
A	4042245	Pte	Oliver, L.G.	30 Jul 44	La Vacquerie
C	4036209	Pte	Taylor, H.	30 Jul 44	La Vacquerie
C	5442615	Pte	Lenney, G.W.	30 Jul 44	La Vacquerie
HQ	4105888	Pte	Sage, E.	30 Jul 44	La Vacquerie
D	4032943	Pte	Phillips, S.C.	30 Jul 44	La Vacquerie
D	4038472	Pte	Pouncett, J.H.	30 Jul 44	La Vacquerie
D	4105209	L/Sgt	Preedy, T.H.	30 Jul 44	La Vacquerie
D	4038143	Pte	Chapman, G.	30 Jul 44	La Vacquerie
D	4042184	Pte	Bowen, I.T.	30 Jul 44	La Vacquerie
A	5256506	Pte	Deleury, D.J.	30 Jul 44	La Vacquerie
B	4105859	Sgt	Millward, R.	30 Jul 44	La Vacquerie
B	14585673	Pte	Wagg, E.	30 Jul 44	La Vacquerie
D	4038235	L/Cpl	Taylor, T.	30 Jul 44	Caen
HQ	?	Pte	Williams, G.	30 Jul 44	Caen

Company	Number	Rank	Name	Date	Location
S	4036821	Cpl	Harding, J.	31 Jul 44	La Vacquerie
S	4041300	Pte	Poole, B.	31 Jul 44	La Vacquerie
S	4104930	Pte	Cartwright, S.G.	31 Jul 44	La Vacquerie
D	5735628	Pte	Amphlett, J.A.	4 Aug 44	La Biste
S	5057799	Pte	Ankers, F.	5 Aug 44	La Biste
S	4038567	Pte	Finnikin, W.G.	6 Aug 44	La Biste
B	4105904	Cpl	Williams, H.H.	9 Aug 44	Presles
S	5623310	Pte	Farmer, G.N.	11 Aug 44	Le Bas Perrier
D	5254336	Cpl	Doughton, A.B.	15 Aug 44	Le Thiel
D	4104469	L/Cpl	Husbands, G.J.	15 Aug 44	Le Thiel
D	4042419	L/Cpl	Worton, L.G.	15 Aug 44	Le Thiel
B	14708317	Pte	Powell, S.	15 Aug 44	Le Thiel
D	4460325	Pte	Cutting, F.J.	15 Aug 44	Le Thiel
S	4040797	Pte	Pope, B.	15 Aug 44	Le Thiel
S	4040785	Pte	Lewis, W.T.	15 Aug 44	Le Thiel
B	5118158	L/Cpl	Hands, A.H.	15 Aug 44	Le Thiel
S	4105770	Pte	Davies, E.E.P.	18 Aug 44	Ecouche
S	4038484	Pte	Plant, J.	18 Aug 44	Ecouche
S	4038431	Pte	Jones, H.J.C.	18 Aug 44	Ecouche
D	5126604	Pte	Howard, D.E.	9 Sep 44	Helchteren
D	14391729	Pte	Tye, A.	9 Sep 44	Helchteren
D	4036688	Cpl	Marks, E.	9 Sep 44	Helchteren
D	4035987	Pte	Robinson, A.A.	9 Sep 44	Helchteren
D	5251394	Pte	Davies, W.	9 Sep 44	Helchteren
B	4042347	L/Cpl	Jones, J.H.	9 Sep 44	Helchteren
B	5259560	Pte	Cattell, W.	9 Sep 44	Helchteren
A	4104876	Sgt	Hunt, G.V.	10 Sep 44	Hechtel
A	4038882	L/Cpl	Langley, J.	10 Sep 44	Hechtel
A	5107452	Pte	Tranter, A.E.	10 Sep 44	Hechtel
A	4080145	Pte	Hemberey, F.W.	10 Sep 44	Hechtel
C	14347613	Pte	Blount, S.J.	10 Sep 44	Hechtel
C	4105769	L/Sgt	Derry, W.	10 Sep 44	Hechtel
C	5126621	Pte	Jeffs, D.	10 Sep 44	Hechtel
C	4042358	Cpl	Lloyd, W.A.	20 Sep 44	Leende
D	4041923	Pte	Wisedale, J.C.	21 Sep 44	Zomeren
B	4034935	Cpl	Lucas, H.	21 Sep 44	Zomeren
B	14428400	Cpl	Nicks, T.G.	21 Sep 44	Zomeren
D	5119682	Pte	Summers, W.	21 Sep 44	Zomeren
D	5255941	Pte	Barrows, W.A.	21 Sep 44	Zomeren
D	14221897	Pte	Gray, M.S.	21 Sep 44	Zomeren
D	14591147	Pte	John, W.R.	21 Sep 44	Zomeren
D	4922299	Pte	Stennett, W.E.	21 Sep 44	Zomeren
B	14210383	L/Cpl	Holland, W.H.	21 Sep 44	Zomeren
B	14714357	Pte	Fowkes, E.	21 Sep 44	Zomeren
B	5248815	Sgt	Tomkins, F.	21 Sep 44	Zomeren
C	4036623	Pte	Todd, W.G.S.	21 Sep 44	Zomeren
C	5113990	Pte	Littler, F.	21 Sep 44	Zomeren

Company	Number	Rank	Name	Date	Location
B	14585314	Pte	Moses, J.H.	21 Sep 44	Zomeren
S	4105730	Pte	Bickerton, G.J.	21 Sep 44	Zomeren
A	4035139	Cpl	Burgess, A.	21 Sep 44	Zomeren
B	4041826	Pte	Bedford, E.R.	22 Sep 44	Asten
B	14210319	Pte	Mellor, F.	22 Sep 44	Asten
C	4036329	Pte	Farmer, J.W.	11 Oct 44	Overloon
B	4103988	Pte	Jones, W.C.	12 Oct 44	Overloon
A	5440378	Cpl	Bailes, S.	17 Oct 44	Ijsselsteijn
D	984286	Pte	Allott, J.H.	17 Oct 44	Ijsselsteijn
A	5120895	Pte	Donovan, V.	17 Oct 44	Ijsselsteijn
D	4922977	Pte	Peck, A.E.	17 Oct 44	Ijsselsteijn
D	4926966	L/Cpl	Sidwell, J.W.	17 Oct 44	Ijsselsteijn
HQ	4036386	Pte	Penn, E.E.	18 Oct 44	Veulen
B	4038897	Cpl	Gregson, R.	18 Oct 44	Veulen
C	4038510	Sgt	Shotton, B.W.	18 Oct 44	Veulen
A	4105865	Pte	Phillips, H.H.	22 Oct 44	Veulen
A	4105468	Pte	Price, G.L.	22 Oct 44	Veulen
D	4042197	Pte	Carden, W.	31 Oct 44	Grientsveen
S	4033786	Pte	Edwards, H.	9 Dec 44	Grubbenvorst
S	5779942	Pte	Loombe, S.	25 Jan 45	Heel
A	14734569	Pte	Wright, C.A.J.	27 Feb 45	Udem
A	3907790	Pte	Walters, D.A.	27 Feb 45	Udem
A	14736896	Pte	Cooper, W.A.	27 Feb 45	Udem
A	5617583	Pte	Aherne, P.	27 Feb 45	Udem
B	4033789	Cpl	Leader, M.T.	27 Feb 45	Udem
B	4031097	L/Cpl	Whalley, A.R.	27 Feb 45	Udem
C	1693276	Pte	Fantham, W.	27 Feb 45	Udem
S	4105204	Sgt	King, W.F.	27 Feb 45	Udem
S	4036308	L/Cpl	Wise, W.J.J.	27 Feb 45	Udem
A	14736935	Pte	Glossop, F.	27 Feb 45	Udem
A	14744697	Pte	Fowles, W.G.	28 Feb 45	Udem
C	5501116	Pte	Holloway, R.P.	1 Mar 45	Kervenheim
B	3854813	Cpl	Stewart, J.	1 Mar 45	Kervenheim
D	4105920	Cpl	Wilkins, H.S.	1 Mar 45	Kervenheim
S	4105639	Sgt	Chapman, S.J.	1 Mar 45	Kervenheim
S	4105866	Pte	Palmer, G.T.	1 Mar 45	Kervenheim
D	14735897	Pte	Rider, A.R.	1 Mar 45	Kervenheim
B	14497254	Pte	Hollyman, R.E.F.	2 Mar 45	Kervenheim
B	14577749	Pte	Sheppard, J.	2 Mar 45	Kervenheim
B	14267818	Pte	Hughes, P.	2 Mar 45	Kervenheim
B	5618491	Pte	Turner, R.	2 Mar 45	Kervenheim
A	5116190	Pte	Bowkett, G.	2 Mar 45	Kervenheim
D	3774848	Pte	Roy, J.E.	2 Mar 45	Kervenheim
S	4105543	Pte	Hutton, A.	2 Mar 45	Kervenheim
A	14733642	Pte	Marshall, L.C.	1 Apr 45	Birgte
A	5113845	Sgt	Raines, L.F. (MM)	1 Apr 45	Birgte
A	14738008	Pte	Smith, W.E.	1 Apr 45	Birgte

Company	Number	Rank	Name	Date	Location
A	14802424	Pte	Judd, D.J.	1 Apr 45	Birgte
D	4920201	Cpl	Young, J.	1 Apr 45	Birgte
	14808349	Pte	Anstey, C.	1 Apr 45	Birgte
	5618727	Pte	Carpenter, F.	1 Apr 45	Birgte
	5618606	Pte	Chapman, G.E.	1 Apr 45	Birgte
	14625202	Cpl	Cole, H.E.	1 Apr 45	Birgte
	14816537	Pte	Dagenhard, L.A.	1 Apr 45	Birgte
	14737899	Pte	Dowler, A.K.	1 Apr 45	Birgte
	5259581	L/Cpl	Foster, T.H.	1 Apr 45	Birgte
	5253487	L/Cpl	Longdon, J.	1 Apr 45	Birgte
	6342207	Pte	Maloney, J.	1 Apr 45	Birgte
	14210323	Pte	Mitchell, S.	1 Apr 45	Birgte
	14795168	Pte	Onions, C.	1 Apr 45	Birgte
	14778632	Pte	Portch, R.F.	1 Apr 45	Birgte
	6292162	L/Cpl	Redstone, L.W.	1 Apr 45	Birgte
	14803351	Pte	Sullens, W.G.	1 Apr 45	Birgte
C	14822242	Pte	Holdnall, C.G.	6 Apr 45	Schlusselburg
B	4037470	Pte	Bushell, J.	6 Apr 45	Schlusselburg
B	14718069	Pte	Hayler, J.W.	8 Apr 45	Mandelsloh
B	14812908	Pte	Hewins, R.E.	10 Apr 45	Schwarmstedt
B	14805550	Pte	Hopkins, D.W.	10 Apr 45	Schwarmstedt
D	5619626	Pte	Cumming, A.H.	10 Apr 45	Grindau
HQ	14740711	Pte	Sealey, G.W.	10 Apr 45	Grindau
HQ	6399601	Pte	Richardson, C.R.	10 Apr 45	Grindau
A	14508555	Cpl	Dooley, J.S.	14 Apr 45	Winsen
C	2572256	Pte	Francis, C.	14 Apr 45	Winsen
A	4919665	L/Cpl	McDermott, J.	15 Apr 45	Muden
C	14754372	Pte	Howard, S.E.	15 Apr 45	Muden
HQ	4035659	Pte	Powis, J.	16 Apr 45	Brambostel
D	14744320	L/Cpl	Gurnett, P.W.	17 Apr 45	Eimke
D	14734513	Pte	Bennell, J.W.	17 Apr 45	Eimke
D	14497070	Pte	Clayden, J.W.	17 Apr 45	Eimke
D	1579901	Pte	Jordon, S.	17 Apr 45	Eimke
D	14804597	Pte	Clarke, C.B.	17 Apr 45	Eimke
B	14729624	Pte	Hill, W.J.B.	19 Apr 45	Ebsdorf
C	14770155	Pte	Panter, J.	21 Apr 45	Winsen
A	14703237	Cpl	Buttifant, S.F.	1 May 45	Havekost
HQ	4039637	Pte	Tarron, W.E.	1 May 45	Havekost
HQ	4105715	Pte	Bailess, G.H.	1 May 45	Havekost
C	14812536	Pte	Bower, G.W.	1 May 45	Havekost

Other ranks who died of wounds received in action:

Company	Number	Rank	Name	Date	Location
HQ	4105780	L/Cpl	Evans, A.C.	20 Jul 44	Ranville
D	4036979	Pte	Jones, A.H.	21 Jul 44	Demouville
HQ	4041870	Pte	Hancock, S.	30 Jul 44	La Vacquerie

Company	Number	Rank	Name	Date	Location
D	4036251	L/Sgt	Jones, F.A.	30 Jul 44	La Vacquerie
A	14228319	Pte	Meadows, G.B.	30 Jul 44	La Vacquerie
HQ	4104173	Pte	Snowzell, G.C.	30 Jul 44	La Vacquerie
HQ	4104417	Pte	Goodman, R.	30 Jul 44	La Vacquerie
D	4042375	Pte	Owen, H.C.	31 Jul 44	La Vacquerie
D	4036652	Pte	Sharpin, A.A.	9 Aug 44	Presles
C	14385082	Pte	Davies, E.H.	18 Aug 44	Ecouche
C	4042802	Pte	Waythe, A.A.W.	19 Aug 44	Ecouche
C	4038451	Pte	Morris, E.	7 Sep 44	Antwerp
C	4038277	Pte	Stevens, P.B.	10 Sep 44	Hechtel
C	4041740	Pte	Jones, F.	20 Sep 44	Leende
B	4039281	L/Cpl	Smith, F.W.	22 Sep 44	Asten
C	4923789	Pte	Tedstone, G.T.	22 Sep 44	Asten
B	14409732	Pte	Wycherley, I.A.	22 Sep 44	Asten
B	4035552	Cpl	Price, H.W.	24 Sep 44	Asten
D	14642716	Pte	Merchant, R.M.	10 Oct 44	Overloon
B	4915792	Cpl	Lightfoot, S.	12 Oct 44	Overloon
C	5116683	Pte	Gee, F.E.	13 Oct 44	Overloon
B	4105362	Pte	Sparkes, W.G.	13 Oct 44	Overloon
A	3911826	Pte	Castree, R.G.	17 Oct 44	Ijsselsteijn
D	3597899	Sgt	Lord, T.P.	17 Oct 44	Ijsselsteijn
D	4041743	Pte	Saunders, R.C.	17 Oct 44	Ijsselsteijn
D	5112024	Sgt	Nicholls, A.W.	17 Oct 44	Ijsselsteijn
A	5126716	L/Sgt	Wale, D.B.	17 Oct 44	Ijsselsteijn
A	4104983	Pte	Hill, A.E.	17 Oct 44	Ijsselsteijn
A	4031984	CQMS	French, J.H.	23 Oct 44	Veulen
A	4041880	Pte	Knight, D.	23 Oct 44	Veulen
C	14735729	Pte	Whittle, J.	1 Mar 45	Udem
C	4460144	Cpl	Shufflebottom, A.	6 Apr 45	Schlesselburg
C	5253540	Pte	Pepall, D.H.	14 Apr 45	Winsen
B	14728774	Pte	Townend, W.	19 Apr 45	Ebstorf
C	14751680	Pte	Enright, J.	20 Apr 45	Winsen

Deaths other than battle casualties:

Company	Number	Rank	Name	Date
REME	7598173	Sgt	Holloway, E.A.	17 Mar 45
HQ	14576892	Pte	Kemp, C.E.J.	31 Mar 45
A	14846157	Pte	Marriott, S.	21 Apr 45

Serving at the time of death with 1st Battalion the Herefordshire Regiment in the North West European Campaign (alphabetical order):

Officers:

Capt.	Barneby, R.P.	Capt.	Boddy, S.H.	Capt.	Bulmer, O.T.
Lt.	Creamer, F.B.	2/Lt.	Hancox, T.E.	Lt.	Hopkinson, G.G.
Lt.	Kotchapaw, W.J.	Lt.	Spittall, A.J.		

Other ranks:

Pte	Aherne, P.	Pte	Allott, J.H.	Pte	Amphlett, J.A.
Pte	Andrews, E.	Pte	Ansell, E.	Pte	Ankers, F.
Pte	Anstey, C.	Cpl	Bailes, S.	Pte	Bailess, G.H.
L/Cpl	Baker, D.	Pte	Barrows, W.A.	Pte	Bedford, E.R.
Pte	Bell, C.V.	Pte	Bennell, J.W.	Pte	Bickerton, G.J.
Pte	Blount, S.J.	Pte	Bowen, I.T.	Pte	Bower, G.W.
Pte	Bowkett, G.	Cpl	Burgess, A.	Pte	Bushell, J.
Cpl	Buttifant, S.F.	Pte	Carberry, W.H.	Pte	Carden, W.
L/Cpl	Carey, R.W.	Pte	Carpenter, F.	Pte	Cartwright, S.G.
Pte	Castree, R.G.	Pte	Cattell, W.	Pte	Chapman, G. (143)
Pte	Chapman, G.E. (606)	Sgt	Chapman, S.J.	Pte	Chivers, G.J.
Pte	Clarke, C.B.	Pte	Clayden, J.W.	Cpl	Cole, H.E.
Pte	Cooke, G.H.	Pte	Cooper, W.A.	Pte	Cumming, A.H.
*Cpl	Curtis, J.A.	Pte	Cutting, F.J.	Pte	Dagenhard, L.A.
Pte	Davies, E.E.P.	*Pte	Davies, E.H. (82)	Pte	Davies, V.J.
Pte	Davies, W.	Pte	Deleury, D.J.	L/Sgt	Derry, W.
Pte	Dodd, W.	Pte	Donovan, V.	Cpl	Dooley, J.S.
*Cpl	Doughton, A.B.	Pte	Dowler, A.K.	Pte	Edwards, H.
Pte	Enright, J.	Pte	Evans, S.C.	L/Cpl	Evans, A.C.
Pte	Fantham, W.	Pte	Farmer, G.N.	Pte	Farmer, J.W.
Pte	Finney, D.L.	Pte	Finnikin, W.G.	Pte	Ford, J.J.
L/Cpl	Foster, T.H.	Pte	Fowkes, E.	Pte	Fowles, W.G.
Pte	Francis, C.	CQMS	French, J.H.	*Pte	Gee, F.E.
Pte	Glossop, F.	Pte	Goodman, R.	Pte	Gray, M.S.
Cpl	Gregson, R.	L/Cpl	Gurnett, P.W.	Pte	Hancock, S.
L/Cpl	Hands, A.H.	Cpl	Harding, J.	Pte	Hayler, J.W.
Pte	Hemberey, F.W.	Pte	Hewins, R.E.	Pte	Higgins, E.R.
Pte	Hill, A.E.	Pte	Hill, J.E.	Pte	Hill, W.J.B.
Pte	Holdnall, C.G.	L/Cpl	Holland, W.H.	*Sgt	Holloway, E.A. (REME)
Pte	Holloway, R.P.	Pte	Hollyman, R.E.F.	Pte	Hopkins, D.W.
Pte	Howard, D.E. (604)	Pte	Howard, S.E. (372)	Pte	Hughes, P.
Sgt	Hunt, G.V.	L/Cpl	Husbands, G.J.	Pte	Hutton, A.
*Pte	Jeffs, D.	Pte	John, W.R.	Pte	Jones, A.E. (548)
Pte	Jones, A.H. (979)	Pte	Jones, F. (740)	L/Sgt	Jones, F.A. (251)
Pte	Jones, H.J.C. (431)	L/Cpl	Jones, J.H. (347)	*Pte	Jones, J.H. (583)
Pte	Jones, W.C. (988)	Pte	Jones, W.J. (451)	Pte	Jordon, S.
Pte	Judd, D.J.	*Pte	Kemp, C.E.J.	Sgt	King, W.F.
Pte	Knight, D.	L/Cpl	Langley, J.	Cpl	Leader, M.T.
Pte	Lenney, G.W.	Pte	Lewis, W.T.	Cpl	Lightfoot, S.
Pte	Littler, F.	*Pte	Lloyd, G.H.	Cpl	Lloyd, W.A.
L/Cpl	Longdon, J.	Pte	Loombe, S.	Sgt	Lord, T.P.
Cpl	Lucas, H.	L/Cpl	McDermott, J.	Pte	Maloney, J.T. (207)
Cpl	Marks, E.	Pte	Marriott, S.	*Pte	Marshall, L.G.
Pte	Meadows, G.B.	Pte	Mellor, F.	Pte	Merchant, R.M.
L/Cpl	Millington, T.E.	Sgt	Millward, R.	Pte	Mitchell, S.

Pte	Morris, E.	Pte	Morrisey, J.H.	Pte	Moses, J.H.
Sgt	Nicholls, A.W.	Cpl	Nicks, T.G.	*Pte	Oliver, L.G.
Pte	Onions, C.	Pte	Owen, H.C.	Pte	Palmer, G.T.
Pte	Panter, J.	Pte	Peck, A.E.	Pte	Penn, E.E.
Pte	Pepall, D.H.	Pte	Phillips, H.H.	Pte	Phillips, S.C.
Pte	Plant, J.	Pte	Poole, B.	Pte	Pope, B.
Pte	Portch, R.F.	Pte	Pouncett, J.H.	Pte	Powell, S.
Pte	Powis, J.	L/Sgt	Preedy, T.H.	Pte	Price, G.L.
Cpl	Price, H.W.	Sgt	Raines, L.F. MM	L/Cpl	Redstone, L.W.
Pte	Richardson, C.R.	Pte	Rider, A.R.	Pte	Ritterband, B.
Pte	Robinson, A.A.	Pte	Roy, J.E.	L/Cpl	Rycroft, W.A.
Pte	Sage, E.	Pte	Saunders, R.C.	Pte	Sealey, G.W.
Pte	Sharpin, A.A.	Pte	Sheppard, J.	Sgt	Shotton, B.W.
Cpl	Shufflebottom, A.	L/Cpl	Sidwell, J.W.	Pte	Skinner, B.
L/Cpl	Smith, F.W.	Pte	Smith, W.E.	Pte	Snowzell, G.C.
Pte	Sparkes, W.G.	Pte	Stennett, W.E.	Pte	Stevens, P.B.
Cpl	Stewart, J.	Pte	Sullens, W.G.	Pte	Summers, W.
Pte	Tarren, W.E.	Pte	Taylor, H.	L/Cpl	Taylor, T.
*Pte	Tedstone, G.T.	Pte	Todd, W.G.S.	Sgt	Tomkins, F.
Pte	Townend, W.	Pte	Tranter, A.E.	*Pte	Turner, R.
Pte	Tye, A.	Pte	Wagg, E.	L/Sgt	Wale, D.B.
Pte	Walters, D.A.	Pte	Ward, F.	Pte	Waythe, A.W.
L/Cpl	Whalley, A.R.	Pte	Whittle, J.	Cpl	Wilkins, H.S.
Pte	Williams, G.	Cpl	Williams, H.H.	L/Cpl	Wise, W.J.J.
Pte	Wisedale, J.C.	L/Cpl	Worton, L.G.	Pte	Wright, C.A.J.
Pte	Wycherley, I.A.	Cpl	Young, J.		

* These names are included in the roll of honour of 11 Armoured Division and/or 1st Battalion the Herefordshire Regiment, but not in the regimental roll of the Herefordshire Regiment.

Herefordshire Regiment serving at time of death with the KSLI:

Number	Rank	Name	Date	Location
4104934	Cpl	Bevan, Edward C.	14 Oct 44	North-west Europe
4104920	L/Cpl	Deen, Walter G.	31 Mar 44	United Kingdom
4033806	Pte	Downes, Robert	12 Dec 44	Italy
53926	Pte	Downing, Ivor	7 Feb 44	Italy
4104847	Pte	Faulkner, William T.	30 Jan 44	Italy
4105506	Pte	James, George C.	8 Feb 44	Italy
4105544	Pte	Jones, Colston	4 Jul 44	North-west Europe
4105503	Pte	Jones, George R.	18 Jul 44	North-west Europe

Herefordshire Regiment, not otherwise recorded:

Officers

Number	Rank	Name
38190/7	Captain	Sir J.H. Croft Bt

Other Ranks

Number	Name	Number	Name
5436834	Allinson, A.W.	14210349	Jones, W.J.
5254114	Barnes, S.H.	4105646	Lewis, W.
4105735	Bateman, G.	5127545	Little, J.E.
4105644	Bath, W.B.	4105512	Melrose, K.A.
14808730	Bowden, C.B.	14645799	Moloney, J.L.
4104659	Capes, R.E.	4031961	Owen, T.S.
4032918	Carthy, F.	4105154	Phillips, W.H.
5383841	Cater, J.F.	2050972	Quincey, E.
4037122	Cumberbatch, L.I.	14438587	Shelton, T.J.
4038165	Eades, G.	4105257	Stevens, W.V.
4036043	Fitzmaurice, H.R.	4040062	Stokes, H.A.
980589	Gibson, R.	3663831	Stoptforth, R.
14814163	Goddard, E.J.	4027918	Stringer, G.
978874	Goodwin, F.C.B.	4038843	Summers, C.W.
4036469	Govier, G.C.	4460272	Warren, A.
4033446	Harding, J.T.	14801646	Wells, J.S.
4029934	Hardman, G.	4036814	Whetstone, F.
4104366	Herbert, T.W.	4037817	Williamson, T.J.
4460411	Jenkinson, T.H.		

Rank	Name	Date	Location
2/Lt.	Fraser, N.J.	November 1941	United Kingdom
Pte	Clarkson, H.	March 1946	North-west Europe
Pte	Evans, L.B.	April 1943	North Africa
Pte	Nuttall, H.	December 1939	United Kingdom
Pte	Rushworth, H.V.	April 1943	North Africa
Cpl	Taylor, T.	July 1944	North-west Europe
Cpl	Wynn, J.W.	July 1945	United Kingdom

The roll of honour of 1st Battalion the Herefordshire Regiment is contained in the history of 11 Armoured Division. There also exists the roll of honour compiled by 1st Battalion on 14 June 1945 relating to the period 13 June 1944–8 May 1945. The list of Herefordshire personnel serving at the time of death with the KSLI is recorded in the Army roll of honour for the KSLI. Illuminated rolls of honour are displayed in the TA Centre, Harold Street, Hereford.

Honours and Awards

The First World War, 1914–1918

Victoria Cross

Capt. Fox-Russell, J. MC RAMC at Khuweilfeh Nov 1917, while serving as medical officer to 1st Herefords *LG* 11 Jan 18

Distinguished Service Order

Maj.	Chipp, W.F.		Maj.	Powell, E.B.
Lt-Col.	Drage, G.		Maj.	Pateshall, H.E.P.
Maj.	Green, A.L.B.		Maj.	Rome, C.S.
Maj.	Lawrence, E.M.			

Military Cross

Capt.	Ashton, P.		Lt.	Fraser
Capt.	Barker		Capt.	Jordan, L.O.
Lt.	Blackmore		Lt.	Lingell
Lt.	Capel, E.A.		Lt.	Moses
Capt.	Chipp, W.F.		Lt.	Mullis
Lt.	Evans		Capt.	Russell
Capt.	Evelyn, C.		Lt.	Sully
			Capt.	Whitehouse, A.G.R.

Distinguished Conduct Medal

Pte	Edwards, R.		CSM	Vaughan *LG* Feb 18
L/Cpl	James		Sgt	Worthing, W.C.G. Sep 19
Pte	Mann, E. *LG* Mar 16		Pte	Parker, H.J. *LG* Mar 20
Sgt	Trapp, H. *LG* May 18		CSM	Coleman, C.S. *LG* Mar 20
L/Sgt	Symonds, J.B. *LG* Aug 17			

Military Medal

Pte	Bannister, J.			
Pte	Brain *LG* Jul 17		Sgt	Harper, W.H.
Sgt	Comer, G.		Sgt	James
Pte	Cotterell, F.A.		Pte	Kettle, F.
Sgt	Dowell		Cpl	Lane, L.
L/Cpl	Evans, H.S.		L/Cpl	Symonds, J.B.
Sgt	Farmer		Sgt	Ward, H.
Pte	Griffiths, F.		L/Cpl	Wheeler

Mention in Despatches

Lt.	Ashton, P.		Sgt	Parker
Capt.	Berney, G.H.		Pte	Pike
Capt.	Capel, E.A.		Capt.	Rogers, E.T.P.
Pte	Downs		Capt.	Sale, R.C.
Sgt	Page		Sgt	Trapp
			Lt.	Whitehouse, A.G.R.

Russian Order of St George

Cpl Mann, E.E.

Croix de Guerre

Lt-Col. Chipp, W.F.
Lt.   Blackmore

The Second World War, 1939–1945

Distinguished Service Order

Number	Rank	Name		Date
87721	Maj.	Barnsley, P.E.	Capt. T/Maj.	LG 1 Mar 45
31905	Lt-Col.	Churcher, J.B.	Maj. T/Lt-Col. A/Brig. KSLI	LG 19 Oct 44
			Bar	LG 24 Jan 46
97801	Maj.	Fripp, R.C.	Capt. T/Maj.	LG 1 Mar 45
(Attached to				
1st Battalion)	Lt-Col.	Turner-Cain, G.R.	R. Norfolk Regiment	

Order of the British Empire, Class V (MBE)

Number	Rank	Name	Date
133786	Capt. (QM)	Brown, E.R.	1 Apr 44
161258	Capt. (QM)	Bryant, T.C.R.	1 Apr 44

Military Cross

Number	Rank	Name		Date
(Attached to				
1st Battalion)	Capt.	Berridge, F.D.	Northamptonshire Regiment	
66667	Maj.	Crofts, W.A.P.	Capt. T/Maj.	1 Mar 45
304130	Lt.	Crockford, K.H.	KSLI	24 Jan 46
(Attached to				
1st Battalion)	Maj.	de Carle, G.R.	and MM	
			South African Defence Force	

Number	Rank	Name		Date
(Attached to 1st Battalion)	Maj.	Gale, M.S.	Q.O.R. West Kent Regiment	
226608	Maj.	Hesketh, R.B.	T/Capt. M.I.D. KSLI	24 Jan 46
(Attached to 1st Battalion)	Capt.	Mills, E.L.	Q.O.R. West Kent Regiment	
(Attached to 1st Battalion)	Maj.	Northey, L.P.	D.C.L.I.	
92394	Maj.	Phillips, A.J.W.	Capt. A/Maj.	21 Dec 44
88390	Maj.	Singleton, G.M.	T/Maj.	24 Jan 46
94975	Lt.	Swayne, R.O.C.	(St Nazaire)	5 Jul 45
	Maj.	Tapper, R.G.		

Distinguished Conduct Medal

Number	Rank	Name		Date
4031694	A/WO2	Evans, A.F.	Sgt A/WO2	21 Dec 44
4035808	Pte	Evans, D.		1 Mar 45
4105061	L/Cpl	Everall, I.R.		1 Mar 45

Military Medal

Number	Rank	Name		Date
—	Pte	Andrew, J.W.		—
4080973	Sgt	Bevan, G.	Cpl A/Sgt	21 Jun 45
4038591	Cpl	Bond, A.C.T.		1 Mar 45
4460383	Pte	Carroll, J.		24 Jan 46
5443575	L/Cpl	Constable, R.E.J.		1 Mar 45
4031735	WO2	Dalton, R.		24 Jan 46
5111940	Sgt	Davies, F.		21 Jun 45
4036204	Sgt	Dunn, H.		1 Mar 45
4034848	Pte	Evans, V.E.		29 Mar 45
—	Pte	Evans, W.G.		—
4104294	Sgt	Fletcher, J.		19 Oct 44
4036078	Cpl	French, A.G.	M.I.D.	1 Mar 45
5618324	Cpl	Green, E.L.		12 Jul 45
6009650	WO2	Hartnett, H.J.		7 Jun 45
4038083	Cpl	Haywood, S.H.		1 Mar 45
14210404	Pte	Howe, R.		21 Dec 44
4035360	Cpl	Millward, G.E.		31 Aug 44
4460191	Sgt	Pearson, H.	Cpl A/Sgt	1 Mar 45
4038249	L/Sgt	Pollard, W.		1 Mar 45
4113845	Sgt	Raines, L.F.		1 Mar 45
4105026	Sgt	Rose, J.T.	Cpl T/Sgt	11 Oct 45
5615505	Cpl	Royster, H.T.		20 Apr 45
4038274	Cpl	Stevens, B.G.	Pte A/Cpl	1 Mar 45
4036809	L/Cpl	Wale, B.		24 Jan 45
—	Pte	Winmill, W.L.		—

Mention in Despatches

Number	Rank	Name		Date
4031362	Sgt	Bell, L.B.		4 Apr 46
4105012	WO2	Benfield, E.J.	A/WO2	4 Apr 46
4105151	Sgt	Cotterell, L.O.		4 Apr 46
5126580	L/Cpl	Dunn, R.F.V.		4 Apr 46
4033463	Pte	Edwards, C.		9 Aug 45
165851	Capt.	France, R.S.	T/Capt. KSLI	4 Apr 46
4036078	Cpl	French, A.G.	MM	22 Mar 45
4105799	Pte	Goodrick, T.		10 May 45
4036210	WO2	Grice, R.R.	A/WO2	4 Apr 46
5441400	Sgt	Hanafin, M.		4 Apr 46
226608	Maj.	Hesketh, R.B.	T/Capt. (KSLI)	9 Aug 45
4105445	Pte	Hiatt, A.C.		22 Mar 45
4034543	Cpl	Hill, S.R.		22 Mar 45
93995	Capt.	Hood-Daniel, J.A.		4 Apr 46
4104087	WO2	Mason, W.		8 Nov 45
4105020	Pte	Newman, J.F.		22 Mar 45
4104664	Sgt	Penson, V.J.		4 Apr 46
4031405	WO2	Roberts, K.H.		4 Apr 46
4104137	WO2	Rollings, H.H.		8 Nov 45
172351	Maj.	Vale, M.A.W.	Capt. A/Maj. (KSLI)	4 Apr 46
4105914	Col.-Sgt	Warrington, F.		9 Aug 45
143476	Capt.	Woolcott, C.W.P. (KSLI)		8 Nov 45

Belgian Chevalier Order of Leopold

Lt. Crockford K.H.

Belgian Croix de Guerre

Lt. Crockford K.H.

French Croix de Guerre

Lt-Col. Turner-Cain
RSM Wells

Lineage of the Herefordshire Regiment

1st Administrative Battalion Herefordshire and Radnorshire Rifle Volunteer Corps

Battalion formed 20 February 1861
Headquarters: Hereford
Comprising: 1st Herefordshire RVC Hereford City @ Hereford formed 10 April 1860; 2nd Herefordshire RVC @ Ross formed 27 March 1860; 3rd Herefordshire RVC @ Ledbury formed 27 March 1860; 4th Herefordshire RVC @ Bromyard formed 15 May 1860; 5th Herefordshire RVC South Archenfield Forest Border Rifles @ South Archenfield formed 15 May 1860, disbanded by January 1873; 6th Herefordshire RVC @ Leominster formed 6 May 1860; 7th Herefordshire RVC @ Kington formed 18 May 1860; 8th Herefordshire RVC Oddfellows @ Hereford formed 27 September 1860; 1864: added 1st Radnorshire RVC @ Presteigne (formed 8 March 1860); 2nd Radnorshire RVC @ Knighton formed 25 April 1860, disbanded 1878 and new 2nd Radnorshire RVC @ Rhayader formed 11 September 1878; 3rd Radnorshire RVC @ New Radnor formed 6 August 1860, disbanded September 1872.

1st Herefordshire (Hereford and Radnor) Rifle Volunteer Corps

Consolidated 1880
Headquarters: Hereford
1881: deemed to form part of the Corps of the King's Shropshire Light Infantry.
Companies: A Company @ Hereford; B Company @ Ross; C Company @ Ledbury; D Company @ Bromyard; E Company @ Ross; F Company @ Leominster; G Company @ Kington; H Company @ Hereford; I Company @ Presteigne (1905: amalgamated with G Company); K Company @ Rhayader; 1881: B Company absorbed E Company; 1889: New E Company formed @ Weobley; 1889: Welsh Border Brigade Bearer Company formed on strength of A Company, transferred to RAMC (V) in 1905; 1905: L (Cyclist) Company formed @ Hereford from Cyclist Section formed in 1888; 1905: M Company formed @ Ruardean
1891: Redesignated 1st the Herefordshire (Hereford and Radnor) Volunteer Rifle Corps.

1st Battalion the Herefordshire Regiment (TF)

Redesignated 1 April 1908
Headquarters: Hereford
Deemed to form part of the Corps of The King's (Shropshire Light Infantry). Designated the Herefordshire Battalion the King's (Shropshire Light Infantry) (TF) until March 1909.

Companies: A Company @ Hereford; B Company @ Ross; C Company @ Ledbury; D Company @ Kington and Presteigne; E Company @ Ruardean; F Company @ Leominster and Bromyard; G Company @ Radnorshire (Rhayader & Knighton); H Company @ Hereford.

The First World War, 3 Battalions: 1st Battalion: embodied 4 August 1914, redesignated 1/1st Battalion, disembodied 24 May 1919; 2/1st Battalion: formed 31 August 1914 @ Hereford, disbanded 10 September 1917; 3/1st Battalion: formed 15 February 1915 @ Hereford designated 1st (Reserve) Battalion 8 April 1916 absorbed by 4th (Reserve) Battalion the King's (Shropshire Light Infantry) (TF) 11 July 1917.

1st Battalion the Herefordshire Regiment (TA)

Reconstituted 7 February 1920
Headquarters: Hereford
Battalion reconstituted less Radnorshire elements, which were converted to artillery to form 332 (Radnor) Battery of 83 (Welsh) Brigade Royal Field Artillery (TA).
Companies: A Company @ Hereford; B Company @ Ross; C Company @ Ledbury; D Company @ Leominster with detachments @ Bromyard and Kington; by 1939: A Company @ Hereford; B Company @ Kington; C Company @ Leominster; D Company @ Leominster; 1 April 1939: formed duplicate unit designated 2nd Battalion the Herefordshire Regiment (TA). Suspended animation 15 July 1946.

1st Battalion the Herefordshire Regiment (TA)

Reconstituted and amalgamated 1 January 1947
Headquarters: Hereford
Formed by the reconstitution and amalgamation of 1st Battalion the Herefordshire Regiment (TA) and 2nd Battalion the Herefordshire Regiment (TA).
Companies: Headquarters Company @ Hereford; A Company @ Kington (1948); B Company @ Ross; C Company @ Ledbury; D Company @ Leominster; Support Company @ Hereford.

1st Battalion the Herefordshire Light Infantry (TA)

Redesignated 1 February 1947
Headquarters: Hereford
Companies: Headquarters Company @ Hereford; A Company @ Kington (1948); B Company @ Ross; C Company @ Ledbury: D Company @ Leominster; Support Company @ Hereford; by 1962: Headquarters Company @ Hereford; A Company @ Cinderford; B Company @ Ross; C Company @ Ledbury with detachment @ Bromyard; D Company @ Leominster with detachment @ Kington; Support Group @ Hereford; 1 April 1967: Unit amalgamated with 4th Battalion the King's Shropshire Light Infantry (TA) to form the King's Shropshire and Herefordshire Light Infantry (Territorials): 1 April 1939: duplicate unit formed by 1st Battalion the Herefordshire Regiment (TA); unit formed part of the Corps of the King's Shropshire Light Infantry.

2nd Battalion the Herefordshire Regiment (TA)

Duplicate unit formed 1 April 1939
Headquarters: Hereford
Companies: W Company @ Hereford; X Company @ Ross; Y Company @ Ledbury with detachment @ Colhall; Z Company @ Bromyard; Suspended animation 15 November 1944. 1 January 1947: Reconstituted and concurrently amalgamated with 1st Battalion the Herefordshire Regiment (TA) to form 1st Battalion the Herefordshire Regiment (TA).

APPENDIX IV

Succession of Honorary Colonels and Commanding Officers 1860–1967

Honorary Colonels

Date	Rank	Name
1893	Col.	Heywood, T. VD
1911	Col.	Scobie, M.J.G. CB VD TD
1932	Col.	Somers, the Lord KCMG DSO MC
1945	Maj.-Gen.	Churcher, J.B. CB DSO
1957	Brig.	Copland Griffiths, F.A.V. DSO MC
1962	Col.	Maclean, J. HML

2nd Battalion

Date	Rank	Name
1939	Col.	Pateshall, H.E.P. CB DSO TD DL

Commanding Officers

The Herefordshire Rifle Volunteers

Date	Rank	Name
1860	Col.	Fieldon, R.
1874	Lt-Col.	Heywood, T.
1893	Lt-Col.	Purser, T.H.
1894	Lt-Col.	Williams, S.W.
1899	Lt-Col.	Scobie, M.J.G.

The Herefordshire Regiment

Date	Rank	Name
1908	Lt-Col.	Scobie, M.J.G. VD
1910	Lt-Col.	Rankin, Sir J.R.L.
1912	Lt-Col.	Gilbert-Harris, J.H.

Date	Rank	Name
1914	Lt-Col.	Drage, G.
20 Aug 1915	Lt-Col.	Rome, C.S.
29 Aug 1915	Lt-Col.	Drage, G.
29 Jun 1916	Maj.	Green, A.L.B.
14 Sep 1916	Lt-Col.	Drage, G.
15 Oct 1916	Maj.	Green, A.L.B.
3 Dec 1916	Lt-Col.	Drage, G.
19 Mar 1918	Maj.	Whitehouse, A.G.R.
26 Mar 1918	Lt-Col.	Lawrence, E.M.
7 Sep 1918	Maj.	Chipp, W.F.
10 Sep 1918	Lt-Col.	Powell, E.B.
15 Sep 1918	Maj.	Chipp, W.F.
25 Sep 1918	Lt-Col.	Lyons
29 Sep 1918	Maj.	Chipp, W.F.
17 Oct 1918	Lt-Col.	Meldon
27 Oct 1918	Lt-Col.	Evans, E.H. MC
1920	Lt-Col.	Pateshall, H.E.P. DSO
1926	Lt-Col.	Sleeman, J.L. CMG CBE MVO
1931	Lt-Col.	Tomlinson, S.C.
1937	Lt-Col.	Sloane-Stanley, L.F.
1940	Lt-Col.	Bryant, A.D.
1942	Lt-Col.	Churcher, J.B. DSO
1944	Lt-Col.	Turner-Cain, G.R. DSO
1945	Lt-Col.	Fripp, R.C. DSO
1946	Lt-Col.	Barneby, H.H.

The Herefordshire Light Infantry

Date	Rank	Name
1947	Lt-Col.	Barneby, H.H.
1951	Lt-Col.	Armitstead, R.C.H.
1954	Lt-Col.	Thornycroft, G.M.
1957	Lt-Col.	Sale, J.D.
1960	Lt-Col.	Hill, T.J.B. MBE
1962	Lt-Col.	Carr, M.P.
1965	Lt-Col.	Gilbert, E.R.F.

2nd/1st Battalion

Date	Rank	Name
1914	Lt-Col.	Gilbert-Harris, J.H.
1914	Lt-Col.	Wood-Roe, W.B.
1916	Lt-Col.	Addie, J.H.
1917	Lt-Col.	Bates, D.

3rd/1st Battalion (1st Reserve Battalion)

Date	Rank	Name
1915	Lt-Col.	Symonds-Taylor, R.H.T.

2nd Battalion

Date	Rank	Name
1939	Lt-Col.	Blake, N.G. MBE
1942	Lt-Col.	Grey, W.A.
1944	Lt-Col.	Barlow, C.D.

APPENDIX V

Camps and Services, 1860–1967

1st Administrative Battalion of Herefordshire Rifle Volunteers to which were united the Radnorshire Rifle Volunteers

Reviews:

Year	Location
1861	Gloucester
1862	Bristol
1863	Oxford
1868	Windsor

Camps:

1871	Broomy Hill, Hereford
1872	Broomy Hill
1873	Warham
1874	Warham
1875	Warham
1876	Burghill
1877	Eastnor (Ledbury)
1878	Belmont
1879	Netherton (Ross)
1880	Elsdon (Lyonshall)

1st Herefordshire Rifle Volunteer Corps (Hereford & Radnor)

Year	Location/Company
1881	Stoke Edith
1882	Aldershot
1883	Brighton
1884	Stoke Edith
1885	Eywood (Kington)
1886	Abergavenny
1887	Garnons
1888	Crewe (Cyclists); review on Castle Green (remainder)
1889	Stoke Edith
1890	Towyn
1891	Aldershot
1892	Conway
1893	Aldershot
1894	Blackpool

Year	Location/Company
1895	Blackpool
1896	Leominster
1897	Aldershot
1898	Conway
1899	Towyn
South African War 1900–1901	1st Volunteer Service Company KSLI
1900	Fleetwood
South African War 1901–1902	2nd Volunteer Service Company KSLI
1901	Towyn
1902	Salisbury Plain
1903	Isle of Man
1904	Salisbury Plain
1905	Windmill Hill, Salisbury Plain
1906	Southampton
1907	Scarborough

1st Battalion the Herefordshire Regiment (Territorial Force)

Date	Location
1908	County march in Herefordshire
1909	Hereford
1910	Aberystwyth
1911	Pembroke
1912	Hereford
1913	Porthcawl
The First World War 1914–1919	1st/1st Battalion, 2nd/1st Battalion, 3rd/1st Battalion

1st Battalion the Herefordshire Regiment (Territorial Army)

Date	Location
The Defence Force 1921	
1921	Rhyl
1922	Aberystwyth
1923	Porthcawl
1924	Porthcawl
1925	Ramsey, Isle of Man
1926	Porthcawl
1927	Porthcawl
1928	Coberley, Cheltenham
1929	Porthcawl
1930	Holyhead
1931	Porthcawl
1932	Weekend brigade camp, Ross
1933	Porthcawl
1934	Penally
1935	Porthcawl

Date	Location
1936	Ilfracombe
1937	Callow, Hereford
1938	Porthkerry
1939	Weston-Super-Mare
1939	2nd Battalion Weston-Super-Mare
Second World War 1939–1946	1st and 2nd Battalions

1st Battalion the Herefordshire Light Infantry (Territorial Army)

Date	Location
1948	Brecon
1949	Penally
1950	Llanbedr
1951	Castlemartin
1952	Bellerby
1953	Gandales, Yorkshire
1954	Castlemartin
1955	Thetford
1956	Castlemartin
1957	Windmill Hill, Salisbury Plain
1958	Plasterdown
1959	Buckenham Tofts (Stanford PTA)
1960	Millom (Army School of Civil Defence)
1961	East Wretham (Stanford PTA)
1962	Plasterdown
1963	Devizes
1964	Gareloch-head
1965	Sennybridge
1966	Otterburn
1967	Vauxhall camp, Monmouth

INDEX OF PEOPLE, PLACES AND CAMPAIGNS